Dedication

We dedicate this decade-plus of investing in simplified accountable structure to the small, medium, and large churches and their leaders from around the country who allow us to walk alongside them—continuing to learn, grow, and witness how God shows up in beautiful ways when leaders become unapologetically mission-focused.

Blake dedicates this resource to …

~ My friend, colleague, and coauthor, Kay Kotan, who graciously invited me into the publishing world and opened doors that reshaped my ministry.

~ Dr. John Farthing, who guided me into faith, encouraged my call, and taught me how to think and write.

~ Rev. Paul Kottke and Rev. Rodney Steele, mentor pastors and district superintendents, who patiently taught me how to lead.

~ Dr. Craig Gilliam, who taught me that conflict should be transformed, not managed.

~ And for my wife, Kerri, who loves me even when book-writing takes over Christmas vacation.

Kay dedicates this resource to …

~ My friend, colleague, and coauthor, Blake, who graciously and generously invited me to conversations and tables that others would not.

~ My friend, colleague, and mentor, Ken Willard, who allowed me to co-labor with him in forging new paths to invest in church leaders and supported me when the forging was tough.

~ My friend and mentor, Ken Nash, who has been a cheerleader, supporter, and advocate for my ministry as a layperson.

~ To my husband, Bob, and my son, Cameron, who have always been encouraging, regardless of the settings God called us to serve in.

MISSION: POSSIBLE

4th Edition | 2026-2028

Simplifying Church Leadership

A Practical Guide to Simplified Accountable Structure

Kay Kotan & Blake Bradford

MISSION POSSIBLE

4th Edition | 2026-2028

books@marketsquarebooks.com
141 N. Martinwood, Suite 2 Knoxville, Tennessee 37923

ISBN: 979-8-9942008-2-7

Printed and Bound in the United States of America

Editor: Sheri Carder Hood

Cover Design: Kevin Slimp

Post-Process Editor: Ashley Burton

Scripture quotations used with permission from:

Contents

Introduction 1

Section One: Discerning 19

Chapter One: Discerning Simplified Accountable Structure 23

Chapter Two: Discernment Plan 33

Chapter Three: The Big Vote: Saying "Yes" to SAS 43

Chapter Four: Right-Sizing Your Discernment Process 57

Chapter Five: Common Challenges in the Discerning Phase 65

Section Two: Designing 74

Chapter Six: Designing the SAS Leadership Board 77

Chapter Seven: SAS (Governance) and Ministry Teams (Impact) 97

Chapter Eight: Leveraging Leadership: Work Teams 103

Chapter Nine: Right-Sizing Your Leadership Structure 109

Chapter Ten: Common Challenges in the Design Phase 125

Section Three: Equipping 135

Chapter Eleven: Equipping Your Nominations Committee 139

Chapter Twelve: Training Leadership Board Leaders 151

Chapter Thirteen: Accountable Leadership Comes First 159

Chapter Fourteen: Adaptive Leadership 169

Chapter Fifteen: Right-Sizing Your Equipping Process 185

Chapter Sixteen: Common Challenges in the Equipping Phase 189

Section Four: Implementing 201

Chapter Seventeen: Leadership Covenant 205

Chapter Eighteen: Guiding Principles 213

Chapter Nineteen: The Meeting Packet and the Agenda 225

Chapter Twenty: Annual Leadership Rhythms 255

Chapter Twenty-One: Year Two and Beyond 269

Chapter Twenty-Two: Communications 275

Chapter Twenty-Three: Right-Sizing Your Implementation 283

Chapter Twenty-Four: Common Challenges in the Implementing Phase 291

Afterword 295

Index 298

Introduction

Reclaiming Missional Purpose in Church Leadership

It was a meeting like most church board meetings. You walked into the room, over to the credenza, grabbed the minutes, the financial report, and whatever handouts had been run off that afternoon, and took your place at the folding tables. The coffee was lukewarm, and so were you. It's been the fifth meeting in five weeks. What was this? Finance? Trustees? Everyone was shuffling their papers. The pastor opened with a perfunctory prayer. Then the reports began. One after another. Read straight from the page. Word for word.

There were no real decisions to be made, so the group faithfully "received" each report, nodded in agreement, and voted to approve what had already happened. No one was quite sure who technically had a vote, so everyone voted. On paper, everyone had a voice.

There was no conversation about how the church was actually living into its mission of making disciples. No mention of goals or growth. No one could recall the last baptism, or when someone new had joined, or how the congregation was connecting with the neighborhood beyond its walls. Those questions never made it onto the agenda or into leadership conversations.

We were there to listen, to rubber-stamp, and get through the meeting.

When it finally ended, a few people slipped out quietly. Others lingered in the parking lot, leaning against car doors, having the *real* conversations—the ones that carried passion, frustration, hope, and sometimes grief. Those conversations never made it into the minutes either.

You drive home wondering whether all that talking and voting actually mattered. You care deeply about the church. You love these people. And yet something about the process feels stuck—as if the structure were built for another time, when "doing church" meant managing reports rather than leading the mission.

For many congregations, meetings like this have gone on for decades.

If this sounds familiar, you are not alone. And here is the good news. It does not have to remain this way.

There is a better way to lead the church.

A Better Way to Lead

Churches of every size are rediscovering that structure is meant to serve mission, not the other way around.

While differences in polity exist across denominations, most United Methodist congregations (and many other mainline churches) have long operated under a similar model: multiple standing administrative committees such as Finance, Trustees, Staff/Pastor-Parish Relations (S/PPRC), and an Administrative Board or Church Council.

Each committee meets separately, often with overlapping membership but little shared direction. Some leaders serve on three or four committees at once, while others wonder where decisions are really made. In the meantime, the actual ministry of disciple-making is pushed to the margins, crowded out by reports, forms, and bureaucracy.

When we consult with churches, we sometimes begin with two simple exercises:

We ask how many leaders your church elects to each committee and office. Forty? Fifty? 150?! I (Blake) still remember the retired part-time pastor just appointed to a small church that worshipped thirty-five on a good day, who told me she had counted almost sixty elected leaders. How that math worked, I never found out!

We ask the gathered leaders to **"Draw your church's organizational chart."** That's when the fun begins. Few leaders have ever actually tried to map their structure. When they do, we usually receive six or eight different versions, each from the same church! Some charts are rectangles and arrows; others are circles and dotted lines. And often, someone finally shrugs and says, "Well, we're small, so we just all meet together and vote after worship."

No wonder our meetings feel confusing. If we don't share a common understanding of how we're organized (who is responsible for what, how decisions are made, and how all of this relates to our mission), it's no surprise that our energy gets scattered, and our leadership loses focus.

The Structure We Inherited

W. Edwards Deming, a postwar engineer and pioneer in organizational systems, once said, "Every system is perfectly designed to get the result that it does."[1] That's true of the church as well. Our inherited governance and leadership structure was perfectly designed to maintain and preserve the ecclesiastical institution—to ensure nothing too crazy (or creative) happens. It did its job well. But what it was designed for is not what the mission requires today.

Our inherited structure was created in the post-World War II era, when churches were rapidly growing, and average attendance ranged from 150 to 300. The mainline churches' congregational governance structure was designed with multiple layers of checks and balances. Each administrative committee had a clear function and a steady pool of volunteers to fill its seats. *It was designed for stability, not agility.*

But over time, the context changed. Church attendance patterns shifted, communities diversified, and volunteer time became more limited. Yet many congregations are still operating with the same number of committees and meetings, with a structure designed for a church three times its size, and, in most cases, for a culture that no longer exists. The structures that worked so well in the American postwar era of church growth and engagement are simply not nimble enough for the missional church of the twenty-first century seeking to fulfill its disciple-making mission.

Even large congregations, with staff and resources, find themselves constrained by systems built for another time. Multiple layers of approval slow innovation. The structure promotes administrative silos. Committees overlap and duplicate efforts. Passionate people get bogged down in the *process* rather than the *mission*.

The result is the same, whether your church has fifty members or

---

1 W. Edwards Deming, *Out of the Crisis* (MIT Press, 1982), attributed.

five hundred: *Leadership meetings focus on maintenance rather than mobilizing ministry.*

The typical church structure is driving the mission rather than the mission driving the structure! We are simply not accomplishing the mission Jesus intended for our churches. Because of the way churches are structured, the mission is sometimes not even possible. To make matters worse, most leaders know this, yet many are unwilling or unable to change it. Our churches get mired down in the "way we have always done things" and find it difficult, if not impossible, to change the "way we have always done it."

All the churches we work with desire to reach new people (of course, mostly young people with children). Yet some are unwilling to implement the necessary changes to make this happen. We cannot count the times churches tell us that they "want to reach people," but when it comes to making the changes to actually do so, many dig in their heels and resist. Most often, this is because the needed changes will affect those personally resisting them. If changes affect only others, they are acceptable. But once they become personal, changes are much more difficult to accept.

Do you believe the mission is possible? Do you want the mission to succeed? Do you *really* want the mission to succeed? If the answer is YES, we must align all that we do and all that we have as churches and individual disciples with the mission of making disciples of Jesus Christ for the transformation of the world. Yes, making disciples is the very reason each and every church exists. Jesus designed the church to continue his work in spreading the Good News. So again, do we want the mission to succeed—really?

We have always appreciated this quote from Tom Bandy about putting the important missional question into perspective:

> *Are you prepared to stake* ***everything****, change* ***anything****, and do* ***whatever*** *it takes—even if it means altering long familiar habits, redeveloping precious programs, and redeploying sacred assets?*

Tom Bandy, from the foreword of *Winning On Purpose*[2]

---

[2] John Edmund Kaiser, *Winning On Purpose: How To Organize Congregations to Succeed in Their Mission* (Abingdon Press, 2006).

Right-Sizing Leadership for Mission

The good news is that our polity allows for a faithful alternative. *The Book of Discipline of The United Methodist Church* ¶ 247.2 provides an alternative path to structure your church leadership uniquely for missional purposes:

> *The charge conference, the district superintendent, and the pastor, when a pastor has been appointed (see ¶ 205.4), shall organize and administer the pastoral charge and churches according to the policies and plans herein set forth. When the membership size, program scope, mission resources, or other circumstances so require, the charge conference may, in consultation with and upon the approval of the district superintendent, modify the organizational plans, provided that the provisions of ¶ 243 are observed.*[3]

And ¶ 243 reads:

> *Primary Tasks—The local church shall be organized so that it can pursue its primary task and mission in the context of its own community—reaching out and receiving with joy all who will respond; encouraging people in their relationship with God and inviting them to commitment to God's love in Jesus Christ; providing opportunities for them to seek strengthening and growth in spiritual formation; and supporting them to live lovingly and justly in the power of the Holy Spirit as faithful disciples. In carrying out its primary task, it shall be organized so that adequate provision is made for these basic responsibilities: (1) planning and implementing a program of nurture, outreach, and witness for persons and families within and without the congregation; (2) providing for effective pastoral and lay leadership; (3) providing for financial support, physical facilities, and the legal obligations of the church; (4) utilizing the appropriate relationships and resources of the district and annual conference; (5) providing for the proper creation, maintenance, and disposition of documentary record material of the local church; and (6) seeking inclusiveness in all aspects of its life.*[4]

---

[3] *The Book of Discipline of The United Methodist Church,* 2020/2024 (United Methodist Publishing House, 2024). Note: All *Book of Discipline* citations reference the 2024 edition.

[4] *The Book of Discipline.*

Because of the generalized wording in *The Book of Discipline* (BOD) ¶ 247, a variety of ways have been created to streamline church structure. There is no universally perfect structure, and there are always contextual factors to consider. We have walked alongside hundreds of congregations across the country to implement simplified accountable structure, and we will share best practices based on those experiences.

A church must still fulfill the responsibilities of Finance (dollars), Trustees (property, assets, and legal affairs), and Staff/Pastor-Parish Relations (personnel), as well as the strategic governance work of the Church Council. However, fulfilling these responsibilities can now be accomplished with more effective, agile, and efficient methods that reflect more modern systems and practices.

The flexibility offered in ¶ 247.2 and ¶ 243 opened the door to what many now call the **"simplified accountable structure" (SAS)**, sometimes nicknamed the "one-board model." SAS consolidates the key administrative functions of Finance, Trustees, and Staff/Pastor-Parish Relations into one unified **Leadership Board** that oversees mission, vision, and stewardship together. Instead of multiple committees working in isolation, the church has one cohesive team that meets regularly to discern, decide, and stay aligned with the mission.

SAS is missional, strategic, purposeful, and adaptive:

- **Missional**, because leadership energy shifts from maintaining structure to advancing impactful discipleship.
- **Strategic**, because meetings become focused on ministry outcomes rather than reports.
- **Purposeful**, because decisions are clear, authority is defined, and communication is transparent.
- **Adaptive**, because it encourages leaders to continually learn, experiment, and adjust the church's methods to best respond to new opportunities, challenges, and changing circumstances.

The COVID-19 pandemic underscored the need for this kind of clarity and adaptability. Churches operating within a simplified accountable structure were able to respond quickly to ever-evolving requirements and expectations, make timely decisions, and engage their communities through creative ministries. Churches with multiple layers of committees and approvals often struggled to adapt. In an ever-changing world, a structure that supports flexibility and faithful decision making is more important than ever.

Authors' Lenses

We have watched churches of all sizes and contexts (rural, suburban, and urban) experience transformation through simplified accountable leadership. This transformation isn't about copying another church's system. It's about right-sizing your leadership to your current reality, context, values, and mission. Simplified accountable structure is not a shortcut or a "lite" version of church governance. It is a faithful realignment of leadership that enables a church's structure to reflect its calling and supports its sacred responsibility to participate in God's mission and the Great Commission of Jesus Christ.

Our motivation for creating this resource stems from years of walking alongside churches and leaders who long to see their structures serve their missions. Between us, we have worked with thousands of leaders in hundreds of congregations, large and small, rural and urban, helping pastors and laity discover new ways to lead faithfully and effectively. Again and again, we have seen how unclear structures exhaust leaders and limit ministry, and how faithful realignment can open space for healthier leadership and renewed missional focus.

This book is written for the church. While simplified accountable structure draws on leadership practices that may be familiar in other settings, it is intentionally created for congregational life and for communities ordered around shared faith, shared discernment, and shared responsibility for mission. The guidance offered here assumes that leadership decisions are not merely technical choices but spiritual ones that shape how a congregation fulfills its mission.

Simplified accountable structure is grounded in a theological understanding of stewardship. Stewardship is not about control but about trust. Churches are entrusted with people, resources, influence, and responsibility for ministry. The way leadership is structured reflects how that trust is received and practiced. Rather than treating structure as neutral or incidental, this resource approaches leadership design as part of the church's faithful response to what God has entrusted to it.

SAS Resource Hub

A fuller articulation of the theological foundations that undergird simplified accountable structure is available in our online **SAS Resource Hub** (QR code to the left). That theological framework informs this book, but it is not repeated in full here. Interested readers are invited to engage that material alongside this resource as they discern, design, equip, and implement leadership structures that are faithful to their calling.

We intentionally invested a great deal of care and effort to streamline the resource and make it as user-friendly as possible while adding the new content we felt was critical to share. Therefore, throughout this resource, you will find various references to particular SAS Resource Hubs. The SAS Resource Hub is a complimentary shared resource community for the readers of this edition of *Mission Possible*. In addition, we also offer a subscription-based Pro+ SAS Resource Hub that includes everything in the complimentary SAS Resource Hub, along with numerous additional resources and editable forms.

Kay Kotan writes from the perspective of a dedicated layperson who has served as a consultant, coach, conference cabinet member, and conference staff member for over a decade. She has guided thousands of lay and clergy leaders across the country through the process of simplifying and aligning their structures for mission. Her deep conviction is that healthy, accountable leadership creates space for every disciple to serve with clarity and joy.

Blake Bradford, a clergy leader, brings the vantage point of a former district superintendent, conference parliamentarian, cabinet dean, and conference staff member, having served in both large and small church appointments. That experience has allowed him to see the church's leadership systems from every level: local, district, and conference. He has witnessed both the promise and the pitfalls of different structures. He writes as a pastor who has seen firsthand how good structure empowers ministry and how poor structure can slowly drain it.

Together, Kay and Blake's work of writing, coaching, consulting, and leading continues to evolve as they learn from the faithful leaders and congregations who are willing to ask difficult questions and reimagine how the church organizes itself for the mission of making disciples of Jesus Christ who transform the world. Simplified accountable structure is not a quick fix or a "one size fits all" model. It is a faithful framework that helps churches clarify purpose, build trust, and lead with grace in compliance with polity.

A Few Disclaimers

Terminology: Simplified vs. Single Board

You may have heard this model described as the "single-board" or "one-board model." Early in our work, that was the common term used. Over time, we discovered that referring to a simplified structure as a single board or one board often created confusion. Some churches assumed that having a single board meant eliminating all other ministry teams or committees, leading to unhealthy outcomes and even the loss of vital ministries.

Kay experienced this firsthand while working with churches that stopped their ministry activity because they misunderstood the term. In one case, a church nearly closed after discontinuing its ministry teams altogether, believing the single board was meant to handle every ministry and administrative function.

To avoid such confusion, we now use the term "simplified accountable structure." This term better reflects the model's purpose: to simplify decision making and ensure strong accountability and clear alignment with the mission of making disciples. Simplifying without accountable leadership rarely produces fruitfulness. Healthy structure requires both simplicity and shared responsibility.

Personal Interpretations

The practices described in this book reflect our interpretation and application of the current *Book of Discipline of The United Methodist Church*. These insights have been shaped through years of coaching and consulting with hundreds of congregations in many different contexts across the country. Your bishop, district superintendent, or annual conference may provide additional guidance or have policies that differ from what is shared here.

Ultimately, the decision to implement this structure rests with your district superintendent (DS), who has the authority to approve or deny local church structural changes. We encourage every church to remain in close conversation with its superintendent and conference leadership throughout the discernment process.

And if your district superintendent has questions or concerns, you might consider buying them a copy of this book. It's always good to have everyone reading from the same page, both literally and figuratively.

United Methodist-Centered

Our work and examples come primarily from United Methodist congregations. If you are part of another denomination, we invite you to adapt these ideas to your own polity and tradition. The principles of clarity, accountability, and grace are universal and can guide any church seeking to align its leadership structure with its mission.

Avoiding Misuse of the Model

Before we go any further, we need to identify a misunderstanding that has grown in the wake of denominational disaffiliations. In some places, people assumed that a one-board or simplified structure enabled pastors or boards to become authoritarian. That assumption is understandable, especially when a church has experienced harm or heavy-handed decision making. But it is not accurate to the intent of SAS or the accountability that is at the heart of this leadership model.

Authoritative or autocratic leadership is the opposite of accountable leadership. SAS is built on transparency, trust, shared authority, and clear lines of accountability. When practiced as designed, it prevents unilateral decision making, not the other way around.

The real problem in several churches was not SAS. The problem was that alternative structures were adopted with little training, oversight, or understanding of the spiritual maturity required for accountable leadership. Any tool can be misused when it is placed in the wrong hands or implemented without support. A hammer can build a house or break a window. The tool is not the issue. What matters is the way it is used.

SAS is not a shortcut that allows a pastor or a small group to take control. SAS is a framework that requires leaders to work together with clarity, humility, and shared responsibility. When the system is healthy, it slows down ego-driven leadership and speeds up mission-driven leadership. When the system is ignored, the risks are the same as for any other structure: confusion, control issues, and conflict.

We state this clearly because we care about the integrity of the mission and the well-being of congregations. Churches deserve a structure that supports healthy relationships, shared discernment, missional alignment, and accountable leadership. SAS, when practiced faithfully, does exactly that.

Laity, We Need to Talk

Simplified accountable structure assumes a particular kind of lay leadership. This model is not designed for Leadership Boards that want to perform governance without exercising real responsibility, for leaders who like titles but not hard work, or for leaders who prefer endless discussion without shared ownership of outcomes. SAS calls for Leadership Boards that practice real discernment, real decision making, and real accountability to the mission of the church.

This structure entrusts laity with meaningful authority, but that authority is inseparable from trust, preparation, and shared spiritual maturity. Leadership Board members are not representatives of special interests or committees. They are stewards of the whole church. This stewardship requires courage, curiosity, and a willingness to engage adaptive challenges and changes rather than retreat to familiar habits. When laity step fully into this role, SAS becomes a powerful means of aligning vision, releasing people for ministry, and strengthening the church's impact and witness.

Clergy, We Need to Talk

This book assumes a particular kind of pastoral leadership. If you are looking for a simplified structure that allows you to move faster without slowing down for discernment, accountability, attentive listening, or shared leadership, this model is not for you. Simplified accountable structure does not reduce the need for leadership maturity. It raises it—A LOT. SAS works best with pastors who can tolerate complexity without controlling it, who are willing to slow the process down so the right people are formed and equipped, and who understand that authority in the church is always exercised within covenant, open communication, and community.

We need to name this clearly because some pastors will feel convicted by this book. A pastor who avoids accountability, hoards authority, or refuses coaching may experience this model as threatening and may project that discomfort onto SAS itself. When that happens, the issue is not the structure. It is the leadership posture. SAS is designed to surface unhealthy patterns early, not hide them behind endless layers of committees. When practiced faithfully, SAS strengthens pastoral leadership rather than diminishing it, but it does require humility, transparency, and a willingness to be accountable alongside others.

A Living Model

Simplified accountable structure continues to evolve and be refined as church leaders across the country learn and adapt. What we offer here represents the most current, field-tested practices we have seen bear fruit. Every congregation's story is unique, so faithful adaptation will always be necessary. We hope this resource serves not only as a practical guide for the journey toward simplified accountable structure but also as a trusted companion for the ongoing work of leadership in the life of the church.

Explaining Simplified Accountable Structure in 10 Minutes

If this is your first introduction to the church leadership structure, we now call simplified accountable structure (SAS), or if you are trying to explain what it is to someone, this section is for you!

In the United Methodist Church (UMC), our polity has historically called for four administrative committees to care for the "business" of the church: the Trustees Committee, Finance Committee, Staff/Pastor-Parish Relations Committee, and the Church Council. These committees usually consist of six to twelve people serving three-year rotating terms. In addition to these generalities, each committee has its particular nuances and requirements as outlined in our United Methodist Church *Book of Discipline* (the official book that constitutes the law, polity, and doctrine of the United Methodist Church). While the structure and numbers vary from church to church, the average congregation has between twenty-five and seventy-five members serving on these four administrative committees.

While our denominational predecessor bodies have approved a *Book of Discipline* for 200 years, the first edition of the United Methodist *Book of Discipline* was published in 1968, when the United Methodist Church was formed through the union of the Evangelical United Brethren Church and the Methodist Church. In 1968, the church's primary responsibility was to receive the continuous flow of people coming in the door from a church-centric culture and make them official members. The legacy structure was designed for continuity and stability in a time when predictable patterns of attendance, volunteerism, and community life were the norm.

Today's world is very different. The culture is not church-centric. In many places, the church is countercultural. The legacy structures were not built for this complexity or rapid change. The primary responsibility of administrative committees is no longer simply adding names to a membership roll. Leadership must be structured for a shifting time and a missional focus.

In the latest edition (2024) of *The Book of Discipline*, ¶ 247.2 gives a congregation, with the approval of the district superintendent, the opportunity to restructure in order to be more missionally focused. While *The Book of Discipline* outlines in detail how the four administrative committees are traditionally formed, this paragraph is intentionally broad and flexible. Over the past two decades, as hundreds of churches and thousands of leaders have worked with this flexibility, a simplified and accountable structure model for leadership has steadily developed through real-world congregational experiences, refinement, and continual improvement.

Today, the simplified accountable structure model, as defined in the *Mission Possible* series of resources, is generally accepted by district superintendents, cabinets, and bishops across the country, with some districts and conferences applying their own contextual nuances. This SAS approach began as a practical response to the needs of local congregations and has since matured into a widely recognized framework for aligning leadership with mission. Churches have now adopted it in multiple conferences across the country.

Originally, ¶ 247.2 was introduced mainly to help small churches that struggled to find enough people to staff the four required administrative committees. Interestingly, many of the first adopters were larger churches that quickly recognized the model's efficiency and effectiveness.

Questions often arise about whether SAS can function in rural, suburban, urban, small, midsize, or large churches. Across the connection, regardless of the demographics, the consistent experience is that it can. The core elements of accountability and the number of board leaders remain relatively stable across settings. The variations appear in areas such as ministry teams, staffing patterns, Guiding Principles, Leadership Covenants, the existence of childcare or preschools, and multi-point charges. The conclusion is straightforward: simplified accountable structure can work in any size of church and in any context.[5]

To simplify the structure, the four administrative committees (Trustees, Finance, Staff/Pastor-Parish Relations, and Council) cease to exist as separate bodies. They are combined into a single Leadership Board of nine people serving three-year, staggered terms. The Committee on Nominations and Leadership Development nominates this Leadership Board, and the election occurs at a church or charge conference. Instead of four separate meetings, there is now one unified board meeting. Leaders apply a holistic and mission-focused lens to every area of governance. Technically, and in fulfillment of *The Book of Discipline*, all four committees still exist, but they exist within this single Leadership Board. The Leadership Board carries the full responsibilities, qualifications, and authority of each administrative committee, consisting of the Church Council, the Trustees, the Finance Committee, and the Staff/Pastor-Parish Relations Committee. One well-structured, unified meeting now accomplishes what once required four agendas, four committees, and four rounds of decision making.

When simplifying the structure, accountability must be a deeply integrated and highly accepted component of simplification. Without accountability, simplification should not be attempted! When transitioning to accountable leadership, the new Leadership Board shifts

---

[5] There is only one exception to this statement. If a church is unable to fulfill the requirements for a simplified structure (six to nine unrelated people), this is not a structure-related issue (although small churches often seek out this model as the answer to the problem). Instead, we believe there is a need (and perhaps a responsibility) to ask different questions and explore other options. If a church can't meet the minimum legal and polity requirements, is it time to consider other options, such as becoming a house church, a society, a class model, merging with another church, or closing?

from managing the church to governing the church. This significant shift should not be minimized or glossed over. While simplifying is a technical shift, accountability is an adaptive one that takes longer and is much more difficult for most churches to embrace. Thus, this is not the "easy fix" some churches might think or even desire.

Accountable leadership changes not only the agenda but also the conversations, focus, and priorities at the leadership table. The nominations process is adapted in this model as well. The role of the pastor will likely need to shift—and sometimes staff roles will, too. While the new Leadership Board governs in the model of accountable leadership, the pastor leads, the staff (paid and unpaid ministry leaders) equips and coordinates ministry, and the congregation is released to serve in ministry.

The primary purposes and benefits of simplified accountable leadership are these:

1. Removes bottlenecks in the decision-making process (e.g., time, energy, resources, multiple committees/layers, silos, disjointed focus and priorities).

2. Established systems, procedures, and policies are implemented and designed to be both flexible and adaptable.

3. More people are released and available for ministry.

4. Leadership Board is responsible for the church's faithfulness to the Great Commission (making disciples).

5. Leadership Board aligns church resources to the mission and vision.

6. Guiding Principles are in place for efficiency and permission-giving, within healthy boundaries.

7. Leaders are held accountable at all levels.

8. Leadership Board is responsible for focusing on the areas of stewardship, strategic alignment, generative future focus, and accountable leadership.

9. Missional focus, priority, and alignment are nonnegotiables.

Remember, this explanation is provided for your convenience as a general overview of simplified accountable structure. It is neither intended nor recommended to be a substitute for a thorough review of this resource and the additional training and recommendations covered herein. Rather, it is a brief overview intended to provide a basic understanding of the model. This resource lays out the four phases of leading with the simplified accountable structure (Discerning, Designing, Equipping, Implementing) in detail, along with tools and samples to ease the transition and foster clarity as your congregation begins operating with this powerful, effective model of leadership.

The Layout and Why of *Mission Possible 4* (MP4) as a Ministry Resource

Unlike previous versions of *Mission Possible*, this resource is offered in four primary sections. Those four sections reflect the **four** phases of moving to a simplified accountable structure: **Discerning**, **Designing**, **Equipping**, and **Implementing**. Each phase involves different players (leaders) and different seasons. Dividing the process and this resource into phases allows the different players to more closely focus on their particular phase involvement. Please note, we do NOT recommend reading only one section of the resource. Rather, we hope each leader will digest the entire resource and be able to refer back to it more easily as needed throughout the process.

At the end of each section (phase), you'll notice we added two new resources—"Right-Sizing" and "Common Challenges." The "Right-Sizing" chapters identify nuances to help navigate the particular phase based on church size. The "Common Challenges" chapters provide insights on the most common challenges churches face in each phase. We hope that by naming the challenges, church leaders can avoid them altogether or be better equipped to work through them.

We were also very intentional in creating a detailed index. In creating this book as a resource and reference for church leaders, our goal was to provide an easy way to find information on a particular topic within SAS. By providing a detailed index, we hope it provides quicker access to assist you with your questions.

The first phase, **Discerning**, is typically completed just once by a church. The remaining phases (**Designing, Equipping,** and

Implementing) are intended to be useful for both new churches moving into the model and for leaders in churches with an established modified structure as a resource and training tool. These phases, resources, and best practices continue to evolve. Therefore, as leaders, there is always more to learn, understand, and practice as maturing disciples and servant leaders.

In addition to these four sections, you will find links to access digital resources. These are **local church resources** for the existing Church Council, the new Leadership Board, the Committee on Nominations and Leadership Development, judicatory leaders, and Authorized SAS Coaches. They include over thirty resources, such as leadership application samples, a checklist for discernment, organizational charts, FAQs, and sample Guiding Principles, to name just a few. (New resources are always being added!)

We also offer digital access to resources and information for **judicatory leaders,** including district superintendents, presiding elders, cabinet members, congregational developers, and directors of connectional ministries. Because these leaders play a role in approving the local church structure, we must all be on the same page. This is especially true of district superintendents. These resources provide checklists, recommendations, and specific resources for church and charge conferences related to local churches moving to a simplified accountable structure. These judicatory resources can be found in the Judicatory SAS Resource Hub (QR code on right).

Judicatory
SAS Resource Hub

Like the previous version of *Mission Possible 3+*, the layout was created so this resource could be used as both a practical guide and an ongoing leadership resource. During the various leadership seasons, you will want this resource handy as a reference, too, to remind you of those best practices and recommendations. This resource is not meant to be read once and then placed on the bookshelf to collect dust. Rather, it was written with the intent of being close at hand for Leadership Board members, members of the Committee on Nominations and Leadership Development, pastors, coaches, and judicatory leaders as a guide, resource, reference, and tool for a simplified accountable structure.

Throughout this book, we'll explore how to make a thoughtful, faithful transition to SAS. You'll learn the theological grounding, practical tools, and best practices that hundreds of churches across the connection have used to move from bureaucracy to mission. Most of all, you'll discover that leadership, when structured around accountability and grace, becomes a source of energy instead of exhaustion.

We hope and pray that this resource will help churches discern carefully before they act, navigate the process wisely when they do, and emerge more fruitful in ministry. Above all, our prayer and desire are that the church structure serve the mission, helping the church lead with grace, accountability, and courage for the sake of Christ and the transformation of the world.

This book will lead you through both the technical and adaptive shifts needed to align your church with the mission of making disciples. If you came to this book looking only for the technical "how-tos" for moving into a simplified structure so you can have fewer meetings, you may find yourself a bit frustrated. We challenge you to move beyond making a mere technical change. Step by step, we will guide you through this large adaptive change to help your church create a whole new trajectory of vitality with a much deeper, transformational impact.

Your next church meeting doesn't have to be another round of reports and rubber stamps. It can be a space where prayer leads to purpose, where decisions build trust, and where structure truly serves the mission of making disciples of Jesus Christ for the transformation of the world.

If you are ready to embark on a bold, brave journey toward faithfulness in fruitful ministries for you and your church, let the journey begin!

Notes

SECTION ONE

Discerning

He said, "Go out and stand on the mountain before the Lord, *for the* Lord *is about to pass by."*

Now there was a great wind, so strong that it was splitting mountains and breaking rocks in pieces before the Lord, *but the* Lord *was not in the wind,*

and after the wind an earthquake, but the Lord *was not in the earthquake,*

and after the earthquake a fire, but the Lord *was not in the fire,*

and after the fire a sound of sheer silence.

When Elijah heard it, he wrapped his face in his mantle and went out and stood at the entrance of the cave.

Then there came a voice to him that said, "What are you doing here, Elijah?"

1 Kings 19:11–13 (NRSVue)

Discerning Phase Introduction

What is the Discerning Phase?

The Discerning Phase is the first foundational step in considering the adoption and implementation of the simplified accountable structure. This phase includes starting the conversation in the local church to explore SAS, requesting permission from the district superintendent to proceed, informing and communicating with the local congregation regarding the model, and ultimately, the discernment of the congregation and its leaders, whether this is the right model in the right season for the church.

Who Is Involved in This Phase?

The phase is initially led by the Council chair, lay leader, and pastor, with an SAS Discernment Team and a Prayer Team added along the way. Your congregation's leadership will need to consult with your district superintendent, and some conferences may have Authorized SAS Coaches (or choose one from our Authorized SAS Coach network) who can journey with you through the process.

What Is the Timing of This Phase?

Ideally, this phase begins in the first quarter of the calendar year if the church intends to move to the model on January 1 the following year. This phase should not be rushed and will last approximately three to six months.

Understanding the Discerning Phase

Moving to a new structure is potentially a transformational change. Consideration for converting your leadership structure into a simplified accountable structure is no exception. Too often, leaders learn about the model, get excited, and then rush to get through the local church and district approval process. It's not a race! When the proper prayer, communication, information, and process are rushed, the new leadership model is launched on an unstable foundation. Rushing the discernment process often creates a lack of trust in the model and the new leadership. Trust us here, please!

Too many churches unknowingly undermine the potential for a new leadership structure and model by rushing to implement it. Therefore, allow approximately six months for the Discerning Phase, depending on the church's size. Because we have witnessed this unfortunate aftermath far too often, we have created a step-by-step process to help churches discern whether to adopt this model in a healthy, transparent way. Following all these steps in the recommended order provides the church with the opportunity to launch this new structure with a strong foundation rather than one fraught with mistrust, anxiety, and mystery.

The Discerning Phase may feel like it slows the process down (and it does), yet it provides a healthier progression that is worth the investment long term. I (Blake) have assisted in leading a few church building programs over the years. Every time, I am amazed by how long it takes the construction team to complete site work and pour a slab to begin building. I'm not a particularly patient person, so I just want to see steel and masonry going up, drywall hung, and fixtures installed. But we all know that excellent foundation work will ensure the building remains for generations of ministry. Likewise, a leadership structure needs time spent on its foundation if we expect it to withstand the challenges and tensions of ministry in today's world.

SAS Resource Hub

Below is a quick overview of the steps in the Discerning Phase. You will also find the overview in the online SAS Resource Hub (QR code on the left). Refer to the list often to ensure each step is covered and in the proper order.

Twelve Steps to Discerning and SAS Transition

1. Determine why a structure change is needed or desired. Church Council votes to explore SAS after assessing the *why*.
2. Letter from Council chair and pastor to DS seeking permission to explore SAS.
3. Approval from DS to explore SAS and assignment of an Authorized SAS Coach.
4. An Authorized SAS Coach works with leaders to establish an SAS Prayer Team and equip an SAS Discernment Team to lead in learning, organizing, and communicating during the SAS Discerning Phase.

5. The SAS Discernment Team implements a communication and information plan to ensure the congregation is prepared for an accountable leadership model of simplified governance. Prepare for and lead congregational conversations about potential changes utilizing two-way communication. Lead with the *why* and then follow with the *what* and *how*. Create a draft timeline and plan for discernment and communication of the proposed change. Report the findings to the Church Council via a Recommendations Report.

6. Based on congregational feedback, leadership discernment, and the Discernment Team Recommendation Report, the Church Council votes whether to request the adoption of SAS. If a favorable vote results, the pastor and Council chair submit a letter to the DS seeking approval to move to SAS (or not).

7. An Authorized SAS Coach works with the Church Council, along with the Discernment Team and the Nominations Committee, as the Church Council crafts a resolution that defines the new simplified accountable structure (beginning the Designing Phase).

8. The district superintendent consults with the congregational leadership and the Authorized SAS Coach. If the DS approves of the alternate structure, a letter is issued authorizing a called church conference to consider the resolution.

9. Authorized SAS Coach begins to work with the Nominations Committee (see Equipping Phase) and continues to work with leaders on communication strategies and timelines.

10. The church conference is held to adopt the resolution to move to an SAS model.

11. The Committee on Nominations completes its work of discerning and nominating leaders to be elected to the Leadership Board.

12. The church/charge conference is held to elect the nominated Leadership Board members and the members needed to fill in the Committee on Nominations and Leadership Development.

Note: After completing the Discerning Phase, move into Phase Two, Designing; Phase Three, Equipping; and then onto Phase Four, Implementing.

We highly recommend partnering with an Authorized SAS Coach through all four phases for the most effective and healthiest outcome!

CHAPTER ONE

Discerning Simplified Accountable Structure

Starting the Journey

Typically, someone discovers the simplified accountable structure from another church leader, attends a workshop or webinar, or reads some information or a book on the subject. This leader begins to share their curiosity and excitement about the model with other leaders. Before long, the idea of changing the church structure comes up in a meeting (e.g., Staff/Pastor-Parish, Council, Finance, Trustees, or Nominations). Those with more information and more time to think about it try to convince others that it is the best thing since sliced bread. Often, there is some looming deadline, like the fall charge conference, that clamors for a rushed decision. This is the moment to pause, because stakeholders matter more than the schedule.

The conversation for discernment should typically begin in the first quarter of the fiscal year (which is also the calendar year for the majority of churches). This allows the appropriate time for healthy discernment, information sharing, and equipping for the typical fall charge conference rhythm. Since this is again a significant change for congregations, the process needs to go before the appropriate leadership body, the Church Council/Board. While conversations might have sprouted in another group, the discerning phase needs to be owned and implemented by the Church Council.

Step One (1 of 12) in the Discerning Phase:

Determine why a structure change is needed or desired. Church Council votes to explore SAS after assessing the why.

The first step of the Church Council is not a vote to approve a new structure. NO! STOP! The Church Council first needs to fully understand the fundamentals of the model and how it will shift the leadership culture of the church. You can start with the ten-minute overview in this book or with the overview videos of SAS on kaykotan.com or blakebradford.org.

Once there is a general understanding of the model, it is now important for the Council to explore *why* this change of structure is needed or desired. The desire to implement a change often fast-forwards us right to the *what*, but the *why* is the most important factor in considering the change. Failing to spend discovery time understanding and articulating the *why* is like pouring concrete for a foundation without first installing footings, gravel, and rebar. The foundation will not provide adequate support for the structure built on it, and the structure will likely crumble and crack.

The *Why*

Before making any change, whether in governance or in implementing a new ministry, we must begin with the *why*. So many times, when organizations go through changes, we lead with the *what* and the *how*. We communicate what we desire or what steps we need to accomplish. However, it is most helpful to lead with the *why*. In other words, *why* is this change needed? *Why* will this change make a difference in the life of the congregation? People are often more motivated by the *why* than the *what*. In our experience, when we lead with the *what*, people come to their own conclusions about the *why*. These self-conclusions are often misleading because they are not well-informed.

Most churches we work with find one or more of the following five elements to be the driving motivators in considering structure changes: efficiency, alignment, missional focus, accountability, and adaptability.

- **Efficiency:** In its traditional structure, many church decisions must run through multiple committees. Not only are there multiple stops on the "permission" train, but the schedule is inefficient as well! One must sometimes wait a month or more for the next scheduled meeting on the permission train schedule. Those trying to work the process often find themselves discouraged, frustrated, and may even give up. Often, churches also have their congregation members tied up in administrative tasks and committees, leaving no one to do the ministry. The more time disciples are dealing with administrative issues, the less time they have for ministry in the neighborhood. By simplifying governing structures, more disciples can put their spiritual gifts to work in ministry rather than spend time in meetings.

- **Alignment:** Most churches find themselves working in silos. One team or committee has no idea what the other is doing. It's like a car with each of the four wheels going in different directions. Sometimes scheduling or resource conflicts arise. There is internal competition for people, power, funding, and staff time. The Trustees move forward with a maintenance plan without consulting the Staff/Pastor-Parish Relations Committee (S/PPRC), the body responsible for the custodial staff budget. The Finance Committee prepares a budget without taking into account the Church Council's new priorities. Groups do not seem to be pulling in the same direction for a common purpose or focus. Some churches operate as multiple mini-churches or groups within one church. Alignment with the mission and vision is about being faithful to our purpose, not about reaching consensus. Alignment with our mission and vision needs to be nonnegotiable.

- **Missional focus:** It still astonishes us that, when you ask the average person in the pew why the church exists, they often answer, "to serve me," "to help me grow in my faith," or "to provide pastoral care to the flock." While those are all great benefits for members, they are not the church's foundational purpose. Somewhere along the line, we have lost sight of our purpose. We have become a nation of churches where so many have an internal focus on being served rather than an external focus on making disciples. A change in structure to fulfill a missional focus usually helps us shift more time, energy, resources, and disciples into ministry while using fewer resources for administration. In my (Blake's) conference, we describe this as "unleashing laity for missional leadership." The more time and effort we spend on governance and strategy, the fewer leaders are available for the impactful work of forming, equipping, and sending disciples.

- **Accountability:** For some reason, there is a belief that because the church consists mostly of "volunteers," no one can be held accountable (As an aside, we prefer "serving disciples" instead of "volunteers"). Think about that for a minute. If this life is preparing us for eternal life, where did we ever come up with the idea that accountability for fruitfulness in the life of the church and as a disciple is not reasonable? Should this not be the place where we are held most accountable? We are Wesleyans, and Methodist Christians have accountability hard-wired into us from our history of class meetings and the early societies and conferences. We need to reclaim this missional accountability today.

- **Adaptability:** For years, most of our changes in congregations were technical in nature. We had tried-and-true tools and methods at our disposal. Innovative and resourceful congregations tested solutions to ministry problems and provided roadmaps for other congregations to follow their recipes for success. Most of these recipes have broken down due to the sheer magnitude and speed of changes over the last decade or two. Adaptive leadership is about creating solutions and conducting experiments where no roadmap or recipe is yet available. Rapid cultural change is not going away. Adaptability calls for us to regain our pioneering roots, which Jesus modeled and Wesley reinforced. We must forgo our habits of being settlers in pews and once again use our pioneering roots to be a movement. Simpler structure must be enthusiastically invited into our congregations for lay leadership to thrive, creativity and innovation nurtured, to maintain accountability, and to be nimbler.

Don't Use a *Book of Discipline* Response For a Matthew 18 Problem

Please, heed this WARNING. If you are considering simplifying your structure but are unable or unwilling to also begin practicing accountability, don't move into simplification. All churches could (and we suggest that they need to) practice accountable leadership. No church should move to simplified accountable leadership without accountability.[6] Time and time again, churches that have moved into a simplified structure without accountable leadership practices have faced severe pushback, conflict, decline, and flat-out ugliness. It is all but impossible to hold a committee accountable. Individuals are held accountable. Accountability keeps us from falling into the traps of being pastor-centered churches, churches of silos, churches that hoard resources, or churches of controlling cliques.

Also, be honest with yourself about your motivations. If the motivation for seeking this change in structure is a pretext or passive-aggressive attempt to get a particularly difficult member off a committee, hit the brakes. In those cases, the congregation needs to work on communication, healthy boundaries, healthy conflict management, and accountability. No structure, no matter how simple or elegant, can fix problems of relational health. Don't use a *Book of Discipline* ¶ 247.2 response to a Matthew Chapter 18:15-17 problem. We will share much more about accountable leadership in Phase Three: Equipping.

Once the *why* has been identified and communicated, the church needs to consider the process to further explore a new structure with accountable leadership through prayer, discernment, and congregational conversations. This process should not be rushed.

Sometimes leaders are anxious to "get going" and rush through to the execution. This is a fundamental mistake! You are better off slowing the process down. Be intentional and thorough as you walk the congregation through this important time of discernment. Clear, complete, and patient preparation will pay generous dividends as you proceed. This intentional process of discernment continues in the next chapter.

---

6 One Exception: The ONLY time a simplified structure without accountability makes sense is when a church is in its final life stages, and the church has intentionally decided to live out its remaining days caring for itself and its facilities. The church has chosen to enter "hospice." The church is sent a "hospice" chaplain to care for the small remnant congregation, hold their hands, and conduct their funerals. A small team of lay leaders is needed to fulfill fiduciary responsibilities and to ensure that a legacy is left to launch new faith communities.

The REAL *Why*

Fewer people making decisions is NOT the goal of moving to a simplified accountable leadership structure. The goal of any structural change must ultimately be to more effectively implement the organization's mission/purpose. For churches, that mission is to make disciples of Jesus Christ who transform the world. All organizations need a governing, strategic structure that will help make this holy mission a reality.

Some churches explore simplified governance because they no longer have enough active members to fill every slot in the required administrative committees. While SAS may relieve that pressure, it must never be the driving purpose. Structural simplification, when paired with accountability, is not about consolidating power. It is about creating a clearer pathway for flexible, mission-focused decisions and unleashing more lay leadership to spend less time in meetings and more time in ministry.

Often, when we share information with church leaders about a simplified accountable leadership structure during a workshop, a critic in the crowd will share the metaphor of moving deck chairs on the Titanic. There is a truth in the statement: a change in structure will not fix a relational dilemma or missional apathy. A simplified accountable leadership structure can, however, provide greater clarity in roles, reconnect responsibility and authority, and bring missional focus and alignment to your congregation and its leadership.

To return to the metaphor about deck chairs on the sinking ship, a simplified accountable leadership structure isn't about the deck chairs; it is about the leadership. A bit of Titanic history: safer navigation was not implemented through the ice field because the White Star Line chairman pressured the ship's captain to make good time (arrive earlier than expected) on the maiden voyage. It is the Titanic's captain, its officers, and its owners who ignored the radio warnings about icebergs, failed to provide lookout officers with binoculars and searchlights, turned the ship the wrong way, decided to travel full speed through icy waters, and under-equipped the ship's lifeboats. The deck chairs were fine. It was the folks on the ship's bridge who caused the trouble. A simplified accountable leadership structure is about who is on the "ship's bridge" and how they are empowered (and held accountable) to lead the church in fulfilling its disciple-making mission. *At its core, a simplified accountable structure changes the leadership culture of a congregation.*

We also offer a warning in our book *Impact! Reclaiming the Call of Lay Ministry*:[7] "Changing the number of people around the leadership table without also changing the leadership culture will only result in an isolated and ineffective board."

Chapters 20 and 21 of the Gospel of John are instructive here. After the resurrected Jesus appeared to Mary, the gathered disciples, and Thomas, Peter returned to what he knew best: fishing in Lake Galilee. He even went back to fishing on the same comfortable side of the boat. And the disciples were catching nothing. It took another appearance of Jesus for them to try fishing from the other side. And this time their net was filled! It was so full that they couldn't even haul their net into the boat. After a meal with the Risen Christ, Peter and Jesus have some words, including Jesus' imperative, "Follow Me!" Peter couldn't go back to his comfortable habits and remain fruitful in Christ. He had to change to become the disciple Jesus needed him to be to fulfill God's mission.

That is why discovering and articulating your *why* is so important. We have both seen many churches that changed their *structures* but did not change their *behaviors* or leadership *culture*. They continued to use the same agenda and the same decision-making processes. And, therefore, they kept on having the same conversations at the leadership table. After becoming frustrated, these leaders either reached out for help or scrapped the modified structure altogether. A clear *why* moves a structural change from just a technical modification into a transformative opportunity.

---

7 Kay Kotan and Blake Bradford, *Impact! Reclaiming the Call of Lay Ministry* (Market Square Books, 2018).

Who Are We Now?

To get to your missional *why* for a new structure and leadership model, you and your fellow church leaders need to fully understand and describe the structure of your current leadership system. How does your church make decisions and set goals *now?* Does your official nominations report, submitted and approved at the charge conference, actually reflect your system of governance? Or are there unwritten rules or unelected people, such as a matriarch or patriarch, that have a de facto veto power over your church's decisions? As a church, be honest with yourselves. If your congregation has lingering issues of mistrust or a history of power-grabbing cliques, then a change in governance structure will not be a magic wand. Instead, a structural change will likely deepen and intensify your internal mistrust. Congregational health and a refocus on Christ's mission for the church must come first.

As you consider the church's current leadership structure, think in terms of a system. Often, when we work with congregations, the current structure is described by the people in terms of their relationships with one another. While relationships are vitally important in ministry, now is the time to think systematically—about roles, responsibilities, limits to authority, policies, and committee job descriptions.

SAS Resource Hub

To fully prepare for discussions about a structure change, perform a Leadership Inventory and Analysis. This resource can be found in the SAS Resource Hub.

Once the *why* has been identified and communicated, the church needs to consider the process to further explore a new structure with accountable leadership through prayer, discernment, and congregational conversations. In the next chapter, we will recommend that your Church Council create a Discernment Team to lead the congregation through this process. We also describe how an Authorized SAS Coach can walk alongside that team, offering guidance, resources, and best practices to support a thorough and healthy discernment journey.

Church Council Vote to Explore

The Church Council's first decision point is to determine whether they wish to enter the Discerning Phase to *explore* a simplified, accountable structure with their congregation. That's it. No decision to adopt the model (yet). It's too soon. There is not enough known or understood to adopt, let alone implement, SAS. It is simply the time to decide whether to enter into a season of prayer and discernment to *explore* the model.

Once the Church Council has taken adequate time to understand the key factors of a simplified accountable structure and explore the motivating reasons (the *why*) to consider SAS, only then is the Church Council ready to vote on whether this is the right season and model for the church to *explore* in dialogue with the entire congregation.

If, after faithfully exploring the model and the *why*, and after obtaining a positive vote from the Church Council to explore, you are now ready for the next step. The next step after a vote to proceed is for the pastor, Council chair, and/or lay leader to write a letter to the district superintendent formally requesting permission to explore the SAS model of leadership structure. The United Methodist Church *Book of Discipline* allows simplification of the governance structure, including the *four administrative committees of traditional structures* in ¶ 247.2, in partnership with the district superintendent. In the letter, include the missional purposes for moving to SAS (your *why*). A congregation can move forward with simplifying its structure only in partnership with, and with the approval of, the district superintendent.

Step Two (2 of 12) in the Discerning Phase:

Letter from Council chair and pastor to DS seeking permission to explore SAS.

During my season as a district superintendent, I (Blake) required a letter from the pastor, the lay leader, and the Church Council chair to confirm that these pre-discernment steps have been followed and that there is buy-in from key leaders. You may proceed in exploring

SAS Resource Hub

the model only after receiving permission from your district superintendent. You'll find the "Initial Consultation with Your DS" form in the online SAS Resource Area. This is the form Blake used with churches exploring SAS for purposes of both documentation and to ensure all bases were covered in the process. This form, along with the "12 Steps to Discerning and SAS Transitions," can also be found online in our SAS Resource Hub.

Notes

CHAPTER TWO

Discernment Plan

You have determined your missional *why*—your purpose in making a structural and leadership change. Amen!

Hopefully, your real *why* goes well beyond simply having fewer meetings and instead focuses more on leading your congregation to impact your mission field. Your district superintendent has approved your exploration of the simplified accountable structure model by entering into the Discerning Phase. Now you and your fellow leaders will need to enter a period of continued discernment and intentional communication.

I (Kay) have a confession to make. When I first started working with pastors and churches, simplifying the church's structure (how decisions are made) seemed like a no-brainer. After all, I had lived this model in corporate America and in my own business. Why wouldn't every church be running towards this structure? I had also lived through the pains and struggles of navigating a cumbersome structure in my own church as a layperson. Again, I could not fathom why churches were not sprinting to their district superintendents' offices to gain permission to move into this structure. And then it happened—reality check! What I have come to understand is that this is a very difficult shift for most churches. It is challenging for a host of reasons. Through my coaching and consulting, I have discovered those reasons include:

- Lack of trust
- Fear of change
- Misunderstanding of the model
- Misunderstanding of the purpose
- Insufficient transparency

- Lack of leadership adaptability
- Unwillingness for leaders to surrender their leadership seat and its real or perceived power
- Fear of the unknown
- The perception of too much power consolidation
- Unresolved conflict
- Nostalgia

Because of these potential or existing barriers, a church must spend time FIRST discerning, preparing, teaching, and communicating about this possible shift of structure and leadership culture. Trust us, trying to do this *after* the new structure is in place is not wise and will likely end in disaster.

As a former district superintendent, I (Blake) had a few additional reasons to ask that leaders take the transition process patiently and intentionally. As readers of this book, you and your team have researched different models of church structuring, downloaded charts and lists, and have spent hours poring through *The United Methodist Book of Discipline.* You have discerned your *why*, and you understand the governance architecture of the structure you are building. However, your average church member has not done this homework nor has spent the time considering and discussing the model as you have. While they may (emphasis on "may") trust you enough to vote their approval of a new structure, a problem will show up a year or two later—after the first set of leaders rotate off the board, or when your pastor is appointed to a new congregation. Then the church is left with a governance system that nobody understands or knows how to run, and it winds up at the DS's office seeking to undo the whole transition. I have spoken with congregational leaders who said they inherited a "sports car of a structure," but nobody in leadership knows how to drive a stick.

So, be intentional and patient in communicating the shift to a simplified accountable leadership structure. We offer the continued steps in the Discerning Phase to assist you in considering this transition. You are now ready for the next step.

Step Three (3 of 12) in the Discerning Phase:

Approval from DS to explore SAS and assignment of an Authorized SAS Coach

It is our hope and desire that your district superintendent has a ministry partner who is an Authorized SAS Coach. If this is the case, the district superintendent will dispatch an Authorized SAS Coach to assist your congregation through the Discerning Phase. Consider your Authorized SAS Coach as a ministry partner, just as the coach is a ministry partner with your district superintendent. If your district does not have an Authorized SAS Coach, check whether your conference has one. If your conference does not have an Authorized SAS Coach, check out our directory of Authorized SAS Coaches.

SAS Authorized Coaches

The Case for Authorized SAS Coaching

Your authors have some of the deepest and longest-tenured experience in the SAS leadership model. It is now a focus of our ministry, and as a result, we continue to invest significant time and energy in equipping leaders in the model and in identifying where congregations struggle most so that helpful tools and resources can be developed. More importantly, we have continued to invest, learn, and evolve the model over more than a decade. As we (Kay and Blake) continue to invest in SAS with hundreds of churches and thousands of leaders across the country, several evolutions and best practices have emerged (and continue to evolve).

Unfortunately, not everyone who claims to coach in the simplified accountable structure has been trained or kept up to date on the evolution, the latest resources, and the current best practices. There are also various interpretations of a modified structure in the church world. Some may not even be familiar with this resource. This is why we have launched SAS coach training and a network for Authorized SAS Coaches. Coaches are authorized for a period of one year at a time after extensive training and coaching with one of us. Authorized SAS Coaches have access to our latest resources and a community of coaches with whom to share ideas and ask questions. Authorized SAS Coaches join quarterly calls with this book's authors for further training, emerging topics, latest learnings from the mission field, and updates on best practices. Churches that invest in Authorized SAS Coaches, by and large, have a significantly healthier experience, launch SAS with greater effectiveness, and avoid common potholes other churches encounter.

To clarify, we HIGHLY RECOMMEND an AUTHORIZED SAS COACH partner with you during all four phases. It is well worth the investment!

Step Four (4 of 12) in the Discerning Phase:

An Authorized SAS Coach works with leaders to establish an SAS Prayer Team and equip an SAS Discernment Team to lead in learning, organizing, and communicating during the SAS Discerning Phase.

Step Five (5 of 12) in the Discerning Phase:

The SAS Discernment Team implements a communication and information plan to ensure the congregation is prepared for an accountable leadership model of simplified governance. Prepare for and lead congregational conversations about potential changes utilizing two-way communication. Lead with the why and then follow with the what and how. Create a draft timeline and plan for discernment and communication of the proposed change. Report the findings to the Church Council via a recommendations report.

Your SAS Discernment Team

With the help of your Authorized SAS Coach, after approval to explore SAS from your district superintendent, it is now time for you to assemble an SAS Discernment Team. This work team has no Disciplinary authority, so its members do not need to be officially nominated by your Nominations Committee. The SAS Discernment Team is generally identified by the pastor, the Council chair, and/or the lay leader. A team size of approximately five to seven people is generally adequate. Those serving on this team should reflect these qualities:

- A clear understanding of the SAS model
- A clear understanding of the motivating reason *why* the Church Council voted to explore the SAS model
- Strong communication skills
- Respected in the congregation
- Awareness of the key congregational, small group, and individual conversations necessary for two-way communication to share information and receive feedback
- Dependability in following through on plans in a timely manner
- Strong listening and discernment skills
- Capacity to create and execute a thorough communication plan

Keep in mind the need to assemble a team that can communicate with the variety of people and groups within your congregation. While the pastor may consult with the Discernment Team, we recommend that the pastor not serve on the team or lead any discernment meetings or conversations. Pastors are often moved to different congregations. In addition, this is a discernment period for congregational structure. The decision to make such a change must be owned by the congregation—not only by the pastor.

The SAS Discernment Team will be tasked with developing and implementing a plan of discernment for the congregation. This plan will include prayer, communication, information, conversations, timelines, feedback loops, and the creation of a discernment report for the Church Council. The Authorized SAS Coach is the resource person and accountability partner for the team. The SAS Discernment Team typically does this work in the first or early second quarter of the year.

Building Your SAS Congregational Discernment Plan

A well-designed SAS Discernment Plan helps the whole congregation understand what is being considered, why it matters, and how they can participate prayerfully and thoughtfully in the process. Here is what the Discernment Team should consider including as they build the Congregational Discernment Plan:

1. Church Council Overview and Rationale

    - The Church Council should craft a short 1–2 paragraph overview articulating what led the Council to its recommendation to enter this Discerning Phase.
    - This overview should clearly express the *why* behind the Council's recommendation, naming the factors and hopes that prompted their vote.
    - The Discernment Team will use the overview during their discerning work with the congregation.

2. Communication About the Decision to Enter Discernment

    - Communicate that the Church Council made the decision to enter the Discerning Phase after careful consideration and conversation.
    - Make it abundantly clear that this is a time of exploration. No decision has been made to adopt the model.

3. Clarification that the Congregation Will Decide

    - Ensure the congregation understands that they will have the opportunity to vote at a church conference if the discernment period leads the Church Council to request such a vote and if the district superintendent approves calling a church conference for that purpose.

4. Centering the Process in Prayer
   - Emphasize that this is a time of prayer and discernment.
   - We suggest forming an SAS Prayer Team to help keep the focus on the church's missional impact.
   - Prayers should intentionally ask for guidance and clarity on the model and the timing.
   - Ask God to provide wisdom and clarity on whether this model will help the church be more faithful and effective in its mission to make disciples.
5. Provide a Clear SAS Overview
   - You may want to use the "10-minute" overview provided earlier in this book.
   - You are also welcome to use the SAS overview video and the FAQ available in the SAS Resource Hub.
6. Plan for Multiple Congregational Conversations
   - Create a plan to conduct multiple conversations with groups within the congregation that share the why, provide an overview of the model, and offer an opportunity for congregants to ask questions.
   - It is most effective to meet with people in their existing groups (Sunday school classes, small groups, choir, United Methodist Men, United Women in Faith, etc.) These gatherings allow for sharing information, answering questions, and receiving feedback.
   - Invite all active attenders and members who are not already part of an existing group to participate in a conversation.
   - Ensure everyone is invited and has the opportunity to attend at least one gathering.
   - Host multiple rounds of conversations, if needed. This builds transparency and trust.
7. Gather Questions, Concerns, and Insights
   - During each conversation, ask what questions or concerns people have.

- Inquire how they think this model might be helpful for the church.
- Offer follow-up opportunities for additional questions or feedback.
- The SAS Discernment Team should keep track of the feedback it receives, including common questions, concerns, and what excites members about the model.

8. Provide Additional Communication Channels

   - Create additional ways for people to receive information and contact the SAS Discernment Team with questions or comments. This can include newsletters, email, text messages, Facebook posts, bulletin inserts, and any other communication tools your church regularly uses.
   - Overcommunicating is all but nonexistent, so err on the side of what may feel like over-communicating!

9. Offer an Equipping Experience for Deeper Learning

   - Consider providing a small-group equipping experience for those who want a deeper dive into understanding SAS, using *Mission Possible 4* as the resource.
   - The Church Council itself may wish to participate in or lead this equipping opportunity to strengthen its own discernment.
   - Your Authorized SAS Coach may be willing to assist with this equipping component.

10. Create a Full Discernment Timeline

    - Develop a clear timeline for congregational conversations, communication efforts, equipping opportunities, and the deadline for the Church Council's decision.

11. Maintain Regular Contact with Your Authorized SAS Coach

    - Continue to be in conversation with your Authorized SAS Coach regarding questions, updates, and progress.

12. Coordinate with the SAS Prayer Team

    - Keep in contact with the SAS Prayer Team.
    - Provide them with the schedule of conversations so they can pray specifically for each gathering.

- Receive feedback, insights, or discernment reflections from the Prayer Team.

13. Invite the Entire Congregation into Prayer

    - Challenge the congregation to be in prayer throughout the Discerning Phase for a faithful next step.
    - You may provide a biblical reference or shared prayer to help guide and unify these prayers.

14. Prepare a Summary Report for the Church Council

    - Provide a summary report of all conversations and feedback for the Church Council.
    - This report should include:
        - The number of congregational meetings and their attendance
        - One-on-one conversations with key stakeholders
        - Common questions, concerns, and affirmations expressed
    - This report presents the team's recommendations and helps inform the Council's decision on whether to recommend adoption of the SAS model.

15. Disband the SAS Discernment Team

    - Once the team has completed all steps in the process and prepared the summary report, the SAS Discernment Team has completed its work, so thank the team for their service.
    - From this point forward, the SAS Discernment is now back in the hands of the Church Council.

Notes

CHAPTER THREE

The Big Vote: Saying "Yes" to SAS

The Council Has the Ball

The SAS Discernment Team has completed its work and delivered the congregational feedback, summary, and recommendations to the Church Council. The SAS Prayer team has been praying for congregational and leadership discernment, as well as clarity on whether SAS is the right model and whether this is the right season for the congregation. We hope the members of the Church Council have also been in an attitude of prayer for discernment in this season.

Step Six (6 of 12) in the Discerning Phase:

Based on congregational feedback, leadership discernment, and the Discernment Team Recommendation Report, the Church Council votes whether to request the adoption of SAS. If a favorable vote results, the pastor and Council chair submit a letter to the DS seeking approval to move to SAS (or not).

It is now time for the Church Council to make its decision on a recommendation. Here are some questions you might consider as you prepare to make this important decision:

- Is simplified accountable structure the right structure and leadership model for the church?
- Is this the right time to move to this model?
- Do we understand that fewer people will be in administrative leadership so that more people can be released for the most important work of the church: ministry?

- Are we prepared for the hard work of learning the new model and leaning into accountable leadership?
- Is the congregation generally supportive and trusting of such a structure change?
- Do we understand that we are embarking on a change in the church's leadership culture, and are we ready to take this important journey?
- Was the congregational discernment process thorough, and did we receive the feedback needed to make the decision before us?
- Are we making this decision with our eyes fully open to the pros and cons of both staying in our current structure and shifting to a simplified accountable structure?
- Are we willing to invest in leadership and coaching if we decide to move forward with SAS to set ourselves up for the best possible outcome?
- Is this the next faithful next step for our church?

It is now time for the Church Council to vote on whether to proceed to the next step and request permission from the district superintendent to officially adopt a simplified accountable structure.

Step Seven (7 of 12) in the Discerning Phase:

An Authorized SAS Coach works with the Church Council, along with the Discernment Team and the Nominations Committee, as the Church Council crafts a resolution that defines the new simplified accountable structure (beginning the Designing Phase).

In coordination with your district superintendent and Authorized SAS Coach, and the Committee on Nominations will walk alongside the Church Council to create the resolution for the change in church structure, which can be found in the SAS Resource Hub. Steps 7 and 8 work in unison so that the resolution can be sent to the DS along with the formal request to move to a modified structure.

Make copies of the completed resolution available for the congregation to review in advance and offer opportunities for questions and feedback. This ensures that questions are addressed before the church conference. *The church conference is not the time for questions to be raised for the first time.*

Decide on a name for the new structure. There is more about this in the Designing Phase, but if you choose to use something other than "Leadership Board" for the name of your new simplified accountable structure, be sure to update the name in the sample resolution to be used at the church conference and the formal request to the DS introduced earlier in this chapter. Both of these can be found in the SAS Resource Hub.

SAS Resource Hub

Formal Request to the DS

If the Church Council votes favorably to request approval to move to a simplified accountable structure, the pastor, Council chair, and/or lay leader will write a letter to the district superintendent formally requesting approval to move to a simplified accountable structure through a called church conference. Use the sample form, "Formal DS Request," that you'll find in the Pro+ SAS Resource Hub to help draft the letter's content.

Pro+SAS Resource Hub

In the second letter to the district superintendent, include the following information:

- A formal request for approval of a modified organizational plan, based on ¶ 247.2 of the *Discipline*
- A listing of the committees that will be combined in the new Leadership Board
- A brief overview of the discernment process used by the congregation to come to their recommendation
- A draft of the resolution that will be used to transition to the new structure

Step Eight (8 of 12) in the Discerning Process:

The district superintendent consults with the congregational leadership and the Authorized SAS Coach. If the DS approves of the alternate structure, a letter is issued authorizing a called church conference to consider the resolution.

Once the DS receives the letter, we strongly recommend that the superintendent consult with the Authorized SAS Coach for feedback on the congregation's process. The DS may also speak with the pastor, Council chair, lay leader, and/or the SAS Discernment team leader for additional clarity.

The district superintendent has full authority to approve or decline the request. Keep in mind that the DS may have information your congregation does not, such as upcoming appointment changes or district-level considerations that impact the decision.

Be aware that each district superintendent has their own unique experience and understanding of SAS. This depends on how widely SAS has been implemented in the district/conference, as well as on their personal experience in local church leadership. Also know that each district superintendent has to work with dozens of different local church structures in their district. So, be clear and concise about your plans, ask plenty of questions during consultation meetings with your DS, and ensure that both the congregation and the DS share the same expectations, understandings, and timelines.

A well-prepared, well-documented request helps build trust and positions the congregation for a smooth transition into the next phase of SAS implementation.

Step Nine (9 of 12) in the Discerning Phase:

Authorized SAS Coach begins to work with the Nominations Committee (see Equipping Phase, Chapter 11) and continues to work with leaders on communication strategies and timelines.

After the Request to the DS

If the district superintendent approves the request, there are four next steps to take right away:

1. Inform the congregation about the decision of the Church Council to request approval and the district superintendent's approval to move to SAS.

2. Schedule the church conference with your district superintendent and provide notice to the congregation.

3. Inform your Authorized SAS Coach of the approval so the coach can begin to work with the Committee on Nominations and Leadership Development. There are two tasks to begin with the Nominations Committee. First, the Nominations Committee and Council need to collaboratively design the official structure that will be voted on by the church conference (there is a lot more to say about this in the Designing Phase section).

4. Second, the coach will need to equip the Nominations Committee on how to discern and nominate the slate of members they will eventually recommend for election. This will allow the Nominations Committee to "hit the ground running" as soon as the new structure is approved. You will read more about this training in the Equipping Phase, but don't wait until after all the votes to begin training and preparing your Nominations Committee.

We know this discernment journey takes effort, and we're grateful for the thoughtful work you've put into it. As you move toward the next step, the next pages will guide you in preparing for the church conference, where members will have the opportunity to vote on adopting the simplified accountable leadership model.

Every step taken during this Discerning Phase has been intentional to build trust, transparency, and a congregational buy-in so that when the new Leadership Board takes shape and begins to guide the church, they can lead from this strong foundation.

Preparing for the Church Conference

The district superintendent has approved your Church Council's formal request to move to a simplified accountable structure. You are now entering the final stages of the Discerning Phase. This final stage is the ultimate discernment of your congregational members as they vote to approve (or not) the SAS model. This part of the Discerning Phase is likely to be completed in the summertime. This ensures the previous steps of informational conversations, feedback loops, Church Council vote, and DS approval have had sufficient time, but it still leaves time for the Nominations Committee to be equipped for their new work before the fall charge conference, which will vote on the nominated leaders for the new simplified accountable structure.

Step Ten (10 of 12) in the Discerning Phase:

The church conference is held to adopt the resolution to move to an SAS model.

This is no time to let up on the communication strategy. Be sure to keep your congregation informed:

- What is the date, time, and location of the church conference?
- Where will the church conference be held (e.g., sanctuary, fellowship hall)?
- How does voting at a church conference work (e.g., only members present can vote)?
- Will the vote be by written ballot or a show of hands?

- Who will preside at the church conference? District superintendent? Presiding elder?
- Be clear that SAS will be the only item voted on at the church conference and that no other agenda items may be considered or added. Don't wait until the charge conference to offer a venue for the congregation to ask questions about the proposed structure. Publish copies of the resolution well in advance and create opportunities for the congregation to fully understand the structure well in advance of the vote.
- Members will vote only to approve the structure. The new leaders will be nominated by the Committee on Nominations and Leadership Development and elected by the regular fall charge conference if/when the structure is approved.
- Ministry teams are selected, not elected, in this new model. Therefore, the only two elected "committees" are the Leadership Board and the Committee on Nominations.

The Approval Two-Step

Please note that we **strongly recommend** a two-step approval process. The first step is for a church conference to approve transitioning to a new structure and leadership model. The second step is to approve the nominees for the new Leadership Board. Let us explain our reasoning for this recommendation.

First, we recommend a church conference (with congregational members voting) rather than a charge conference (with only specific leaders voting). We are often asked, "Why require a *church* conference, not a *charge* conference?" I thought we were trying to make things simpler?" We recommend that the meeting to transition to a new structure be a church conference, as we believe as many people as possible should be involved in a decision of this magnitude. Numerous people are about to be removed from elected office in the church. Both the operation and the process to adopt SAS require enormous trust. A church conference allows every present professing (baptized and confirmed) member, not just the board, to make this important decision.

There needs to be a clear sense that a small minority of the leadership never pushed through this change to cling to or gobble up power for themselves. A church conference provides the greatest participation and transparency in the decision-making process. Of course, any calling of a charge or church conference must be done in consultation with your district superintendent or presiding elder, but we highly recommend a churchwide vote to adopt this model to increase transparency and accountability and to ensure the new Leadership Board's legitimacy.

Secondly, we recommend that only the new structure itself be considered at the church conference. It is presumptuous to present both the new structure and the names of the new leadership at the same time. Voting on both at the same time also does not allow the Nominations Committee sufficient time to be trained on the new model.

Preparing and Customizing the Resolution

SAS Resource Hub

We recommend that either the pastor or the Church Council chair work with the DS to prepare the process and the resolution to present to the congregation for the vote to move to SAS. A Sample "Church Conference Resolution for Structure Transition" can be found in the online SAS Resource Hub.

The resolution for the structure change should be made available ahead of time for members to review. This might provide the opportunity to answer questions ahead of time and clear up any misconceptions. If it is not made available in advance, consider whether the members will be provided a copy of the resolution or whether the district superintendent or presiding elder will read it aloud. An editable resolution can be found in the Pro+ SAS Resource Hub, which offers all the resources in the SAS Resource Hub, plus numerous additional premium resources.

Pro+SAS Resource Hub

The Church Council moves the charge/church conference adoption of a resolution to modify our organizational plan of governance, utilizing the simplified accountable structure:

Sample Church Conference Resolution for Structure Transition

The ______________________________ Church Council moves the charge/church conference adoption of a resolution to modify our organizational plan of governance, utilizing the simplified accountable structure:

Resolution to Change Congregational Organizational Plan to Simplified Accountable Governance Structure

WHEREAS, ¶ 247.2 of the 2024 *Book of Discipline for the United Methodist Church* allows alternative models of governance; and

WHEREAS, the simplified accountable leadership structure is utilized as an alternative model throughout the denomination and fulfills the provisions of ¶ 243 of the 2024 *Book of Discipline for the United Methodist Church*; and

WHEREAS, the Church Council of ________United Methodist Church prayerfully voted on ________(date) to explore the simplified accountable structure for local church governance; and

WHEREAS, the congregation provided feedback concerning a potential change in governance structure on multiple occasions; and

WHEREAS, the congregation was motivated to convert for reasons of stewardship of our resources, efficiency, alignment with our mission and vision, accountability, and missional focus; and

WHEREAS, the Church Council, Committee on Nominations and Leadership Development, the Discernment Team, and the pastor, after months of discernment, have crafted an alternative organizational structure for ________United Methodist Church and offered this proposal to the district superintendent for approval; and

WHEREAS, the district superintendent approved the alternative organizational plan on ________(date);

and NOW, THEREFORE, BE IT RESOLVED THAT:

1. On January 1, 20____, the authority and various responsibilities of the Church Council, Staff/Pastor-Parish Relations Committee (S/PPRC), Finance Committee, Endowment Committee, and Board of Trustees, as outlined in the current Book of Discipline, will be combined into a single governing body called the Leadership Board. Existing elected leadership of all classes of all constituent committees that make up the new Leadership Board will conclude their terms of service on December 31, 20_____, as the church transitions to the new organizational plan.

2. The Committee on Nominations and Leadership Development of ____________ United Methodist Church is directed to submit a list of officers and members of a simplified accountable structure known as the Leadership Board and a Committee on Nominations and Leadership Development, divided into appropriate three-year classes, as outlined in *The Book of Discipline,* for election by the charge conference. All members of the Leadership Board and the charge conference will be professing members. The chair of the Board of Trustees will be elected from among the voting Trustee members of the Leadership Board at the first board meeting of each year, in accordance with the Discipline, and s/he may also serve as the Leadership Board chair.

3. Beginning on January 1, 20____, the charge conference of the United Methodist Church will be composed of:

   a. Members of the Leadership Board, appointed clergy (ex officio)

   b. Retired ordained ministers and retired diaconal ministers who elect to hold their membership in our charge conference

   c. Lay member(s) of annual conference

   d. The lay leader

   e. The treasurer (if non-staff)

   f. Elected membership of the Committee on Nominations and Leadership Development

4. The lay member of annual conference and the lay leader are ex officio members of the Leadership Board, if not already elected to a membership class of the Leadership Board.

All Disciplinary requirements and qualifications for each of the constituent committees (Church Council, S/PPRC, Finance Committee, Endowment Committee, and Board of Trustees) will continue to apply to the combined Leadership Board, including Trustee age-of-majority qualifications and S/PPRC household membership limitations.

All references to the Church Council, Board of Trustees, S/PPRC, and Finance Committee, in all existing church policies, as of December 31, 20____, shall be understood to refer to the Leadership Board beginning January 1, 20____.

The Board of Trustees is directed immediately to make appropriate amendments to the congregation's bylaws to reflect the new plan for organization and submit an update to the Secretary of State's office in a manner defined by state law for nonprofit corporations.

In service to our common mission to make disciples of Jesus Christ for the transformation of the world, all existing ministry teams will be accountable to the pastor and the Leadership Board in administrative matters and in fulfillment of ¶ 243. The Weekday Childcare Ministry Advisory Board (¶ 256.2.c) will be amenable to the Leadership Board in all matters and is responsible for regular reporting to the Board. Recommended Approach: The Weekday Childcare Ministry Advisory Board (¶ 256.2.c) will serve as a ministry team and will be accountable directly to the pastor.8

The charge conference affirms the continuation of all existing financial, child protection, building use, and personnel policies. The Leadership Board is hereby authorized and directed to create, maintain, and amend Guiding Principles, policies, and a Leadership Board Covenant, and to submit updated Guiding Principles and policies to the charge conference on an annual basis.

APPROVED________(date)

____________________ ____________________

Secretary Charge Conference Presiding Elder

---

8 If the Weekday Childcare Ministry is a separate 501(c)(3) entity, an altogether different approach to the relationship is required. Please see Chapter 9.

¶ 247.2 The Charge Conference, the district superintendent, and the pastor, when a pastor has been appointed (see ¶ 205.4), shall organize and administer the pastoral charge and churches according to the policies and plans herein set forth. When the membership size, program scope, mission resources, or other circumstances so require, the charge conference may, in consultation with and upon the approval of the district superintendent, modify the organizational plans, provided that the provisions of ¶ 243 are observed. Such other circumstances may include, but not be limited to, alternative models for the conception of a local church, such as coffee house ministries, mall ministries, outdoor ministries, retirement home ministries, restaurant ministries, and other emergent ways in which people can gather in God's name to be the church.

¶ 243. Primary Tasks - The local church shall be organized so that it can pursue its primary task and mission in the context of its own community - reaching out and receiving with joy all who will respond; encouraging people in their relationship with God and inviting them to commitment to God's love in Jesus Christ; providing opportunities for them to seek strengthening and growth in spiritual formation; and supporting them to live lovingly and justly in the power of the Holy Spirit as faithful disciples.

We also recommend that any entities associated with the church that are not separately incorporated be brought into the new structure. For example, if the endowment is not a separate 501(c)(3) foundation or legal entity, the endowment is now part of the responsibility of the new leadership structure. This allows the best alignment, flexibility, adaptability, and focus.

Another example might be a childcare program or preschool that is not separately incorporated (i.e., shared Employer Identification Number). Again, if this is not a separate legal entity, this ministry is under the authority and responsibility of the SAS Leadership Board (and the pastor) and should be aligned accordingly. While advisory (ministry) teams can always be created to support their ministry, this is the time to clean up governance silos and align for accountability. The Designing Phase section will walk your team through the options to consider and help you learn more about them, and then you can craft a resolution and design a structure that fits your unique contextual needs.

The Church Conference Votes to Adopt SAS

The day has finally arrived. The church conference gathers, and the decision is now in the hands of the professing members of the congregation. Make sure the SAS Prayer Team is praying in the days leading up to the vote. With the permission of your district superintendent, someone from the Prayer Team may offer a prayer before the vote begins.

The vote will be taken using the method agreed upon with the district superintendent, whether by paper ballot or by a show of hands. Unless your DS instructs otherwise, a simple majority of those members present and voting is required to adopt the resolution to move to a simplified accountable structure. The district superintendent will typically announce the results once the count is complete.

After the vote, communicate the results clearly and promptly to the entire congregation. This reinforces transparency, builds trust, and ensures that members who were unable to attend are fully informed. If the vote is favorable, the next season of work shifts toward preparing the church for the new structure. The Nominations Committee now goes into overdrive!

As you complete the final two steps in the Discerning Phase, the Designing Phase is on the horizon:

Step Eleven (11 of 12) in the Discerning Phase:

The Committee on Nominations completes its work of discerning and nominating leaders to be elected to the Leadership Board.

Step Twelve (12 of 12) in the Discerning Phase:

The church/charge conference is held to elect the nominated Leadership Board members and the members needed to fill in the Committee on Nominations and Leadership Development.

If the vote does not pass, the Church Council will need to reflect prayerfully on the reasons behind the decision. Sometimes the concerns reveal underlying trust issues or unresolved conflict. Sometimes the communication or feedback loops were insufficient or congregants felt uncertain about the process. In many cases, the underlying issues are not actually about structure but about congregational relationships. These concerns deserve patient attention and pastoral care.

We Voted, Now What?

With the congregational vote complete, the Discerning Phase comes to a close, and the church is ready to move forward. Much of the Designing Phase has already been underway in the background, and now that the structure has been approved, this work becomes the primary focus. This is the point when design conversations deepen, details are finalized, and the congregation begins preparing for its first Leadership Board.

At the same time, several elements of the Equipping Phase begin to take on greater importance. Throughout Discerning and Designing, the Authorized SAS Coach should already have been working with the Committee on Nominations and Leadership Development. Even though the new leaders are not nominated until after the church conference approves the structure, the Nominations Committee needs time to learn a new approach to discernment, understand its responsibilities, and prepare its process. Beginning this work early gives the Committee on Nominations and the larger leadership the clarity and capacity it needs as the church moves toward implementation.

Now that the structure is officially adopted, the Nominations Committee completes its remaining design responsibilities and begins preparing the slate of Leadership Board members for election. Once the congregation elects that slate, the Authorized SAS Coach will equip the Leadership Board members for their new role, helping them understand accountable governance, Guiding Principles, and the ministry outcomes that will guide their leadership.

Trust the groundwork laid during this Discerning Phase. It has prepared your congregation to enter the Designing and Equipping Phases with clarity and confidence as you take the next faithful steps together.

CHAPTER FOUR

Right-Sizing Your Discernment Process

Every congregation can engage in faithful discernment. Not every congregation can (or should) engage its discernment work the same way. The heart of the Discerning Phase remains constant across churches of all sizes: prayerful listening, clarity about the *why*, honest assessment of strengths and challenges, and transparent communication. *Church size affects the scale of discernment, not the substance.* Right-sizing your process means your church can embrace SAS in a way that fits your story, your resources, your unique context, and your mission so the structure serves the gospel instead of the other way around.

Whether your church averages 30 people in worship or 3,000:

- Communicate more than you think necessary.
- Engage your *why* before touching your *how*.
- Think adaptively, not just technically.
- Name your hopes and your anxieties.
- Honor the roles of the DS, pastor, and laity.
- Let prayer open the windows of the process.
- Did we already encourage you to communicate? Do it some more!

Discernment is not about speed. It's about encouraging congregational health. Here are some church size factors that may impact your discernment process.

Right-Sizing for Large & Multisite or Multi-Staff Churches

Larger churches and multi-staff congregations bring complexity. Multiple ministries, specialized staff roles, more internal "lanes" of communication, and a wider diversity of expectations all influence discernment. In these settings, clarity is oxygen.

First, make sure staff members understand the SAS model and their roles within it. A single confused staff member can unintentionally derail the process, not because they're resistant, but because they're trying to make sense of the system without sufficient context. Teaching the distinctions between governance and management of the ministry teams and reinforcing who supervises them will save you a world of headaches. Earlier, we noted a common challenge for long-term committee chairs who may see SAS as an attack on their authority and identity. There may be staff who feel they are losing their "voice" with the governing board or a special contact on a vital committee. Listen and help them discover how they still have connections with leaders, even as the structure changes.

Second, build a Discernment Team with broad representation of the larger congregation and knowledge of the governing work of administrative church committees. This ensures that the Discernment Team can speak to the lived experience of the whole congregation: worshipping communities, generations, major ministries, and stakeholders who carry the church's culture in their bones.

Third, communication requires a multi-layered, multi-format plan in a larger congregation. You will likely need written materials such as FAQs, graphics, multiple town halls, Q&A videos, and intentional conversations. Larger churches should expect the Discerning Phase to last the full six months. That time isn't wasteful; it's pastoral.

Right-Sizing for Midsize Churches

Midsize churches (with a full-time pastor and a mix of part-time and full-time paid and unpaid staff) often need a hybrid approach. You have enough people to warrant a structured process, but not so many that every communication needs a graphic designer and a three-week production timeline.

These churches tend to benefit from:

- A Discernment Team that includes both board leaders and a few newer voices
- A handful of town halls, rather than a more complex presentation

- Clearly written materials, such as an FAQ document and a simple handout for worship
- Scheduled updates in newsletters and from the pulpit

Midsize congregations often complete discernment in four to six months—quick enough to maintain momentum, slow enough to stay healthy.

Right-Sizing for Small Churches

Small churches bring their own gifts to this work. Before continuing, a definition is helpful. Traditional metrics such as budget, worship attendance, or membership are no longer reliable indicators of what makes a congregation "small." Instead, we have found a more useful guide in the pastoral appointment itself. When a congregation shares a pastor with another church or is served by a bi-vocational or part-time pastor, the relational and organizational dynamics of that congregation are markedly different from those of a congregation served by a full-time licensed or ordained clergy. This context shapes both the challenges and the opportunities in implementing SAS.

A Smaller Board is Not Automatically Simplified Accountable Structure

When the whole congregation fits in the fellowship hall, and most folks are related, information spreads quickly. That's a blessing—and occasionally a challenge. Their Discerning Phase will be shorter, perhaps only a few months. Often, the leaders of a small church glance through the resources and exclaim, "We are already doing this!" but don't really follow through on both the technical changes (an SAS Leadership Board that fits all *The Book of Discipline* requirements) and the adaptive changes (accountable leadership and intentional planning).

Right-sizing for small churches includes two suggestions and a warning about two temptations. First, the two suggestions:

1. In small churches with part-time or bi-vocational pastors, the laity take on even greater ministry accountability, not simply governance responsibility, which makes the clarity and health

of the SAS model especially important. In a small church, the laity—and certainly not the pastor—needs to drive the process. We have seen too many clergy lead the charge for a simplified model with such speed that the laity do not fully understand the implications or even the *why*. Then appointments change, and laity are left with a leadership structure that seems foreign to their culture and understanding.

2. The communications plan in a small church is much simpler: fewer gatherings, fewer printed pieces, and more relational conversations. But don't skip the informational meeting. At least one gathering is essential to explain:

    - Why SAS is being considered
    - What SAS actually is
    - How SAS will strengthen discipleship and mission
    - What will change (and what won't)
    - How the process will unfold

Even in small churches, clarity is kindness!

And now the two temptations:

1. The first temptation is to skip steps in the Discerning Phase. While the schedule and communication plan are simplified and compressed, small churches still need to follow through on ALL the steps. When a church has only a few leaders doing the heavy lifting, it's easy to think, "We all know what we mean, so let's just move ahead." Please don't! The why conversation is not optional. It is the spiritual heart of discernment. Skipping the why conversation usually means that the congregation "simplifies" into a one-board model but doesn't actually adopt a simplified ACCOUNTABLE structure. The discernment tools help congregations (yes, even smaller ones) move beyond technical motivations of "fewer meetings" and "simpler paperwork" to deeper, missional reasons for adopting SAS: purpose, accountability, missional alignment, and the stewardship of limited energy.

2. The other temptation for small churches during the Discerning Phase is to slap the SAS label onto your current Church Council, converting it into the new SAS Leadership Board ("DS, there aren't many of us!"). In a small church, the Discernment Team may be identical to the Church Council. If possible, add a couple of voices not currently in leadership. You'll avoid "the usual suspects making the usual assumptions." This self-discipline will also create some sacred space for other voices and perspectives as your new SAS Leadership Board takes shape.

Real Talk for Small Churches

Some churches ask, "What if we can't find enough leaders for the minimum Leadership Board and Nominations Committee?"

This is not an uncommon question, and it deserves both compassion and honesty. In the Designing Phase, you will see that the simplified accountable structure can be right-sized for small churches. This includes a fully compliant six-member Leadership Board with three members on the Nominations Committee. This adaptation honors both *The Book of Discipline* and the realities of congregations served by part-time, shared, or bi-vocational pastors.

But if a church cannot identify even this smaller number of unrelated laity, it is almost always a sign that the church needs a deeper conversation than one about structure. And this is where faithful stewardship requires courage.

A congregation unable to seat a six-person Leadership Board is certainly unable to staff the much larger slate required by the traditional structure. At this point, the question is no longer, "Should we move to SAS?" because the issue isn't SAS versus traditional governance. The issue is ministry capacity.

This raises several deeper discernment questions:

- **Are there enough people left to do ministry, not just governance?**

  Leadership positions are not the purpose of the church. Serving through ministries for missional effectiveness is the purpose. If leadership slots are empty, ministry teams are likely struggling as well.

- **Is maintaining a *Book of Discipline*–compliant corporate structure still faithful?**

  A building, a nonprofit legal status requiring bookkeeping, insurance, utilities, and all the expectations of a chartered United Methodist Church, may no longer align with the gifts, capacity, and energy of the current congregation.

- **Is there a more mission-appropriate expression of the church for this season?**

  Could the Holy Spirit be inviting you toward a different form of gathering and discipleship? Perhaps your church would be better served by engaging in a ¶ 212 or ¶ 213 conversation about congregational potential.

Micro-Churches and Simplified Governance

In our introductory section, we noted a single exception to the principle that SAS fits churches of every size. If a congregation cannot meet the minimum legal and *Book of Discipline* requirements (even in the simplified model), then the issue is not governance. Again, the deeper issue is identity, mission, and stewardship.

At that point, other faithful expressions of the United Methodist community may be worth discerning with your district superintendent or other judicatory leader:

- **A Wesleyan Class Meeting or House Church Model**

  A return to our Wesleyan roots, emphasizing discipleship, accountability, and mission without corporate overhead. This small, covenantal gathering is centered on worship, prayer, and service without the administrative and facility burdens of a traditional church. Sometimes the class meeting is held under the umbrella of another congregation.

- **Merging with Another Congregation**

  Not a defeat, but a strategy of multiplication. Many thriving churches today were born from holy mergers.

- **Adoption by a Larger Church**

  Becoming a second site or ministry extension of a nearby congregation can bring pastoral care, stewardship accountability, and renewed mission. I (Blake) recently led an adoption process for a smaller, faithful congregation within my larger downtown church. We have launched a second "East Campus" using the facility. The adopted church's members were sacrificial stewards with missional hearts. The adoption is exciting and hope-filled for both congregations.

- **Graceful Closure and Resurrection**

  Sometimes, the most faithful decision is to finish a chapter well so that future ministry can rise from the gifts entrusted to the church.

Every congregation has seasons and a lifespan, so understand that none of these questions represents failure. They represent faithful stewardship, the willingness to see the truth of your situation and respond with courage, humility, and hope. Small churches are often the most spiritually mature communities we meet, precisely because they know how to trust God when resources are thin.

If your church finds itself asking these questions, take heart. You're not alone, and you're not in trouble. You're doing the work every congregation must do: listening for what God wants next.

Notes

CHAPTER FIVE

Common Challenges in the Discerning Phase

Every church can engage in faithful discernment. What trips us up is usually not theology or good intentions. More often, the obstacles are timing, lack of information and training, communication, and misunderstandings. The good news is that each one can be identified early and overcome with clarity, patience, and the right support.

This chapter gathers the most common obstacles we see in congregations across the country. These patterns show up in large churches, midsize congregations, cooperative parishes, and small rural churches served by part-time clergy. Consider these less as warnings and more as invitations to prepare wisely.

Starting Discernment Too Late Or Trying To Rush the Phase

The most frequent mistake is starting discernment in the second or third quarter of the year and expecting to get the new structure ratified and implemented by January 1. The transition into simplified accountable structure requires prayerful discernment, thoughtful teaching, broad communication, and a full congregational decision. Compressing discernment into a few weeks almost always creates confusion, suspicion, and resistance.

The *Mission Possible* four-phase rhythm is designed to begin the Discerning Phase early in the year. When the church starts late in the year and attempts to short-circuit discernment, several problems follow:

- There is not enough time to discover, articulate, and conduct the full *why* conversation.
- The new governance structure is steeped in mistrust.
- Leaders feel pressured to make decisions before understanding the model.

- Congregants feel rushed into a structural change they did not help shape.
- The district superintendent's timeline becomes unworkable.

Beginning early in the year (early first quarter) honors the congregation's emotional and spiritual pace and allows for discernment to proceed alongside the important ongoing ministry of the church.

Discernment is not a sales pitch. Even when churches begin at the right time, some try to move too quickly. This usually happens for one of three reasons:

- Lay leaders believe SAS is simply a merger of committees.
- The pastor is tired of the current structure (or maybe the glut of committee meetings!)
- The congregation has "change fatigue" and wants to "get it over with."

Rushing skips the adaptive work of *why* the change is needed and how accountable leadership functions. Without this work, churches often adopt a modified structure that fails to deliver the true missional benefits. That is how you get a "one-board model" that is simplified but not accountable.

Discernment is not about speed; it is about congregational health. If people cannot articulate the mission behind the structure, you are not ready to vote.

Not Including the Whole Congregation

SAS succeeds only when the congregation understands what is changing and *why*. When communications remain locked inside the committee meeting room, the congregation fills in the blanks with fear or suspicion:

"This is a power grab."

"We will never have a say again."

"The pastor will run everything."

"This is a takeover by that committee."

You can prevent this by:

- Offering town hall meetings
- Publishing FAQs
- Giving clear worship announcements
- Posting graphics, charts, or short videos
- Hosting small group Q&A sessions
- Providing written summaries after each Discernment Team meeting

Successful *Mission Possible* congregations over-communicate. If you are not tired of communicating, the congregation has not heard enough yet.

Choosing a Charge Conference Instead of a Church Conference to Vote on the New Structure

The Book of Discipline allows for modification of the organizational structure under ¶ 247.2 with the approval of the district superintendent and a vote of the charge conference. However, our best practices strongly recommend that congregations use a church conference—not a charge conference—for this important vote.

Why? Because a church conference invites all professing members to participate in the decision. A Discerning Phase that involves the whole congregation should conclude with a decision made by the whole congregation. Using only a charge conference bypasses that shared ownership and commitment and often leads to suspicion or resentment, even if the Church Council acted in good faith.

The new simplified accountable structure means that several people who have been voting on various committees will no longer be elected leaders. Having only the Church Council approve a structure change that gives a small group (perhaps even the same individuals) such an enormous amount of authority can be perceived as self-dealing. SAS relies upon trust. Trust grows when the entire membership is invited to vote.

Misunderstanding SAS as an Authoritarian Leadership Model

One of the most damaging misconceptions is that SAS gives power to a small group of people. This misunderstanding usually comes from congregants who hear "nine-member board" and assume "centralized authority." SAS is not an authoritarian model. It is an *accountable* one.

Authoritarian leadership concentrates power. Accountable leadership disperses responsibility, clarifies roles, and keeps the mission at the center. The Leadership Board is held accountable by:

- Jesus' mission and the congregation's vision and goals
- *The Book of Discipline*
- The Guiding Principles
- The Leadership Covenant
- The Nominations Committee
- The Charge and Church Conference
- The District Superintendent

In accountable leadership, good authority is exercised transparently, with clear boundaries and spiritual maturity. When people understand this, anxiety goes down, and commitment goes up.

Misunderstanding the Role of Staff

The shift to simplified accountable structure often surfaces anxiety among staff. This is true for both paid and unpaid staff, and especially for long-serving volunteer leaders who have carried major ministry responsibilities for years. Most of these concerns do not come from policy changes, but from the ways leadership has functioned informally in the past.

Typical misunderstandings include:

- A staff member who used to attend board meetings or present reports feels excluded.

- A staff member assumes they will lose direct access to the S/PPRC.
- A longtime employee fears the board will begin to "micromanage."
- Ministry team leaders think their team must now "report to the board."
- Staff confuse the pastor's supervisory role with unchecked authority.

These misunderstandings make sense when you remember that many Church Councils have historically operated with a blurry mix of elected leaders, program staff, administrative staff, and unofficial influencers all sharing decision-making authority at the leadership table. Clearly defining the roles of different leaders prevents the stakeholders from returning to old habits. Shifting to accountable leadership does not create confusion; it reveals the confusion that was already present.

The good news is that accountable leadership brings clarity!

In a church that practices accountable leadership:

- The pastor supervises staff and ministry team leaders.
- The pastor aligns staff and ministry teams with the mission.
- The board evaluates the pastor's leadership and the ministry outcomes, not individual staff performance.

Teaching these lines of responsibility early and often lowers anxiety. It also helps staff understand that SAS is not designed to reduce their voice, but to strengthen their alignment with the church's mission and protect them from inconsistent or informal oversight.

Leadership Boards need training as well. SAS is not a model where the Leadership Board becomes the employer or manager of staff. The Leadership Board does not direct daily ministry or supervise personnel. Individual board members do not have supervisory authority unless specifically assigned this authority by the Leadership Board in the Guiding Principles.

Clear lanes build trust. When staff know who leads, who supervises, and how decisions flow, they can do their work with confidence, creativity, and alignment.

The Human Cost of Change

One of the most underestimated dynamics in leadership restructuring (change) is *loss*. Even faithful change carries a cost, and that cost is often felt most deeply by faithful people who have served the church well for a long time. This is where trust is either strengthened or quietly eroded.

When committees disappear, people can lose more than a meeting. They can lose a sense of identity, purpose, and belonging. For decades, some leaders have understood their discipleship through service on Church Council, Trustees, Finance, or Staff/Pastor-Parish. Those roles mattered. Their work mattered. Simplification does not erase that legacy, but it can feel like it does if leaders fail to account for the human cost of change.

Longtime leaders will probably feel sidelined or replaced, even when the intent is to equip leadership differently. What looks like efficiency to one person can feel like erasure to another. We once worked with a very large church that had the same Trustee chair for more than thirty years. He quietly hoped to surpass the record of his predecessor, who served forty(!) years in that role. For this Trustee chair, the role was not simply a position or a line in the nominations report. It was his identity, vocation, and place within the church's relational ecosystem. And it is not only the Trustee chair that would have to adjust in a transition to SAS. Imagine the cultural shift required when a congregation has known only two Trustee chairs since the Eisenhower Administration! It would be incredibly hard for the church to imagine a different way of stewarding property and leadership. That emotional gap deserves care, not coercion.

Grief is real, even when change is right. Healthy discernment makes room for sacred lament alongside hope. Churches that name loss honestly tend to move forward with greater trust, deeper unity, and less resentment than those that rush past it.

Not Using an Authorized SAS Coach

This item is both the most overlooked and the most easily avoided. Churches often believe they can implement SAS without outside help. Some can. Many cannot.

An Authorized SAS Coach brings:

- Experience with multiple congregations
- No emotional or relational attachment that can sometimes blur decisions
- Updated best practices from across the connection
- Equipping resources for members of the Leadership Board and the Committee on Nominations
- Access to updated templates, Guiding Principles, covenants, and sample agendas
- The ability to mediate tensions before they escalate
- Neutrality when leaders disagree
- Accountability to make sure nothing is skipped
- Observe Leadership Board meetings to offer course correction and blind-spot recognition

Without a coach, churches often:

- Reinvent broken wheels
- Skip critical steps
- Use outdated versions of SAS or even "one-board" models
- Misinterpret Book of Discipline requirements
- Drift back to (or never detach from) old habits and structures

Authorized SAS Coaches have completed the authors' training, attend quarterly calls for ongoing training and updates on best practices, have access to a plethora of SAS tools and resources, and can contact the network of Authorized SAS Coaches and the authors via a message board for guidance and advice.

An Authorized SAS Coach is not a luxury. It is an investment in long-term leadership and congregational health. To locate an Authorized SAS Coach in your area, use this QR code:

SAS
Authorized Coaches

Meeting the Challenges

Every obstacle in this chapter shares a common theme. None of these issues arises from bad intentions. They arise from assumptions, congregational cultural practices, and the natural anxiety that accompanies significant change. Discernment succeeds when:

- The process begins early to provide sufficient time, prayer, discernment, and understanding.
- Communication is constant and clear.
- The entire congregation is invited to learn and vote on a structural change.
- Leadership is accountable rather than authoritative.
- Staff and ministry team leader roles are taught and aligned.
- An Authorized SAS Coach helps guide the congregation.

SAS is not a shortcut. It is a faithful journey into healthier leadership for more effective ministry. When churches anticipate and address these common challenges, they move through the Discerning Phase with more confidence, deeper trust, and clearer purpose.

Notes

SECTION TWO

Designing

Jethro, Moses' father-in-law, brought a Whole-Burnt-Offering and sacrifices to God. And Aaron, along with all the elders of Israel, came and ate the meal with Moses' father-in-law in the presence of God. The next day Moses took his place to judge the people. People were standing before him all day long, from morning to night. When Moses' father-in-law saw all that he was doing for the people, he said, "What's going on here? Why are you doing all this, and all by yourself, letting everybody line up before you from morning to night?"

Moses said to his father-in-law, "Because the people come to me with questions about God. When something comes up, they come to me. I judge between a man and his neighbor and teach them God's laws and instructions."

Moses' father-in-law said, "This is no way to go about it. You'll burn out, and the people right along with you. This is way too much for you – you can't do this alone. Now listen to me. Let me tell you how to do this so that God will be in this with you. Be there for the people before God, but let the matters of concern be presented to God. Your job is to teach them the rules and instructions, to show them how to live, what to do. And then you need to keep a sharp eye out for competent men – men who fear God, men of integrity, men who are incorruptible – and appoint them as leaders over groups organized by the thousand, by the hundred, by fifty, and by ten. They'll be responsible for the everyday work of judging among the people. They'll bring the hard cases to you, but in the routine cases they'll be the judges. They will share your load and that will make it easier for you. If you handle the work this way, you'll have the strength to carry out whatever God commands you, and the people in their settings will flourish also."

Exodus 18:12-23 (MSG)

Designing Phase Introduction

What is the Designing Phase?

The Designing Phase creates an intentional time and focus to design the official SAS model, clarify roles, and draft the resolution that will later go before the congregation for approval. Beginning this work early prevents last-minute confusion and ensures that the proposed structure is both Disciplinary and mission-aligned.

Who Is Involved in This Phase?

The Designing Phase is a collaborative effort among the Church Council, the pastor, and the Committee on Nominations.

What Is the Timing of This Phase?

The Designing Phase overlaps the tail end of the Discerning Phase and is typically completed late in the first quarter or sometime in the second quarter of the year.

Understanding the Designing Phase

Over the years, as we have coached congregations across the country, we have discovered that designing the new structure requires far more attention than we originally anticipated. Again and again, leaders told us they had to revisit the structure multiple times before they fully understood how the Leadership Board, pastor, staff, and ministry teams relate within SAS. We also noticed that Nominations Committees were often unprepared for the shift to accountable leadership and unsure how to discern the nomination of a slate that reflected the mission, Guiding Principles, and spiritual maturity required by the model. These patterns led us to create a dedicated Designing Phase in *Mission Possible 4*. By giving focused time to collaborate, clarify, and learn the structure before the vote, churches make better decisions, avoid common mistakes, and enter the Equipping and Implementing Phases with far greater confidence and unity.

The Designing Phase is the second step in the SAS process, but it does not wait until after the congregational vote to begin. In *Mission Possible 4*, the Designing Phase begins during the Discerning Phase, as soon as the Church Council informs the Authorized SAS Coach that it intends to explore SAS. This early start allows the Coach to begin working with the Committee on Nominations and Leadership Development long before any vote is taken.

During this Discerning-Designing overlap, the Authorized SAS Coach guides the Church Council, in collaboration with the Nominations Committee and the Discernment Team (when contextually appropriate), in creating the initial governance structure that will be presented to the church conference in the form of a formal resolution (a sample resolution is in Chapter 3). In this phase, the Nominations Committee collaborates with the pastor, Church Council, and key leaders to design the official SAS model, clarify roles, and draft the resolution that will later go before the congregation for approval.

As the process moves forward, the Designing Phase also overlaps with the Equipping Phase. While the congregation is still discerning, the Authorized SAS Coach equips the Nominations Committee to identify, evaluate, and recommend the first slate of Leadership Board members should SAS be adopted. This training helps the committee understand the qualities, competencies, and spiritual maturity required for accountable leadership, enabling them to nominate the most suitable leaders at the right time. Beginning this equipping work before the congregational vote allows the Nominations Committee to "hit the ground running" once the structure is approved. You will read more about this work in the Equipping Phase, but it is essential not to wait until after the vote to begin preparing and equipping your Nominations Committee.

Once the church conference adopts the simplified accountable structure, the Designing Phase continues with focused preparation of the Leadership Board itself. The Authorized SAS Coach equips the newly nominated Leadership Board members in November or early December, so they are ready to begin their work on January 1. Because one-third of the Leadership Board and the Nominations Committee rotate off each year, annual equipping remains essential for sustaining healthy, accountable leadership.

Notes

CHAPTER SIX

Designing the SAS Leadership Board

No Half Measures in Simplification

Because the wording of BOD ¶ 247 is broad, churches across the connection have experimented with a variety of simplified structures. Blake has occasionally referred to these as "exotic variants." There is no single perfect model. Yet after walking alongside hundreds of congregations, we have helped implement a modified structure that fulfills all BOD requirements and conditions while avoiding many of the common pitfalls found in these other approaches. Our recommended model not only complies with the *Discipline* and is trusted by bishops and district superintendents across the country, but it is grounded in best practices and shaped by the (sometimes very hard) lessons learned from congregations that struggled with partial or improvised designs.

Local context and values will always matter as you establish a new structure. Still, our best-practice recommendation is to adopt full simplification whenever feasible, using simplified accountable structure. In this model, all four administrative committees are rolled into a single Leadership Board of nine members, with the pastor serving in an executive capacity. The Church Council, Trustees, Finance Committee, and S/PPRC still exist in terms of their functions, but they now operate as a single combined group, taking on the responsibilities and authority of a single administrative committee we refer to as the Leadership Board.

Leadership Board = Council + Trustees + Staff/Pastor-Parish Relations + Finance

A Nine-Member Board

To move into the most simplified structure, you will need a Leadership Board of nine lay members. We didn't pull this number out of thin air. *The Book of Discipline* (BOD) establishes nine as the standard (and sometimes maximum) size for the committees on Trustees, Finance, and Staff/Pastor-Parish Relations (S/PPRC). Using nine members allows the Leadership Board to assume the Disciplinary authority of all three committees without needing separate bodies. In other words, nine members provide the cleanest way to meet every BOD requirement while keeping the structure simple and accountable.

Technically, a church may expand the Leadership Board beyond nine members. *However, doing so reintroduces significant complexity.* Only a limited number of members can legally count as Trustees or as the voting members of S/PPRC. When a Leadership Board grows larger than nine members, the chair and secretary must track which individuals hold which Disciplinary roles, who may vote on specific matters, and how those votes must be recorded in the minutes. This becomes especially cumbersome when taking legal actions that require precise documentation. In short, larger boards recreate the very confusion SAS is designed to eliminate.

What Are Classes?

In the United Methodist Church, most elected administrative leaders serve three-year terms, which are grouped into what we call classes. A "class" is simply the year in which a leader's term ends. For example, if someone is part of the "Class of 2028," their term concludes on December 31, 2028. This means their 3-year term of service begins in January 2026, continues throughout 2027, and concludes at the end of 2028.

Most United Methodist Church administrative committees (including the SAS Leadership Board) have three staggered classes of three people each, for a total of nine board members. One class of three members rotates off every December while a new class begins service in January. This pattern means one-third of the board turns over each year, which creates a healthy rhythm of continuity and renewal.

Using classes creates a predictable cycle for leadership development, nominations, and transitions. It also keeps a balance of continuity and change on the Leadership Board, since not all members rotate off at the same time. This is the basic system across the United Methodist Church, whether you are using the traditional committee model or a simplified accountable structure.

The Book of Discipline outlines how to begin a rotation when the church is implementing a change in structure. Here is an example from the S/PPRC section (¶ 258.2.b): "To begin the process of rotation where such a process has not been in place, on the first year, one class shall be elected for one year, one class for two years, and one class for three years."

In addition to all the requirements for rotating classes in *The Book of Discipline*, state laws often require that boards of directors for incorporated nonprofit entities have set terms. While terms can usually be repeatable, or succeeding classes, the terms of office are legally required to be set and published.

Therefore, we recommend keeping the Leadership Board at three rotating classes totaling nine lay members unless there is a compelling reason to change that number. We will offer options to meet contextual requirements later in this Designing Phase. For example, the adapted six-person model described later in this chapter is a faithful and fully compliant option for small churches. Yet, whenever feasible, adopting the nine-member Leadership Board provides the most seamless, least confusing, and most widely trusted implementation of the simplified accountable leadership model.

Once elected, the nine-person Leadership Board carries out all the functions assigned in the BOD to:

- The Trustees (and Endowment Committee)
- The Finance Committee
- The S/PPRC
- The Church Council

The pastor serves as the executive leader who aligns staff and ministry teams with the mission and vision and is evaluated by the Leadership Board in accordance with SAS best practices.

The Leadership Board also includes the required individual roles of lay leader, lay member of annual conference, board chair, and one youth member (when contextually appropriate). A single individual may (and likely will) hold more than one of these roles. For example, one member may serve as both lay leader and the lay member to the annual conference. In fact, we highly recommend that the Leadership Board chair also be elected by the board in January as the Board of Trustees chair or president. What matters is not the number of roles but that the Leadership Board remains a single, unified leadership body. For those who like lists, here is a quick rundown of the basic Leadership Board in SAS.

The SAS Design Basics:

- The Leadership Board consists of nine lay members, elected by the Charge Conference and organized into three classes of three members each.
- All nine members (plus the pastor) serve simultaneously as a unified S/PPRC, Trustees, Finance, and Church Council.
- Certain positions must be included among the nine lay members of the board:
    - Board chair
    - Lay member to annual conference
    - Lay leader
- Chair, lay member of annual conference, and lay leader can be combined positions (and is highly recommended).
- Trustees must be 18+ years of age.
- Note that a separate and independent Nominating Committee is still required.
- Our recommended SAS Leadership Board has nine members, as the Trustees and S/PPRC each have a maximum of nine members per *The Book of Discipline.*
- The pastor serves as the executive leader and is an ex officio member of the Leadership Board. The pastor is not, however, a Trustee and may not vote in Trustee matters or be listed in legal documents as a Trustee or a voting member of the legal board of directors in nonprofit corporation records.
- Since the pastor is not a voting member of the S/PPRC, the pastor should not vote on any matters when the Leadership Board is

acting in its capacity as the S/PPRC.[9]

- We *strongly* caution churches against placing representatives *from* chartered groups such as United Women in Faith, United Methodist Men, or the United Methodist Youth Fellowship on the Leadership Board. This practice tends to shift the Leadership Board's work toward representational governance rather than missional leadership and often reintroduces the very silos that a simplified accountable structure is designed to address. It also blurs the lines between governance work and ministry teams. In other words, using representatives *from* groups (often selected by the group or, as a default, based on their position/title within the group) falls into the "we strongly do not recommend" category.[10] That said, your authors are realists. In some congregational cultures, relationships between chartered groups and church leadership are deeply and historically valued, and an outright prohibition can create unnecessary resistance. If a church determines that a Leadership Board connection with chartered groups is necessary, the healthier option is to assign a Leadership Board member to act as a liaison *to* a chartered group rather than receiving a representative *from* that group. In this model, the liaison is an existing, fully nominated and elected member of the Leadership Board, not an additional seat; it is advisable that the liaison would not even be a member of the group. The liaison role may be combined with other responsibilities and should be clearly defined as a communication and support role, not a representative or advocacy role on behalf of the group. If this approach is used, it should be explicitly named in the SAS resolution so expectations and boundaries are clear from the beginning and not forgotten in future years. For example, an additional item in your church conference resolution could say:

  > *The Leadership Board may, as needed, assign one or more of its elected members to serve as liaisons to chartered groups of the congregation, including United Women in Faith, United Methodist Men, and United Methodist Youth Fellowship. Any liaison shall*

---

9 See Judicial Council (UMC) Decision 500.

10 If a "representative" approach is inescapable in your church context, the potential leader should still go through the exact same nominations process and discernment as all other board members. A compromise is the "board liaison" approach outlined above. While still not optimal, the "board liaison" approach does provide an accommodation which does not compromise the Nomination Committee's best practices.

be a duly nominated and elected member of the Leadership Board and shall not constitute an additional seat. The purpose of such liaisons is to support communication and shared understanding between the Leadership Board and chartered groups.

What's in a Name?

Language matters! A common mistake in describing simplified accountable structure is saying, "The church got rid of all four administrative committees." Actually, all your administrative committees still exist, and, in their united form, all their combined responsibilities constitute the authority of the new Leadership Board. In other words, the Leadership Board IS the Finance Committee, IS the Staff/Pastor-Parish Committee, IS the Trustees, and IS the Church Council. Nothing in *The Book of Discipline* is ignored or removed. Instead, the functions, roles, authority, and responsibilities of each of the constituent committees are all placed upon your new Leadership Board. You still have a Finance Committee—it is the nine-member Leadership Board. When asked, "Who is on your Board of Trustees?" the answer should be, "It's our nine-member Leadership Board."

The BOD Nonnegotiables
(Staying Legal with the SAS Leadership Board)

In this new edition of *Mission Possible*, we thought it might be helpful to pull back the curtain a bit. As we designed simplified accountable structure, we spent a great deal of time navigating the nonnegotiables of the United Methodist *Book of Discipline*—not because we enjoy fine print or footnotes (well, maybe Blake does), but because we wanted to ensure congregations could actually use the structure we were teaching without creating legal problems down the road.

What follows is a brief look at several *Book of Discipline* requirements that shaped our design decisions.[11] These are the realities we had to work within, the questions we had to answer, and the lines we could not cross.

---

[11] Please note that these nonnegotiables only fully apply to United Methodist congregations. District structures, conference structures, and the polity requirements of other denominations carry different sets of nonnegotiables.

Some of them are obvious. Others only surface once multiple committees are combined into a single Leadership Board. By sharing this "behind the scenes" work, we hope to help you and your congregation stay on track (or perhaps even course correct) as you design a simplified leadership structure that is faithful to our denominational commitments, legally sound, and focused on the mission God has placed before you.

First, a separate Committee on Nominations and Leadership Development is required.

The Leadership Board cannot be self-nominating. *The Book of Discipline* is clear that nominations for administrative leadership must come from a separate Nominations Committee and be approved by the charge or church conference. In addition, the pastor is required by the *Discipline* to chair the Committee on Nominations and Leadership Development. That requirement alone makes it impossible for the Leadership Board to absorb the nominations function, particularly since the Leadership Board chair is a layperson. This single non-negotiable eliminates many otherwise creative "one-board" approaches. The Nominations Committee is one of the checks on the Leadership Board. By maintaining healthy rotations and discerning the best leaders for each season, the Nominations Committee ensures excellent servant leadership.

Second, *The Book of Discipline* requires the use of three-year terms and classes.

While we have seen a wide range of creative approaches attempted, *The Book of Discipline* is clear that administrative committee and board members serve three-year terms, organized into classes. There is some allowance for renewal, but the use of terms and a rotation of leadership is required. Any simplified structure must retain this rhythm of continuity and rotations.

Third, when committees are merged in SAS, the most restrictive qualifications apply.

This is one of the most misunderstood aspects of simplified structure. The qualifications of the different administrative committees listed in the BOD differ, and therefore, all the most restrictive qualifications apply simultaneously to the Leadership Board. Trustees may include nonmembers, but the Staff/Pastor-Parish Relations Committee may not. Because the Leadership Board functions simultaneously as Trustees, Finance, S/PPRC, and Church Council, it must follow the most restrictive requirements of each of those committees. That means all Leadership Board members must be professing members of the congregation. Similarly, while not all committees prohibit family members serving together, S/PPRC does. So your new Leadership Board cannot have more than one immediate family member from a household serving on it. The same is true for age requirements. Because Trustees must be able to sign legally binding documents and function as members of the board of directors of an incorporated or unincorporated nonprofit entity, Trustees must be at least eighteen years old. The BOD also recommends that the Trustees be composed of at least one-third laywomen and at least one-third laymen. As a result, all those BOD restrictions apply to the entire Leadership Board membership.

Fourth, the Leadership Board must elect a chair of the Board of Trustees.

Even though Leadership Board members are nominated by the Committee on Nominations and Leadership Development, *The Book of Discipline* and state requirements for nonprofit corporations require that the Board of Trustees (Board of Directors) elect its chair annually, typically in January at the Leadership Board's first meeting. Since the Leadership Board is the Board of Trustees, it must elect a chairperson in January. In practice, this person is almost always the Leadership Board chair whom the Nominations Committee already selected, which helps avoid confusion and unnecessary complexity. Passing the gavel around gets old really quickly. So while the rule of electing a Trustee chair is nonnegotiable, a best practice is to assign the existing Leadership Board chair that additional role.

Fifth, confidentiality requirements must be honored through an executive session.

The Book of Discipline includes clear, enforceable confidentiality requirements for the Staff/Pastor-Parish Relations Committee in its work. Because the Leadership Board assumes that role within a simplified accountable structure, it must also utilize those confidentiality practices whenever S/PPRC work is conducted. This is not a matter of culture or courtesy. It is a Disciplinary obligation.

This issue is also one of the primary reasons district superintendents often pause before approving a congregation to enter SAS discernment or to authorize a transition to a simplified accountable structure. For many district superintendents, S/PPRC work is the committee function they interact with most regularly, and they have often experienced incredible harm when confidentiality is breached. During my season as a district superintendent, I (Blake) was occasionally concerned that a church's leadership lacked the discipline and maturity to follow the protocols for an executive session, especially when discussing difficult or sensitive matters. After all, past behavior is usually the best indicator of future actions, and a shift to SAS does not magically resolve existing boundary issues.

To honor this requirement for confidentiality, the Leadership Board must move into executive session at appropriate times, excuse staff and guests, and adjust its note-taking practices accordingly. S/PPRC confidentiality applies fully even when S/PPRC is embedded within a larger governing board. When handled well, the executive session protects pastoral trust, safeguards the congregation, and strengthens accountability. When handled poorly, it quickly undermines confidence in both SAS and the leadership using it.

Because confidentiality is such an intricate and vital part of the Leadership Board's S/PPRC role, we highly recommend that it be addressed in the Leadership Board's Leadership Covenant. In addition, the importance and expectations of confidentiality need to be explored with potential leaders during the Nominations Committee's discernment (see Chapter 11).

Sixth, the district superintendent must be involved in the process.

Approval from the district superintendent to change the administrative structure is not optional. To honor this requirement, we intentionally place DS involvement in two places: at the beginning of the Discerning Phase and again as part of the church conference request to approve a resolution transitioning to simplified accountable structure.

Seventh, the pastor's role is defined by the United Methodist Church's *Book of Discipline*.

While this book focuses primarily on lay governance, the pastor's role is essential. The pastor serves as the executive leader, manager of staff and ministry teams, and chief articulator of the congregation's mission and vision. The pastor serves ex officio on the Leadership Board as defined by *The Book of Discipline*. Voting authority is limited and context-dependent, particularly in matters related to the S/PPRC and Trustees, and must be handled carefully within the combined structure.

Eighth, the charge conference may delegate quite a bit of authority, but it cannot abdicate its responsibilities.

Simplified accountable structure does not eliminate the authority of the charge or church conference, nor does it grant the Leadership Board powers reserved to those bodies. The Leadership Board is always amenable to the charge conference. Some "one-board" models quietly slide into congregational governance without the authority of the congregation. Remembering this nonnegotiable protects you from congregational overreach.

Ninth, Trustees hold property in trust for the denomination.

The Book of Discipline is clear that local church property is held in trust for the United Methodist Church. Even within a simplified accountable structure, the Trustees' responsibility remains unchanged.

There are a few nuances: Trustees, and therefore the Leadership Board acting in that capacity, may not interfere with the pastor's use of church property for worship, ministry, or other purposes recognized by the Discipline and the established practices of the church. This principle has been reinforced in multiple recent United Methodist Church Judicial Council decisions.

In addition, certain property actions require approvals beyond the Leadership Board, such as leases and other property-related decisions, which may require charge or church conference action and the involvement or approval of the district superintendent and perhaps the District Board of Church Location and Building. Simplified structure does not remove these requirements or consolidate them into board-level authority alone.

It is also important to be clear about who the Trustees are. In simplified accountable structure, the Leadership Board *is* the Board of Trustees. This does not mean that one member or a small subset of the Leadership Board serves as Trustees. The entire nine-member Leadership Board, not including the pastor, carries that Trustee responsibility together.

This distinction matters because when boards are combined, some leaders assume they now have unrestricted authority over church facilities. They do not. Holding property in trust is a sacred and legal responsibility, not a managerial privilege. Honoring these denominational boundaries protects the congregation, the pastor, and the wider connection, and it ensures that SAS governance does not drift into congregational isolation or legal risk.

Finally, quorum requirements still apply.

In most cases, the quorum for Leadership Board action is the members present. However, when the Leadership Board exercises the legal authority and responsibility of the Trustees, a majority of Leadership Board members who are eligible Trustees must be present to conduct business (this quorum restriction is both a legal and BOD requirement).

Beyond Requirements and on to Best Practices

Once these nonnegotiables were clear, we were able to make a series of design decisions that go beyond minimum requirements and reflect best practices for accountable leadership. Along the way, we had to work through several practical questions, and those decisions show up throughout this book. For example, how should a charge conference be composed in a simplified accountable structure? While the Leadership Board could also function as the charge conference, with a few ex officio members, we had to ask whether it truly reflected the spirit of accountability in SAS, given that there was no broader congregational body to which the Leadership Board was answerable. We also had to ask whether the Committee on Nominations and Leadership Development could serve as an effective check on the Leadership Board if it were not included in the charge conference membership at all. Those questions led us to develop clear best practices for charge conference composition.

Similarly, we needed to unpack both the meaning of *The Book of Discipline* and the wide range of congregational practices related to the roles of treasurer and financial secretary. We share a bit more about this later in this chapter.

This newest edition of *Mission Possible* is filled with recommendations and best practices designed to help simplified accountable structure become a powerful tool for congregational vitality and mission. We share these recommendations not as rigid formulas, but as evolved and hard-earned wisdom shaped by real congregations in real contexts across the nation. And all along the way, we have stayed grounded in the expectations and nonnegotiable boundaries of the United Methodist *Book of Discipline*, not as a constraint, but as a gift that helps keep our shared work faithful and accountable, offering the clarity and safeguards that allow leaders to act responsibly and respond well to the real needs of the congregation and community.

Once you understand the nonnegotiables, the design work gets much easier. Now you are no longer guessing or reinventing the wheel. You are simply building a Leadership Board that is faithful to polity, clear in its authority, and strong enough to carry the mission. This is also where the Committee on Nominations and Leadership Development begins to move from theory to practice. It is one thing to understand how SAS works on paper. It is another thing to put names beside roles, organize leaders into classes, and present a slate that will actually function. So before we go any further, we want to show you what this looks like in the real world. What follows is a sample officiary, or nominations report to the charge conference, that illustrates how a Nominations Committee can present the Leadership Board and other required roles in a clear, Disciplinary, and congregation-friendly way.

Sample Nominations Report

2027 Anytown UMC Leadership

- Anytown United Methodist Church is governed according to the denomination's prescribed structure as found in *The Book of Discipline of the United Methodist Church.* All *Book of Discipline* and congregational policy references to the Church Council, Board of Trustees, Staff/Pastor-Parish Relations Committee, Endowment Committee, and Finance Committee shall be understood to refer to the Leadership Board. Where years are listed, they represent the final year of an individual's term.

- The Committee on Nominations and Leadership Development has undertaken a careful, discerning process to prepare the slate below for approval by the charge conference. The committee aims to match persons with open positions according to the following considerations:

- Maturity as a disciple of Jesus Christ

- Alignment with the church's mission: "Making disciples of Jesus Christ for the transformation of the world."

- Length of membership tenure at Anytown UMC, with a balancing of experience in leadership with welcoming and engaging new leaders

- Actively fulfilling member expectations (United Methodist *Book of Discipline* ¶ 217): prayers, presence, gifts, service, and witness

- History of leadership in small groups, classes, ministry teams, committees, and secular settings

- Balance and diversity of the committee, particularly with age, gender, and ethnicity

- Ability to fulfill board requirements, the Board's Leadership Covenant, and attend meetings

Anytown First UMC Charge Conference

- The charge conference includes the members of the Leadership Board, the Nominations Committee, pastors appointed to the congregation, the lay leader, a lay member to annual conference, the treasurer (if not a paid staff member), and all active and retired clergy who have designated our congregation as their home charge conference.
    - Pastor: Rev. Penny Preacher
    - Lay Leader: Ben Black
    - Lay Member of Annual Conference: Carol Clark
    - Treasurer: Cindy Cash
    - Retired Clergy Charge Conference Member: Rev. Gloria Goodpastor
- The Leadership Board serves as the incorporated institution's board of directors and serves as the executive committee of the charge conference.

Anytown UMC Leadership Board

RECOMMENDED version with a NINE-member Leadership Board:

Class of 2027	Class of 2028	Class of 2029
John Jones, T/F/SPR	Jennifer Jackson, T/F/SPR	Sue Smith, T/F/SPR/UWF
Carol Clark, T/F/SPR/LM	Ben Black, T/F/SPR/LL/C	David Dent, T/F/SPR/UMM
Yolanda Youngperson, F/SPR/Y	Larry Lee, T/F/SPR	Maria Martínez, T/F/SPR

Ex-Officio Clergy Member:
Pastor: Rev. Penny Preacher

Key

T - Trustee (minimum of five and a maximum of nine members, and includes at least 1/3 men and at least 1/3 women)

SPR - Staff/Pastor-Parish Relations (minimum of three and a maximum of nine members, not including the lay leader and lay member to annual conference who are members)

F - Finance

LM - Lay member to annual conference

LL - Lay leader

C - Chair

UMM - United Methodist Men

UWF - United Women in Faith

Y - Youth (Note: members under 18 cannot serve as an elected Trustee)

Notes on the Leadership Board:

- The appointed pastor is ex officio, serving with a vote only in matters defined in *The Book of Discipline.*
- At the January meeting, the Leadership Board will elect a Trustee chairperson, who will usually be the Leadership Board chairperson.
- The Leadership Board operates as a single, governing body encompassing the responsibilities and authority of the S/PPRC, Finance Committee, Endowment Committee, Church Council, and Trustees.
- Only one person from an immediate family residing in the same household shall serve on the Leadership Board.
- Members of the Leadership Board shall engage in and be attentive to developing and enhancing their own Christian spiritual life in light of the church's mission.
- The Leadership Board will not include any paid staff members or their family members.

Anytown UMC Nominations Committee (BOD ¶ 258)

Class of 2027	Class of 2028	Class of 2029
Carl Clark	Rollie Rich	Sally Smith
Belle Brady	Gene Galloway	Rob Roberts

Ex-Officio Members:

Lay Leader: Ben Black   Pastor: Rev. Penny Preacher

Notes on the Nominations Committee:

- The chairperson is the appointed senior pastor.
- A lay person elected by the committee shall serve as vice chair.
- Minimum of 3 and maximum of 9 members, not including the pastor and the lay leader.
- Retiring members of the committee shall not succeed themselves.
- Vacancies during the year shall be elected by the Leadership Board with the district superintendent's permission.

- Only one person from an immediate family residing in the same household shall serve on the committee.
- The charge of this committee is to identify, develop, deploy, evaluate, and monitor Christian spiritual leadership for the local congregation.
- Members of the committee shall engage in and be attentive to developing and enhancing their own Christian spiritual life in light of the mission of the church.
- Paid church staff and household members of paid staff will not serve on the committee.

Pro+SAS Resource Hub

Note: The online Pro+ SAS Resource Hub has an editable version of this document that also includes an example of a Childcare Ministry Advisory Board.

The Nominations Committee in SAS

We have been there, and we are sure you have, too. You have attended meetings that seem like absolute wastes of time. You have likely also attended very important meetings where people seemed elusive, unplugged, afraid to speak up, or even absent. There are other times when people take offices so they can have the title but have no interest in doing the work. On occasion, we have experienced situations in which people have a seat at the committee table for honor or prestige rather than for responsibility.

You may have even worked on committees where committee members bring personal agendas to the table or feel that their job at the leadership table is to "fight for their constituents" (a particular ministry team, the quilting circle, scouts, their beloved Sunday school or worship time, the endowment) when it comes time to prioritize staffing and finances. We have all served on dysfunctional committees at some point. Changing the structure is only part of the solution. We must also reconsider how we identify, nominate, elect, and equip the people sitting at the table. That is the work of the Committee on Nominations and Leadership Development. See Chapter 11 for more information on this important work.

We Didn't Forget the Treasurer

A common question we hear when introducing simplified accountable structure is, "What about the treasurer and the financial secretary?" It is a fair question, and an important one. Depending on the church size and context, these fiduciary roles are filled by staff members, elected laypersons, or even contracted bookkeepers.

Their work is essential, but their roles are functional and operational, not governing or strategic. Their primary responsibility is to ensure accurate records, sound financial practices, faithful stewardship of resources, and faithful execution of the Leadership Board's financial decisions, rather than to provide strategic leadership or exercise governing authority. The financial health, integrity, and transparency of the congregation depend on their skill and consistent service. Paid or unpaid, the treasurer and financial secretary serve in staff or staff-like roles.

For that reason, we strongly recommend that the treasurer and financial secretary not serve as ex officio members of the Leadership Board. If a Leadership Board member, who just happens to be the treasurer, serves a three-year term, that is okay as long as everyone is clear that they serve on the Leadership Board for their spiritual leadership, not for their math skills, and during Leadership Board meetings, this leader is seated as a Leadership Board member and not as the treasurer.

So, instead of the individuals in these roles serving ex officio in a governing capacity, the responsibility for understanding, interpreting, and stewarding the church's finances rests with the nine members of the Leadership Board, who work and lead together. The treasurer and financial secretary are responsible for providing accurate records, clear reports, and professional expertise, but the *work of financial discernment and leadership belongs to the Leadership Board as a whole.*

We have seen too many churches allow or encourage the "finance person" to be the sole decision-maker for the spending and budgeting. When financial understanding is concentrated in a single individual, Leadership Boards tend to defer rather than discern. Healthy boards develop shared financial fluency so that stewardship becomes a collective fiduciary responsibility, owned by the entire Leadership Board rather than delegated to one or two people.

This does not mean the treasurer and financial secretary are excluded from the leadership of the church. They are occasionally invited to report to the Leadership Board, participate in appropriate work teams, and provide the tools and reports needed for informed decision making. In churches where these roles are held by church members rather than staff, they may also serve as ex officio members of the charge conference, along with members of the Nominations Committee, if the congregation so chooses.

In some contexts, this approach represents a significant cultural shift. The goal is not to diminish the importance of financial leadership, but to place it within the congregational system where it best supports both accountable leadership and the church's mission and vision.

Organizational Chart Example

The following is an example of the recommended organizational chart, outlining a simplified structure with accountable leadership. This chart illustrates clear lines of authority, responsibility, and accountability. It provides clarity on who reports to whom, the role for each, and the communication channels. The chart will remain consistent from the pastor and everything above that position.

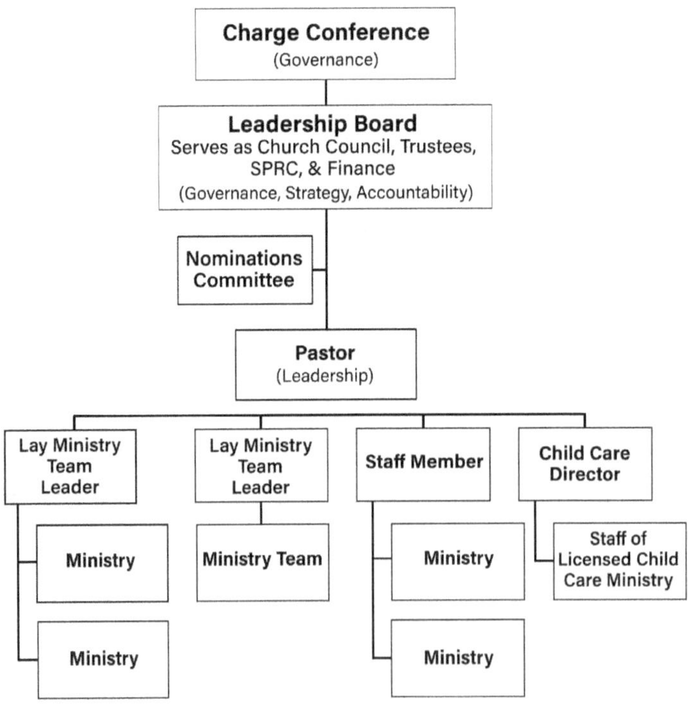

Moving to a simplified accountable structure model (consolidating the four administrative committees into one) is only a portion of the decisions you will need to carefully discern in terms of structure. You will need to make additional decisions, such as whether to adopt the recommended nine-member Leadership Board, how UMM and UWF affiliations will be handled, the role of youth on the Leadership Board, how staff will interact with the lead pastor, whether the chair will also serve as the lay leader, and so on. This is yet another reason to have an Authorized SAS Coach alongside you on this journey to help you navigate the decisions that are best for your congregation and context.

Take the time to carefully discern the most effective structure for your context. All the Disciplinary requirements for all the committees apply to your new Leadership Board, which means that you will be flipping through multiple sections of *The Book of Discipline*. A photocopy of the structure is not enough preparation. You will need to understand and communicate the mechanics of your new structure. Remember, don't create a sports-car-style structure in a context where no one knows how to drive a stick. Keep it simple. Keep it flexible. Don't create a precedent based on a particular person who is now in the picture that will create issues later when that person is no longer present.

Notes

CHAPTER SEVEN

SAS (Governance) and Ministry Teams (Impact)

Steering and Pedaling Toward Impactful Ministry

Dan Entwistle, the senior executive director and COO at the United Methodist Church of the Resurrection in Kansas City, uses the excellent metaphor of a bicycle to describe the difference between the strategic work of a governing board and the mobilization work of ministry teams. Imagine a bicycle; there are two major points of interaction with every bike. You have your handlebars and your pedals. The handlebars are for steering. Through the handlebars, you set the direction you want to go. The pedals are for locomotion—to create the power that takes the bicycle where you are steering it. A bike with no pedals goes nowhere. A bike without a working set of handlebars will land you in a ditch. The Leadership Board's job is to provide **steering**—to set direction through strategic visioning, strategic planning, mission alignment, accountability, and administration. For ministry **mobilization**—to actually get to the place Christ is calling your church—you will need some pedals. Mobilization is the work of ministry teams.

Ministry Teams and SAS Governance

The ministry team leaders and staff who report to the pastor can change from time to time based on the needs and ministries of the season and the church (more on this later in the teams section). Ministry teams are created to meet a ministry need and may disband when the need is met or the ministry is accomplished. For example, a ministry team to plan, implement, and evaluate Vacation Bible School can be assembled and in place for a few months and then disbanded once VBS has been conducted and evaluated.

There will likely be a few standing ministry teams due to ongoing ministry needs. For example, almost every church has a ministry team responsible for hospitality. Almost every church has a team responsible for ongoing building maintenance (more on that later in this chapter). For those ongoing ministry teams, team members can serve for a few days or weeks or for a decade, depending on the team's needs, the person's availability, and their sense of calling. This type of model affords great flexibility and adaptability.

Members of ministry teams are not nominated and elected by the charge conference for specific terms, unlike the members of a governing committee of the church (the Leadership Board). Instead, ministry team leaders and team members are identified by their gifts and passion for a particular area of ministry, with no predetermined length of service. Teams are usually led by a serving disciple (unpaid staff) or a paid staff member and should ultimately be accountable to the pastor.

We suggest that a move to a simplified structure include changing the names of various ministry committees (such as Worship Committee) to names that more appropriately describe a ministry team's defined work, such as Worship Planning Team, Worship Design Advisory Team, Praise Team, or Worship and Hospitality Team. This helps define expectations for team members and clarifies the differences between the governance of committees (steering) and the ministry of teams (mobilization).

The Building Maintenance Team is Different from the Board of Trustees

Let us take a moment to discuss Trustees and building maintenance. This is another area where churches stumble in moving to the simplified structure. Obviously, building and grounds maintenance needs do not go away in the new structural and leadership model. The church property still needs to be maintained. Using the bicycle metaphor, there is still pedaling to do. In our experience, the people who enjoy hands-on work do not necessarily enjoy fiduciary and strategic work or attending meetings. The hands-on work is their ministry using their gifts, experience, and passion! In many churches, the trustees are seen as the people who perform the actual hands-on work on the facility and grounds. They maintain the grounds, change the light bulbs in the sanctuary, and fix the running toilet. They also take care of the fiduciary responsibilities of the Trustees (such as property insurance, facility policies, lease agreements, filing bylaws and articles of incorporation with the state). But in most cases, the majority of Trustees' time and energy is spent on building and parsonage repairs and maintenance. By and large, they have become great caretakers of the facilities.

Toolbox or Briefcase Work?

Meanwhile, other important work is left undone. We believe that "briefcase work" is the intended function of the Board of Trustees, even within the inherited committee-based structure. Like other administrative committees, such as Finance, S/PPRC, and Church Council, the Board of Trustees was originally designed to carry governing responsibility and purpose, not maintenance or hands-on work. Over time, however, this division of responsibility has shifted, and the lines between governance and building maintenance have become blurred.

Early in my ministry, I (Blake) remember a Trustee meeting when the topic of a running toilet came up. We actually paused the meeting, and the chair of the Trustees grabbed his tools from his trunk and, moments later, was on the bathroom floor with a wrench while the rest of us looked on and offered unsolicited advice. The toolbox versus briefcase lines were not only blurred, they were obliterated!

Review the work currently handled by your traditional Trustee Committee.

- What part of the work really belongs to a building maintenance team, the toolbox work?
- What portions of the work remain the fiduciary responsibilities of the Trustees as the corporate officers of the nonprofit organization, the briefcase work that, in SAS, becomes the responsibility of the Leadership Board?

Building Maintenance Team: Get Started Now

Churches can separate the toolbox (Building Maintenance Team) and briefcase work (the Trustees) without moving to a simplified structure. Your church can immediately begin the transition towards creating a Building Maintenance Team to handle day-to-day facility functions. This shift also includes moving this work from an administrative function to a ministry team. Empower this team through the Guiding Principles and assign it to report to the current Trustees (while still in the traditional structure before transitioning to SAS) as an interim step towards future simplification and to place the types of work in the appropriate lanes. This step not only frees up your Trustees for more appropriate "briefcase work," but it also helps the congregation imagine doing its ministry differently. Along the way, the toolbox-toting disciples are having a blast caring for the facility.

The answers to those questions have led us to recommend, based on experience across many congregations, the establishment of a Building Maintenance Team. This specialized *ministry team* is given some authority and responsibility to handle budgeted improvements, repairs, and routine maintenance within the clear boundaries set by the Leadership Board in written Guiding Principles (see the suggested sample of Guiding Principles in the online SAS Resource Hub). When those boundaries are clear, the Building Maintenance Ministry Team can focus on the facilities work they love without being pulled into fiduciary, policy, or governance responsibilities and meetings that belong to the Leadership Board in their role as Trustees.

How all this works depends on context:

- In small and midsize churches, a Building Maintenance Team often functions with spending limits and priorities and is responsive to the pastor, just like any other ministry team. In these congregations, the Building Maintenance Team is trusted, empowered, and given reasonable authority to address day-to-day maintenance needs. For many people, this is meaningful ministry. They love fixing things. They love improving the space. Give them a wrench and a ladder, and they are happy.
- In larger congregations, particularly those with paid maintenance staff, custodians, and maybe a director of operations or business administrator, the role of the team changes dramatically. The church does not need a maintenance team unpredictably roaming the campus, starting projects, or unintentionally bypassing staff leadership. In these settings, Building Maintenance Team members function more like volunteer facilities workers than an independent, proactive team. They work within a clear reporting structure, coordinate through the appropriate facilities staff supervisor, and operate in accordance with Guiding Principles that outline established spending limits and approval parameters.

And, yes, writing these Guiding Principles actually matters! I (Blake) learned that the hard way. I once worked with a church where a new Building Maintenance Team was commissioned to handle simple tasks like changing lightbulbs and replacing stained ceiling tiles. Perhaps the team might, if they were feeling productive, freshen the paint in a classroom in the aging education building. It all sounded reasonable enough, so no Guiding Principles were crafted. Somewhere along the way, however, the Building Maintenance Team's appetite quietly expanded. Acting in good faith and with incredible enthusiasm, the team actually hired their own contractor to remodel the church bathrooms. No permission. No vetting. No approved plans. No permits. They also scheduled the work themselves, without checking the church calendar, nearly colliding with a major congregational event.

Everyone involved had good *intentions...probably.* The problem was that none of the people, committees, or staff involved were clear about boundaries, and they never documented their expectations.

That experience taught all of us an important lesson. Building Maintenance Teams should be empowered to repair and maintain facilities to their original use. They should not initiate renovations, redesign spaces, or commit the church financially without authorization. Clear reporting relationships, a defined scope, and spending limits protect everyone involved: the congregation, staff, and volunteers. When boundaries are clear, Building Maintenance Teams thrive. Their work becomes a genuine ministry rather than an accidental case study in why Guiding Principles exist.

When creating a Building Maintenance Team, select a trusted team leader and give them some authority to select team members as needed. In midsize and larger congregations, this ministry team would most likely report to a staff person or to the pastor. You will also want to specify the limits of the team's spending authority in your Guiding Principles. Here is an organizational chart. Note the circled Building Maintenance Team:

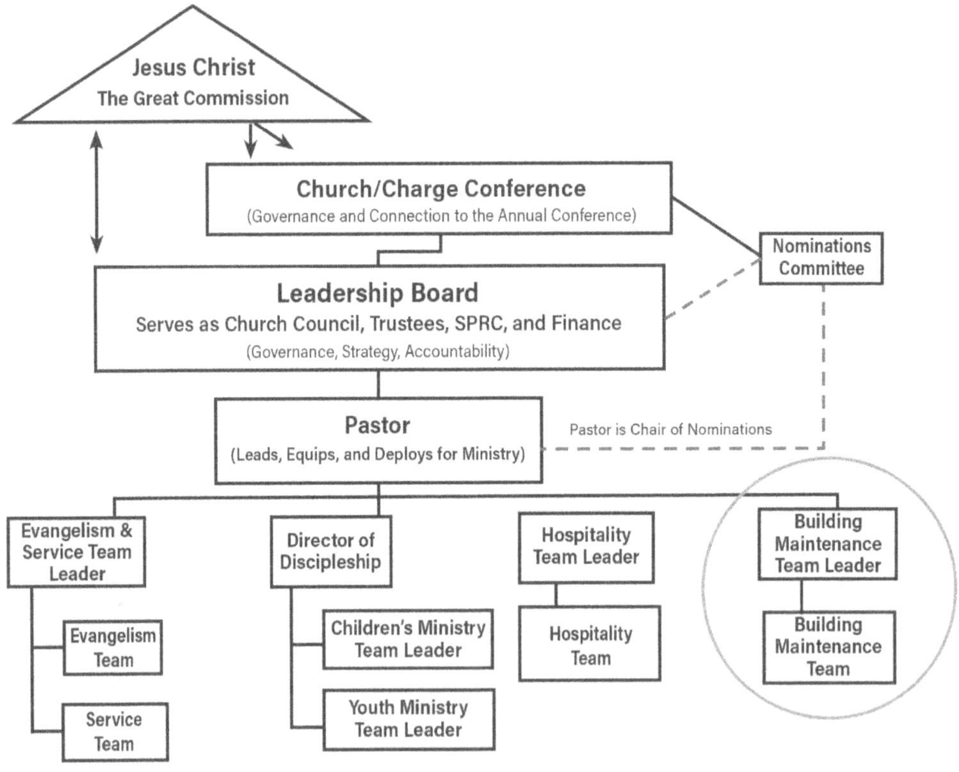

CHAPTER EIGHT

Leveraging Leadership: Work Teams

Using Work Teams

As stated earlier, the Leadership Board will at times initiate work teams. The use of work teams provides the most efficient and effective leadership approach. Examples of effective use of work teams include preparing a preliminary budget or a personnel policy update to report back to the Leadership Board for discussion and approval. Another example might be a work team conducting an in-depth study of a new multisite concept and bringing its findings to the full Leadership Board for discussion and consideration. A third example might be a work team partnering with the pastor on a proposed stewardship campaign and bringing the proposal back to the Leadership Board for discussion and approval.

Do you see the theme here? A work team is a small team (maybe one to five people). They are a small team coming together for a specific task or project for a specific, short period of time. Work teams do legwork, detail work, or preliminary work on behalf of the Leadership Board. They work on in-depth projects outside the larger Leadership Board and then bring them back to the Leadership Board for discussion and potential approval.

Work teams do not have the authority to make decisions independently. We (Kay and Blake) have both worked with congregations in which the three "SPR specialists" (not the recommended model) completed the pastor's evaluation and submitted it to the district office without the knowledge or approval of the full Leadership Board (who has the authority and responsibility for S/PPRC matters). Obviously, this is an unacceptable procedure. Three people working on behalf of the Leadership Board do not have the responsibility or authority to make these types of decisions. Unfortunately, we have witnessed this type of organizational structure lead to very unhealthy and unfortunate consequences.

Creating a Work Team

Each work team will have at least one Leadership Board member assigned by the Leadership Board chair. This provides continuity, alignment, and communication between the work team and the Leadership Board. We recommend that the rest of the work team consist primarily of non-board members. This spreads the work out and allows more people to share their gifts and experience. Being a part of a work team does not require attending a Leadership Board meeting. The Leadership Board member(s) on the team can likely carry the team's message and work back to the Leadership Board. However, it is certainly fine for work team members to attend a board meeting if it would be helpful to the work under consideration by the Leadership Board.

Utilizing work teams provides the Leadership Board a fruitful opportunity to widen the circle of leaders, experience, expertise, and gifts. The Leadership Board is not constrained to using only Leadership Board members for work teams. In fact, we greatly encourage the inclusion of work team members beyond the Leadership Board. People from the congregation with expertise or passion around certain topics or projects can be integrated into work teams. It is amazing how many subject-matter experts are present in our congregations yet are never tapped to use their gifts and experiences in the life of the church. You may also have folks from your congregation who would love to work on a short-term project but are not yet ready or able to serve as a leader, particularly if the leadership demands a three-year term of office.

Additionally, work teams provide a great opportunity for former Leadership Board members to offer their expertise, historical information, and experience, and for upcoming leaders to engage at the next level as part of a larger philosophy of equipping the next generation of leadership. And, as we suggested earlier, this is also a fantastic opportunity to pull in people from the community to speak into the work and discernment of the Leadership Board. This would be especially helpful for strategic and generative work in connecting the church with the community.

Work Team Assignments

Work teams are a great option when creating or editing numerical or text-rich documents. Wordsmithing at the Leadership Board table is not a good practice. In fact, it is often a terrible distraction from the Leadership Board's most important generative, strategic, and mission-accountability work. Wordsmithing in a group is time-consuming and often yields suboptimal results. For example, when a guiding principle needs to be created, the Leadership Board chair can assign a Leadership Board member to form a small work team to draft it for placement on the consent calendar at the next meeting. Don't spend time perfecting the exact wording at the Leadership Board table once the spirit of the guiding principle has been determined. The exact wording can be massaged by a work team of one to two people. The best use of the Leadership Board meeting time is working from drafts or final versions for approval—not from scratch.

Work teams are assigned "projects" by the Leadership Board chair when the need arises. The Leadership Board chair calls on one member of the Leadership Board to take responsibility for the project and for assembling the work team. The Leadership Board chair stipulates the exact purpose, the desired work to be completed by the work team, and a timeline for completing the work. That Leadership Board member is responsible for completing the project but can delegate or collaborate as they see fit.

The Leadership Board member assigned to the project can pull another leader or two from the Leadership Board or, better yet, pull people from the congregation to assist. This allows others to be involved, expands the pool of resources available, and enables those who are unable to make a longer-term leadership commitment to still serve in a shorter-term capacity. Even community members may be pulled into a work team to share their expertise, knowledge, or experience related to the project.

Work teams do not have the authority to make decisions. They work within the confines of the assignment and disband once the assignment is completed. Work teams are not standing teams. They are assigned a project, complete it, and then disband. Work teams may be together for a few days to a couple of months, but typically, the project window is very short-term.

What types of projects are assigned to work teams? This will vary from congregation to congregation and for the various seasons of the year, but here are a few examples of the typical types of projects work teams are assigned:

- Create a rough draft of the initial Guiding Principles.
- Review the personnel handbook and provide suggested edits and additions.
- Research and provide information on the new subdivision being built in town or arrange for the developer or builder to present to the Leadership Board to provide a clear understanding of the new neighbors who will be moving into the area and how best to connect with them.
- Create an initial budget draft.
- Place the final touches on the goals from the strategic ministry planning retreat and ensure they are SMARTER goals. Present the final draft for approval by the Leadership Board.
- Create an initial draft of technology and security policies.
- Explore information and the possibility of a multisite ministry.

Work teams allow for the most efficient use of time during Leadership Board meetings while still encouraging efficient forward momentum. Often, drafts of projects being developed by work teams can be shared electronically between meetings for the Leadership Board's input, preventing progress from stalling. In addition, there are times when projects are assigned and fully completed in a shared document and never have to return to the Leadership Board agenda—if the project's scope already includes that authorization.

Work Teams Are NOT Specialists

Leadership Boards are encouraged to create work teams as needed to complete specific tasks or assignments within a certain time frame and bring the work back to the Leadership Board. We recommend shifting the people and work involved amongst the different Leadership Board members. Otherwise, we find, for example, that one or two people become the de facto "finance specialists" because they are always called upon to lead budget writing.

Please note that we consider work teams to be an entirely different, much healthier approach than permanently assigned specialists or representatives. We believe that task-focused work teams function more readily as we initially envisioned for specialists or representatives in earlier versions of SAS and as sometimes found in other single-board models. However, by eliminating the titles and not assuming spheres of responsibility, it becomes much clearer to the leaders and the congregation alike that all nine Leadership Board members have full responsibility and authority for the combined four administrative functions. Our approach supports the axiom that boards can delegate but never abdicate responsibility.

We have found that using work teams creates less confusion for both leaders and congregations than using the titles "specialist" or "representative." Flexible, task-focused work teams allow for a much more effective, organic use of time, energy, experience, and passions by the Leadership Board members, as well as by those in the larger congregation and community who might be pulled into a work team. We will share more about our concerns regarding specialists in Chapter 10, which covers common challenges later in this section.

Notes

CHAPTER NINE

Right-Sizing Your Leadership Structure

Right-Sizing for Large, Multi-Staff Churches

In larger congregations with multiple clergy and paid program staff, the Designing Phase requires special attention to roles and boundaries. Associate pastors and executive pastors are vital partners in ministry, yet they (usually) serve in the management lane rather than the governance lane. Their primary relationship is with the senior pastor, not the Leadership Board. Multi-staff churches often drift into dual pastoral hierarchies when associate pastors operate as de facto board members or when long-tenured staff begin speaking for or around the senior pastor in Leadership Board conversations. SAS requires simplicity and clarity. Staff attend Leadership Board meetings only when needed for information or context—*as an exception, not as a rule.* Decision-making authority rests with the elected Leadership Board and the senior pastor, who then aligns staff and ministry teams with the mission, vision, and Guiding Principles of the church. This clarity becomes even more important when senior leadership changes, since associate roles can subtly shift depending on personality rather than structure. Right-sizing keeps everyone in the proper lane.

When I (Blake) served as an executive pastor of a large church, the senior pastor and I intentionally organized our work so that I spent much of my time with governing officers, helping translate the missional goals of the Leadership Board and the senior pastor. He wanted me in the Leadership Board meetings, but I had to be incredibly careful not to overshadow his leadership. With any other pastoral team and board, it might have been a disaster, but because we were purposeful, clear in our roles, and willing to let one another lead without competition, it worked. Again, context matters.

For these reasons, we strongly recommend that executive pastors and other staff not be listed in official documents or the defacto practice as ex officio members of the Leadership Board. When staff participation is needed, the chair and lead pastor may invite an executive pastor or another staff member as a guest for a specific purpose or season. This preserves clarity without creating confusion about authority. Large churches do not suffer from a lack of leadership; they suffer from blurred authority and responsibility. Especially in large, multi-staff churches, written clarity matters more than good intentions. *Leadership structures that rely on personalities rather than roles tend to have difficulty during pastoral transitions.* Remember, setting clear boundaries upfront based on roles, not people, prevents setting unhealthy precedents in years to come.

Clear lanes protect everyone. They protect the authority of the Leadership Board, the leadership of the senior pastor, and the ministry focus of the staff. Right-sizing the Designing Phase is not about limiting leadership. It is about ensuring that leadership remains accountable, durable, and aligned with the church's mission.

Right-Sizing for Multisite Churches

We are seeing many congregations discover the benefits of becoming *multisite*. This word encompasses a variety of models, including (but certainly not limited to) multiple worshiping campuses, fresh expressions, "mother-daughter" configurations, and resourceful congregations that have been handed the keys of closing churches and are attempting to rebrand and relaunch as multisite. For example, the congregation Blake serves adopted a smaller church on the verge of closing and relaunched it as its East Campus of First United Methodist Church.

We believe a simplified accountable structure is especially important in these complex congregations because there is an inherent challenge in bringing missional alignment across multiple worshiping communities. When a multisite congregation uses the legacy structure of multiple committees with assigned "representatives" from each campus, it creates silos within silos, and the integrity of mission and alignment is usually the first victim.

Contextual factors can greatly influence the design of your simplified accountable leadership structure in multisite congregations. First, if a congregation has been asked to take responsibility for a closed church or merge a smaller church about to close into a larger church, there will be some voices asking (and occasionally demanding) that the remnant from the merging congregation have representatives on the receiving church's governing committees. We know of a large congregation, with thousands of members, that automatically delegated one or two seats on every Leadership Board to the worshipers of a declining church that had fewer than fifty members when it closed. The new Leadership Board members were used to a family-sized church and had no experience leading in a church system as complex as the receiving church, with dozens of staff, multiple clergy, and hundreds of small groups and ministries. Designating these seats disrupted the congregation's trajectory and impeded its leadership development pathway.

We understand the human need to be included, and we hope that the remnant will be welcomed, discipled, and cared for as valued members of the receiving congregation. However, this welcome is not required to include a precious seat on the Leadership Board. We therefore recommend that no automatic ex officio seats be designated for the merging or closing congregation. The receiving congregation needs to be able to focus on its mission and vision. Including members on the Leadership Board who have not bought into the vision and have not been enculturated and equipped by the congregation's leadership development pathway will damage the church's leadership culture and its ability to be vital and fruitful.

In multisite church models, a question often arises: Do the campus pastors belong on the SAS Leadership Board? The answer to that question is highly contextual, but we can quickly imagine a situation in which there are more clergy at the table than board members. So, we recommend starting with just the lead pastor on the board and inviting campus pastors as guests, when appropriate.

In congregations with an intentional multisite strategy, we recommend that the Nominations Committee consider campus location along with other diversity factors when building a healthy, diverse Leadership Board. This means identifying the best leaders with an eye for including leaders beyond the "home campus." This may evolve over time. Since the lead pastor works with the congregation's Leadership Board and (ultimately) oversees all the campus pastors, accountability flows through the congregation's Leadership Board, via the lead pastor, to the campus pastors. The Leadership Board will also need to be intentional about listening and ensure that their two-way communications opportunities include all campuses.

Right-Sizing for Midsize Churches

Midsize congregations often experience the most confusion when redesigning their leadership structure, not because they lack leaders, but because "managerial" leadership is everywhere. Over time, these churches develop a dense web of influence made up of long-serving disciples, program leaders, staff, committees, and informal decision-makers. Authority is widely shared but rarely clarified. Many decisions are made through relationships, momentum, or precedent rather than through a clearly defined governance process.

As a result, a Leadership Board meeting in a midsize church can look like a jumble of laity and part-time staff who are also frequently members of the congregation. Often, the meeting is co-led by the pastor and the Leadership Board chairperson. Agendas tend to zip from strategy to the program calendar, ministry discussions, then to curriculum choices, and finally to custodial concerns, all in the same meeting.

Because midsize churches are accustomed to broad participation in decision making, the shift to a simplified accountable structure can feel like a loss of voice or a narrowing of leadership. In reality, SAS is asking a different question. Instead of asking who has influence, SAS asks who has authority, responsibility, and accountability for the mission. This shift requires intentional design work, especially in congregations where leadership has historically functioned through overlapping roles and informal agreements. Doing this design work for SAS may, in fact, avoid future obstacles in church growth and vitality that old leadership practices would have otherwise unintentionally blocked.

One of the most common challenges in midsize churches is the assumption that effective leadership requires broad representation at the governance table. When a simplified board is introduced, leaders who previously shaped decisions through committees or program roles may feel displaced or sidelined. Without careful communication, this new structure can be misinterpreted as a consolidation of power rather than a *clarification and redistribution of responsibility and authority.*

Right-sizing the Designing Phase for midsize churches means acknowledging this leadership jumble without trying to preserve it structurally. SAS does not eliminate leadership. It reallocates it. Governance is concentrated in the Leadership Board, while ministry leadership is intentionally expanded through teams and program leadership. This distinction allows more people to lead meaningfully without confusing management, ministry, and governance.

Midsize churches benefit from designing clear pathways for leadership development that help leaders understand where their gifts are best exercised. Some leaders are called to governance and strategic discernment. Many more are called to lead programs, ministries, and teams. When these pathways are named and honored, midsize churches often discover that SAS actually increases participation and ownership rather than diminishing it.

The Designing Phase is also the moment to name cultural assumptions that may resist clarity. Long-standing patterns of shared decision making, informal authority, or "how we've always done it" will not disappear on their own. Right-sizing at this stage requires patient education, clear language, and repeated reassurance that accountability and collaboration are not mutually exclusive. When midsize churches do this work well, they are often surprised by how much energy is released, how flexibility is born, and how momentum is created once leadership roles are clarified and aligned with the mission.

Right-Sizing for Small Churches

Small churches require particular care in the Designing Phase, not because they are incapable of accountable leadership, but because they are often asked to do too much with too few people. Simplified accountable structure can be a gift to small congregations, but only when it is right-sized to their real capacity rather than imposed as a one-size-fits-all model.

To move into the most simplified structure, a congregation will need six to nine Leadership Board members, plus the pastor. Because nine is the standard (and maximum) size required by *The Book of Discipline* for Trustees and Staff/Pastor-Parish Relations, this remains the recommended size whenever possible. However, for smaller congregations, a six-member Leadership Board is a permitted and faithful option. Six members, with two in each class, fulfill the minimum *Book of Discipline* requirements for the S/PPRC while offering a more realistic and sustainable leadership structure for churches with limited lay capacity.

Again, the BOD provides the flexibility for small churches to design a board with six members, with two in each class. Yes, rotating classes are nonnegotiable. Even when leadership pools are shallow, intentional rotation creates space for rest, prevents burnout, creates natural off-ramps when leaders become ineffective, and reminds the congregation that leadership belongs to the whole body, not a few faithful saints. When the same few leaders remain in governance roles indefinitely, accountability weakens, and fatigue sets in. Terms of office feel a lot more like life sentences.

It is important to note that even in this most simplified form, one other required elected committee remains in place. The Committee on Nominations and Leadership Development must still be elected by the charge conference, with a minimum of three members serving in three-year classes, along with the pastor and lay leader. Often, because of limited membership, we have seen spouses of Leadership Board members serve on the Nominations Committee. We offer no ideal solution here, only an honest acknowledgment of the realities many small churches face when staring at a blank charge conference nominations form.

Many small-church Leadership Boards struggle because they try to manage and govern simultaneously. Trying to do both at the same time is like asking one person to be the referee, cheerleader, coach, and player all at once. Each role matters, but none can be done well when they are collapsed together. This is why it is recommended that no one who is actively leading a ministry area also serves on the Leadership Board whenever alternatives exist. When Leadership Board members attempt to govern while also managing ministry, they inevitably drift out of their governance lane and begin planning programs, "calling plays," and solving operational problems rather than setting direction, maintaining accountability, and aligning resources with mission.

Because of this governance/management ministry overlap, small churches must think less in terms of separate ministry "lanes" and more in terms of "roles" or "hats," the different kinds of work that must be done in the life of the church. When no distinction is made between these roles, leaders default to ministry management simply because it is the most visible and urgent work. Left undone is the strategic (governance) work that invites the congregation to ask harder, deeper questions about its calling and its future. This dynamic exists in churches of every size, but it is especially common in small congregations where devoted leaders have to wear so many ministry, operational, and leadership hats.

Small churches also require adjustments in how ministry team leadership is supported and supervised. In mid-sized and larger congregations, staff and ministry teams typically report to the lead pastor or to a designated clergy or staff supervisor. That assumption does not hold in churches with part-time, shared, or bi-vocational pastors. It is often unrealistic for every ministry team leader to report directly to a pastor who may serve multiple congregations, is appointed part-time, or lives in another county. In these contexts, some ministry team leaders (particularly the Building Maintenance Team) may report directly to the Leadership Board rather than to the pastor. This is not a failure of implementing SAS. It is a necessary and faithful adaptation to the realities of small church life. One guiding principle matters here: every ministry team leader should know, in writing, to whom they are accountable, whether that is the pastor, the Leadership Board as a whole, or a specific Leadership Board member serving as a liaison. Note below an organizational chart showing how some ministry teams could report to the Leadership Board rather than the pastor.

Finally, the Designing Phase calls small churches to have an honest conversation about informal leadership. Long-tenured members, former administrative committee members, major givers, or the person who "has always handled that" often carry significant influence, even when they hold no formal role. Every congregation has these leaders, and their voices matter. Their history and commitment should be honored. At the same time, informal influence should not quietly replace accountable leadership and governance. When decisions are made in hallways, parking lots, or private conversations, the Leadership Board is left to react rather than lead. Identifying informal influence early allows the Leadership Board to design healthy communication pathways, clarify how input is gathered, and reduce triangulation. This clarity protects relationships, strengthens trust, and allows leadership to function with transparency and integrity.

Right-sizing the Designing Phase for small churches means accepting that some overlap is unavoidable while still protecting the integrity of accountable leadership. When roles are outlined, expectations are realistic, and adaptations are embraced, small churches will find that simplified accountable structure brings greater clarity, healthier leadership, and renewed energy for ministry rather than an added burden.

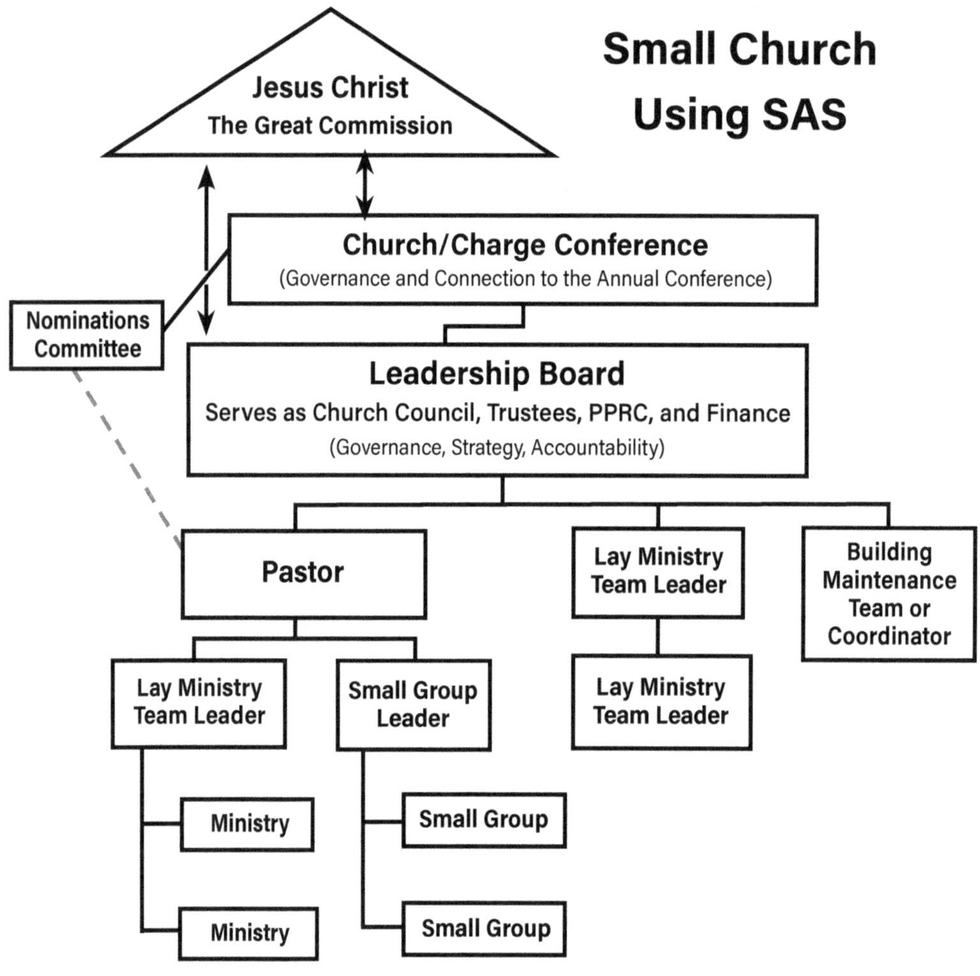

Right-Sizing for Cooperative Parishes and Multi-Point Charges

In the United Methodist Church, smaller congregations are often linked together as a multi-point charge/circuit, a cooperative parish, or as a single charge. If your congregation is considering moving toward a simplified accountable leadership structure, but you are linked with a congregation that follows a more traditional structure, be sure to include your district superintendent in the conversation about the conference's expectations for sharing the work of the Staff/Pastor-Parish Relations Committee (S/PPRC).

If churches in a multi-point charge are considered a single charge, it is appropriate to have a single S/PPRC composed of members from each church to represent the interests and ministries of all congregations. One solution is for the Nominations Committee to assign a few members from your Leadership Board to serve as representatives on the combined Charge S/PPRC (including the lay leader) and to have those assignments approved as part of your charge conference.

In cooperative parishes, wide latitude is given for structuring relationships among multiple congregations. Your Leadership Board may serve as the congregation's S/PPRC and relate to the other S/PPRCs in the cooperative parish, or a separate parish-wide S/PPRC may need to be created by your charge conference. Your district superintendent will certainly have expectations around these options. Additionally, in some flavors of cooperative parish, there are options to create a single parish or charge council to oversee the ministries of all the worshiping and ministry locations.

In all these options, a multi-point charge or cooperative parish will want to ensure representation from all the congregations. For instance, if three congregations of similar size are on a charge together in a cooperative parish model, then the Parish Leadership Board of nine people would be made up of three from each congregation (preferably one from each class).

You will note that, in the sample diagram below, each congregation has a local Board of Trustees. It can be small, with a minimum of three people in successive classes. Due to legal and property issues, local churches will need separate Boards of Trustees. Remember, unless the churches merge into a single legal entity, each church remains a separate nonprofit corporation. However, if all the constituent congregations have experience in the simplified accountable leadership structure and are willing to share a combined Board of Trustees made up of members from each local church, you may decide to take the final step in simplification, where the entire parish has one single governing board with accountability and one Nominations Committee made up of members from all the ministry sites. Whichever model you and your DS choose, be sure to fully document it!

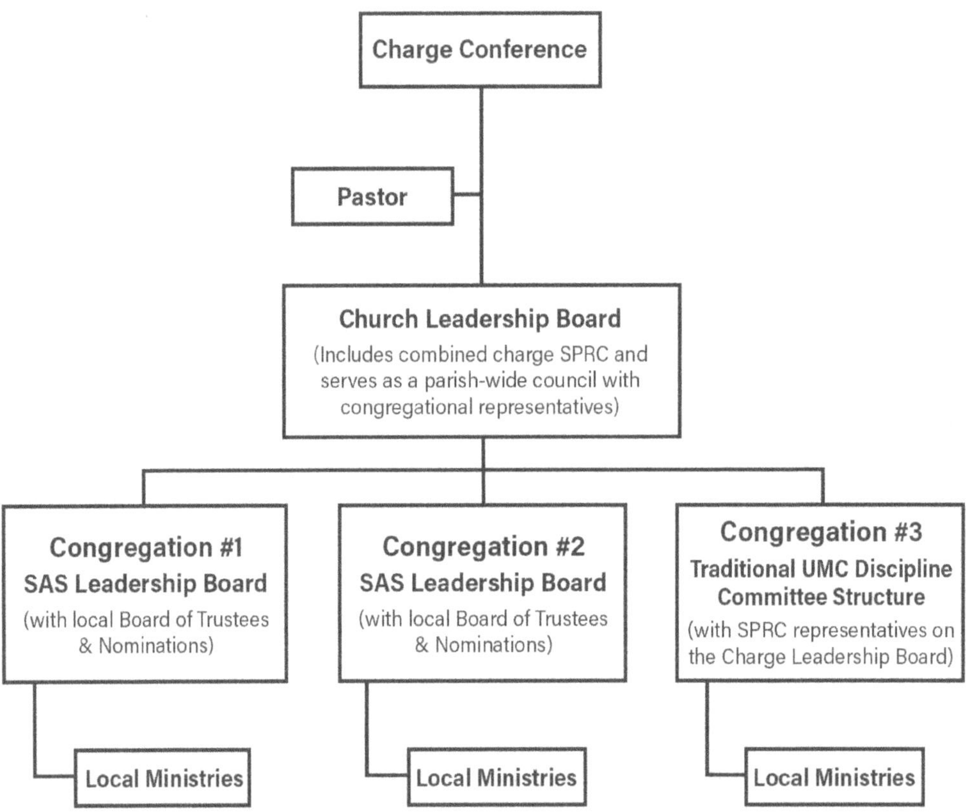

Right-sizing for Childcare, Endowments, and Associated Nonprofits

Some congregations operate ministries or related entities that do not neatly fit into a simplified governance structure. Childcare programs, endowments, and associated nonprofits often carry their own boards, licenses, governing documents, and financial systems. These relationships require particular care in the Designing Phase so that simplification does not unintentionally create additional legal, financial, or missional risk. It is important to remember that these ministries or associated nonprofits often operate using the church's name and reputation, sometimes for decades.

We begin with church-based childcare ministries, which generally fall into one of two categories—and the distinction matters.

Childcare Programs that Share the Church's Incorporation Status

In some churches, the childcare ministry (including preschools, parents' day out, learning centers, etc.) operates as a tuition-based ministry program of the congregation, sharing the church's legal identity, employer identification number, insurance coverage, and liability exposure. In these cases, the Leadership Board, acting in its role as the legal Board of Trustees, officially holds the childcare license and carries ultimate legal and fiduciary responsibility and authority for the ministry. Any BOD ¶ 256.2(c) childcare board (not required, but optional) in this arrangement must be clearly understood as *advisory* in nature. We strongly recommend that you include the word *advisory* in the team's title and highly recommend that you refer to them as an advisory *team* rather than a *board* (similar to and aligned with ministry teams) to eliminate any mistaken perceptions of having governing authority or responsibility.

We have seen situations in which a childcare ministry board, never formally designated as *advisory*, effectively held the license and exercised authority independent of the church's governing board. The liability exposure in such arrangements is significant and spans multiple areas of concern: insurance, personnel, tax liabilities, facility use, and child protection rules, to name a few. For this reason, we strongly recommend that when a childcare program is *not* separately incorporated, the Leadership Board retains clear authority while delegating contextually appropriate operational management to the pastor, director, and an advisory team.

This delegation of authority should be named clearly in the original SAS resolution approved by the church conference (remember that back in Chapter 3?), and then later accompanied by a clearly defined reporting structure and written boundaries, procedures, and Guiding Principles, particularly related to finances, staffing, insurance, compliance, and accountability. Advisory teams may offer expertise and guidance, but they do not replace the governing authority and responsibility of the Leadership Board. *A Leadership Board may delegate authority, but it cannot abdicate it.*

Separately Incorporated Childcare Programs

When a childcare ministry (including preschools, parents' day out, learning centers, etc.) is separately incorporated, with its own employer identification number and governing board, the relationship changes significantly. In these cases, the church and the childcare entity should establish a formal legal relationship, often through a master service agreement, memorandum of understanding, and/or a lease agreement, even if the lease amount is nominal.

Separate incorporation does not eliminate the need for communication or alignment. A reporting structure can and should be established so that both governing boards remain informed and connected. The Leadership Board may also work with the pastor to assign one or more staff members to manage day-to-day coordination between the church and the childcare ministry. These arrangements help protect both entities while preserving clarity of authority and shared mission.

In our experience, separately incorporated childcare programs or preschools operate with their own missions and goals (e.g., preparing children for kindergarten, fostering experiential learning, and supporting social-emotional development). While this is an extremely important and needed mission, it is not the same as the church's disciple-making mission. With no legal connection and no authority over one another, we often find that the childcare center or preschool quickly becomes a *tenant* in the church facility (sometimes without a lease or a liability insurance policy of its own). The congregation often wears the childcare center as a badge of honor, reflecting the number of children who come and go from their facility on weekdays. They label this as a vital ministry (solely because of the activity and number of people) when there is no missional alignment, let alone missional fulfillment through this program.

Working with congregations across the country that have preschools, mothers' day out, and childcare centers, I (Kay) rarely find healthy, vital, missionally-aligned weekday children's programs. This is especially true when the programs are separate legal entities. If the mission field needs weekday children's programs, the best approach is to be one legal entity, with intentional ministry integration practices and sound financial practices that do not damage the childcare marketplace (as so many churches have and are doing). Kay is engaged with a Lilly Endowment grant to help parents and caregivers become more confident and equipped to be faith leaders in their homes through church childcare centers and children's ministries. For more information, go to https://creationincubator.org/thetable and take a look at her book coauthored with Michael Scott, *Inside Out: Everting Ministry Models for the Postmodern Culture.*[12]

Endowments and Other Associated Nonprofits

Endowments and related foundations present similar challenges. Some congregations maintain endowment committees that report to a Church Council, Trustees, or another legacy body. Endowments often operate under complex governing documents that limit how quickly responsibilities can be consolidated into a simplified structure.

As a best practice, when an endowment is not separately incorporated, we strongly recommend disbanding the endowment committee and bringing fiduciary responsibility fully under the Leadership Board. This approach aligns legal accountability with governance authority and reduces unnecessary complexity. For example, when I (Blake) was working with one congregation, we discovered that dozens of additional rules governed its endowment and that even minor changes required a charge conference with a supermajority vote. No one could remember when or why it had been organized in such a complex manner. That level of rigidity made immediate simplification impossible, and so Leadership Board oversight of the endowment had to be phased in gradually over most of a year. During this transitional period, the endowment committee should report directly to the Leadership Board rather than to a legacy committee or council.

---

12 Kay L. Kotan and Michael J. Scott, *Inside Out: Everting Ministry Models for the Postmodern Culture* (Market Square Books, 2022).

If the endowment is a separately incorporated foundation, the relationship between the foundation and the congregation must be clearly outlined in the foundation's governing documents, with the Leadership Board named as the successor executive authority of the church. Similarly, if the congregation has other subsidiary or associated nonprofits (e.g., cemeteries), the Leadership Board should be appropriately named in those entities' bylaws to ensure clear accountability, continuity, and alignment with the church's mission.

I (Blake) have seen endowment committees operate at odds with a congregation's governing leadership. In one church, the council was required to submit a formal grant application to the endowment committee to request the release of funds. At the same time, that same endowment committee raised funds and distributed money for projects within and outside the church without communicating with the governing board or the pastor, and without alignment with the congregation's well-defined priorities and goals. Situations like this create parallel authority structures that undermine accountability, confuse leadership, and weaken missional alignment. Simplified accountable governance exists precisely to prevent this kind of missional drift.

Guiding Principles for Complex Relationships

- Whether dealing with childcare ministries, endowments, or other associated nonprofits, several guiding principles apply:

- The Leadership Board may delegate authority, but it cannot abdicate fiduciary responsibility. Ultimate accountability always rests with the governing board.

- The legal and missional relationship between entities must be clearly articulated, documented, and regularly reviewed and approved.

- The Leadership Board is responsible for stewarding the purpose and vision God has given the congregation. These associated ministries exist to support that mission, not to redefine it.

- In short, do not allow the tail to wag the dog. Childcare ministries and endowments can be powerful expressions of a congregation's calling, but only when they remain aligned with and accountable to the church's mission, vision, and governance. Designing clear accountability structures and reducing unnecessary complexity help protect the congregation's witness, strengthen trust, and ensure that these ministries serve the mission rather than compete with it.

Notes

CHAPTER TEN

Common Challenges in the Design Phase

It's a Paradigm Shift

The first challenge most congregational leaders encounter is simply explaining a simplified accountable structure to fellow church members who have been shaped by a very specific, very committee-centric understanding of how a United Methodist church is organized. For many people, this traditional structure is not just familiar; it feels like *the way church works.*

Simplified accountable structure asks people to rethink some long-held assumptions about committees, authority, and decision making. This process can raise honest questions, concerns, and sometimes a bit of anxiety. The good news is that most of these questions are thoughtful and predictable.

We have gathered Frequently Asked Questions and offer those questions and answers in the SAS Resource Hub.

SAS Resource Hub

Can You Draw It?

Don't overlook the importance of an organizational chart. Creating and maintaining an updated chart is essential for understanding the proper flow of information, communication, accountability, and authority in a simplified accountable structure.

A good rule of thumb is this: can your leaders draw the structure on a napkin or a sheet of notebook paper? Bonus points if their charts don't contradict each other. If they can't draw it, the structure is probably more complicated than it needs to be. Simplified accountable structure is meant to bring clarity, not complexity, and the organizational chart is one of the best ways to test whether that clarity is actually there.

An up-to-date organizational chart also helps prevent confusion about who reports to whom, how decisions are made, how communications should flow, and where accountability rests. When everyone can see the structure and explain it simply, the church is far more likely to trust it and use it well.

Does the Pastor Have a Vote in SAS?

Yes—and also, no.

Formally speaking, in a simplified accountable structure, the pastor is a voting member of the Leadership Board in most circumstances. The primary exceptions occur when the Leadership Board is functioning in its role as the Board of Trustees and therefore acting as the church's legal board of directors or when the Leadership Board is functioning in its role of S/PPRC. In those settings, the pastor does not have a vote, as is the case in the Trustees or S/PPRC in a legacy multi-committee structure.

This distinction is clear enough on paper. The challenge comes in practice. Because the Leadership Board "wears multiple hats," it can switch quickly from one Disciplinary role to another within the same meeting—and often during the same conversation. One moment, the Leadership Board is functioning as S/PPRC. The next moment, it acts as Finance or Trustees. Rather than asking the Leadership Board to constantly track which hat it is wearing in order to determine whether the pastor should vote, and to track all of that in the minutes, we recommend a simpler and healthier practice:

We encourage pastors to refrain from voting altogether.

When presenting in workshops, we usually get a ton of grief over this recommendation (coincidentally enough, always from clergy and never from laity). Pastors, we are trying to do both you and the lay leadership a favor here! This recommendation is not about diminishing pastoral authority. Quite the opposite. In SAS, the pastor already carries significant authority in vision, leadership, staff supervision, and ministry alignment. Choosing not to vote helps preserve clarity, trust, and unity at the table. It allows the pastor to lead the conversation without being perceived as controlling the outcome. It also reinforces the shared accountability of the Leadership Board. When the lay leadership makes decisions, the Leadership Board fully owns those decisions. I (Blake) remember an important meeting early in my ministry during a building program. When the senior pastor raised his hand and made a motion that had a financial impact in the mid-six figures, I saw one of our wise, established leaders tap him on the shoulder and say, "Pastor, I've got this. This is one of those motions that needs to come from laity."

There's another bit of wisdom in this practice:

If a decision hinges on a single vote from the pastor, that is usually a signal that the Leadership Board is not yet ready to decide. Close votes often indicate unresolved questions, insufficient discernment, or unspoken concerns. In those moments, slowing down, asking deeper questions, and creating space for further conversation is almost always the more faithful path.

SAS works best when the pastor leads with influence rather than votes and when the Leadership Board exercises its authority with clarity and confidence. This simple practice helps keep those roles distinct and the system healthy.

Tend to the Culture, Not Just the Structure

Create a culture of launching work teams to promote a healthy, effective, and efficient approach for sharing workloads, engaging more people, leveraging people's gifts, wisdom, and experience, and becoming more missionally vital.

Develop a permission-giving ministry culture that enables ministry team leaders and their teams to creatively align ministries to the mission, vision, and goals of the church. However, that may mean that some ministries may need to stop to provide the bandwidth to engage in ministries that are more vital, fruitful, and/or missionally aligned.

Design the structure and leadership culture with a nonnegotiable missional focus. When leaders of a missionally focused church need to make tough decisions, the culture is much more likely to support them. Otherwise, decisions are made (or not) that instead focus on relationships, personal preferences, and conflict avoidance.

Don't "Phase In" SAS

We realize (and have encountered) that sometimes this full-model simplification is just not possible for some churches. For example, sometimes there is just too much of a political powerhouse in place within the current role or members of the Trustees Committee, so the Trustees Committee desires to operate separately for a while until more trust can be built. What could go wrong?

In our early work helping churches transition to a modified structure, several churches decided not to unify all four administrative committees into a single, simplified governance structure. Those experiences provided us with plenty of evidence to examine the results of this attempted "phase-in." *In all the churches we have worked with that have not unified completely, the results have never been favorable.*

If your church is not ready for the full implementation model, we suggest addressing the underlying issues before proceeding with *any* structure modification. When more than one entity (committee or board) is responsible for governance, the alignment, focus, communication, leadership culture, momentum, and missional impact are at risk. In our earlier work, we would point out these concerns and risks but continue to walk alongside churches when they chose a less-than-complete simplification. In every case, the mission fulfillment and congregational health were jeopardized. Because of these experiences, I (Kay) no longer work with churches that choose a less-than-full implementation. Here are some of the reasons why:

- Full trust in and through leadership is low or nonexistent.
- There is no complete buy-in to accountable leadership.
- While there is a stated intention to complete the final steps of simplification later, "later" never comes. The opportunity is missed and is nearly impossible to regain.
- There is a stronghold of unhealthy power or influence.
- There is no leadership in place to create a healthy leadership culture that will result in effective missional impact.
- The congregation is unwilling or lacks the capacity to make the necessary changes to become more missionally vital.
- There are unhealthy or maligned practices taking place that are unknown or that people are unwilling to address.

- If new leadership were to be elected, long-held or undiscovered secrets would be revealed.

Don't miss the opportunity to align everything with the new structure. Leaders often believe that the harder decisions can be made later, but we have found that delayed decisions become more difficult to address rather than easier—if they are ever addressed at all.

Please Stop Using "Specialists" or "Representatives"

In the early years of churches converting to the simplified structure, a common practice was for the Nominations Committee to assign Leadership Board members the titles of "specialists" or "representatives" for Finance, S/PPRC, or Trustees. In those early days, we both taught the common wisdom of the day that specialists were an optional and temporary part of the model, believing it might ease the transition into the simplified accountable structure. Those shifting to this new model struggle to envision how the work of the traditional administrative committee structure would be carried out in the simplified structure. Having these titles assigned provided relief, knowing that the particular area of ministry would still have a point of contact and a point person to perform the tasks associated with the old four-committee administrative structure.

While some still appreciate issuing these titles with certain areas of responsibility, such as Finance, Trustees, and S/PPRC, *we no longer recommend this practice.* The problem we discovered over the last fifteen years is that assigning these titles of "representatives" or "specialists" is corrosive to the Leadership Board's accountability because, over time, the Leadership Board ceases to retain responsibility and authority for the specialists' or representatives' work. The specialists became mini-committees, often making decisions or taking actions without authority, and fighting turf wars against the rest of the board. The resulting structure is neither "simplified" nor "accountable."

Staff Supervision and SAS

Few areas create more confusion during a transition to simplified accountable structure than staff supervision. This is especially true in congregations that have long relied on informal workarounds to manage relationships, concerns, and conflict. When these patterns are carried forward into a simplified accountable structure, they often undermine the very accountability SAS is designed to restore.

Two specific challenges must be addressed during the Designing Phase:

- Eliminating Leadership Board (S/PPRC) liaisons to paid staff
- Clarifying the supervisory authority and responsibility of the pastor

Eliminating Board Liaisons to Staff

In many churches, a long-standing practice has developed in which members of the Staff/Pastor-Parish Relations Committee are assigned as liaisons to individual staff members. The intent is usually pastoral and supportive. The liaison is meant to serve as a trusted listener, a communication bridge, and a relational point of contact between the staff person and the committee. In practice, however, this liaison model consistently fails.

I (Blake) was introduced to the liaison concept nearly thirty years ago as a student pastor. I have encountered it repeatedly across conferences, training materials, and local church cultures. Despite its good intentions, neither Kay nor I have ever seen it actually work in a healthy or sustainable way. The reason is simple. The liaison model is always destined to lead to unhealthy triangulation.

I (Blake) first learned about family systems theory and triangulation when reading Rabbi Ed Friedman's *Generation to Generation* early in my doctoral studies.[13] Triangulation occurs when two people pull a third person into a situation or conflict between themselves to relieve tension or avoid direct communication. Instead of A talking to B, A talks to C about B. Instead of resolving the issue, the triangle muddies up responsibility, increases anxiety, and creates unhealthy alliances.

This is exactly what happens when S/PPRC members serve as liaisons to staff. In every setting we have observed, the liaison quickly becomes the staff member's advocate and informal ombudsman. Concerns that should be addressed directly between the staff member and the staff

---

[13] Edwin H. Friedman, *Generation to Generation: Family Process in Church and Synagogue* (Guilford Press, 1985).

supervisor or pastor are instead routed through a board member.

The consequences of this pattern are predictable. Eventually, the Leadership Board evolves into a collection of staff advocates rather than a unified body focused on mission, accountability, and strategy. The pastor is no longer supervising the staff alone. The pastor is now supervising the staff while also managing a Leadership Board full of intermediaries. Authority becomes blurred. Communication becomes indirect. The accountability system flips upside down.

This is not a minor structural issue. It is corrosive to healthy leadership. For this reason, if you are currently utilizing the staff liaison model in your S/PPRC, we strongly recommend discontinuing the use of staff liaisons during the transition and implementation into simplified accountable structure (if not sooner)! The Leadership Board Covenant should make this explicit. Staff members report directly to the pastor.[14] Leadership Board members should discipline themselves not to allow staff to triangulate against them through ex parte communications and should agree not to insert themselves into staff relationships or day-to-day supervision.

This clarity protects everyone. It protects staff from mixed messages. It protects pastors from undermined authority. It protects Leadership Boards from being pulled into operational management. Most importantly, it restores direct communication and appropriate accountability and clarifies the pastor's supervisory authority and responsibility.

Clarifying Staff Supervision and Pastoral Authority

The second challenge is closely related and equally important. Leadership Boards must clearly define who has authority for hiring, supervision, evaluation, discipline, and termination of staff.

Congregations tend to approach this question in two primary ways. In the first model, the Leadership Board expects the pastor to supervise staff and build a clear accountability system around that expectation. The pastor is authorized to hire and terminate staff in accordance with

[14] Of course, any staff concerns involving inappropriate pastoral behavior, misconduct, or policy violations should be addressed immediately through your conference's established processes and your congregation's personnel and Safe Sanctuaries policies.

the church's established personnel policies. The pastor (and the pastor's designees) supervises, evaluates, and disciplines staff. Meanwhile, the Leadership Board holds the pastor accountable for doing so faithfully, legally, and in alignment with the church's mission, policies, and procedures. When it comes time for staff compensation decisions, the Leadership Board might approve an aggregate compensation pool for COLA (cost-of-living adjustment) and/or merit raises, and the pastor is responsible for deciding how to distribute the funds. In this model, the Leadership Board does not manage staff; it governs by creating the policies, procedures, and Guiding Principles and holds the pastor accountable to them. The Leadership Board stays focused on mission, strategy, and accountability, while the pastor leads the staff day to day.

We believe this first model is the healthiest and cleanest accountability system. That said, we also recognize that contextual factors such as size, history, and culture may lead some congregations to choose the second model.

In the second model, the Leadership Board retains authority over hiring and termination, while delegating supervision, evaluation, and daily management to the pastor or the pastor's designee. The Leadership Board approves staff positions, recommends job descriptions and compensation. The pastor supervises performance, provides feedback, and manages the staff team. This model can work, but only when roles are clearly defined and carefully honored, and written policies and procedures are in place. Leadership Boards using this approach must be especially vigilant to avoid drifting into day-to-day staff management or informal supervision.

There are also hybrid versions that delegate most supervisory responsibilities to the pastor and supervisory staff, but state in the Guiding Principles that the Leadership Board retains authority over hiring and termination of staff at the director and executive director tiers.

What matters most is not which option is chosen, but that the choice is explicit, written, and consistently practiced. The Guiding Principles must clearly articulate where authority and responsibility rest. The employee handbook and personnel policies must also reflect these expectations. Specific, written processes and procedures for hiring, supervision, evaluation, and termination must be in place and consistently reviewed for potential updates. Ambiguity in staff supervision does not create flexibility. It creates anxiety. Regardless of whether a church uses SAS or a legacy committee structure, ambiguity around supervisory authority is remarkably good at dialing the district superintendent's office.

The Leadership Board must resist the temptation to manage staff work under the guise of care or concern. Governance is neither pastoral nor managerial. Oversight is not supervision. Simplified accountable structure works best when everyone stays in their lane. When Leadership Boards govern, pastors supervise, and staff coordinate ministry, the system becomes not only simpler but healthier.

Notes

SECTION THREE

Equipping

He himself granted that some are apostles, prophets, evangelists, pastors and teachers to equip the saints for the work of ministry, for building up the body of Christ, until all of us come to the unity of the faith and of the knowledge of the Son of God, to maturity, to the measure of the full stature of Christ ... but speaking the truth in love, we must grow up in every way into him who is the head, into Christ, from whom the whole body, joined and knit together by every ligament with which it is equipped, as each part is working properly, promotes the body's growth in building itself up in love.

Ephesians 4:11-13, 15-16 (NRSV)

Equipping Phase Introduction

What Is the Equipping Phase?

The Equipping Phase is the third step in the process, following the Discerning and Designing Phases. This phase focuses on training the members of the Nominations and Lay Leadership Development Committee and the Leadership Board to prepare and support them in their leadership roles in the simplified accountable leadership.

Who Is Involved in This Phase?

The Authorized SAS Coach first equips the Nominations Committee in their work on the adaptive approach to holy conversations and the discernment of new leaders for the Leadership Board and Nominations Committee. Once the Leadership Board is elected, the Authorized SAS Coach will work with the members of the Leadership Board to begin equipping them for their new leadership roles.

What Is the Timing of This Phase?

This Equipping Phase begins as soon as the church conference adopts the simplified accountable leadership structure. Ideally, this is midyear when the Nominations Committee's equipping begins. The equipping of the Leadership Board is generally completed in November or early December so they are ready to start on January 1. Remember, each year a third of the members roll off the Leadership Board and the Nominations Committee, so ongoing, annual equipping is crucial. In addition, moving to SAS is typically a complete shift in leadership culture. Therefore, leaders find repeating the training is extremely helpful to pick up on the deeper leadership teachings that did not resonate during the first training.

Understanding the Equipping Phase

The Equipping Phase in the simplified accountable structure process builds directly on the foundational work completed in both the Discerning and Designing Phases. Even though some early preparation begins during the Designing Phase, the Equipping Phase provides the deeper formation leaders need to serve with clarity, accountability, and spiritual maturity in the new structure. The goal of this phase is simple:

equip the people who will guide the church so they understand the SAS model and are ready to lead within it.

The first emphasis in the Equipping Phase is the Committee on Nominations and Leadership Development. Because their work is central to shaping the initial Leadership Board, the Authorized SAS Coach begins equipping the Nominations Committee during the Designing Phase and continues that formation after the congregational vote. This training helps the Nominations Committee understand the structure and culture for which they are developing and identifying leadership, along with the qualities, competencies, spiritual commitments, and expectations of accountable leadership, so they can discern and nominate the best-aligned slate of servant leaders for the new structure.

Once the church conference adopts the simplified accountable structure and the congregation elects its first Leadership Board, the Equipping Phase turns toward Leadership Board preparation. The Authorized SAS Coach guides the newly elected Leadership Board through the responsibilities and expectations of their role, including how accountable governance works, how the pastor's alignment function supports mission, how to stay in appropriate lanes, and how to lead faithfully through Guiding Principles and mission outcomes. Most churches complete this focused equipping in November or early December so the Leadership Board is ready to begin its work on January 1.

Because one-third of both the Nominations Committee and the Leadership Board rotate off each year, equipping is not a one-time event. Healthy SAS churches embrace ongoing, annual leadership development. Returning members need refreshed clarity, and new members need a solid foundation so the Leadership Board can function as a unified, accountable, missionally focused body. The Equipping Phase, therefore, is not simply preparation for launch. It becomes part of the annual rhythm that sustains healthy, accountable leadership for years to come. In addition, it is important to remember that adopting a simplified accountable structure creates an entirely new leadership culture. Changing culture requires time, nurture, and consistent equipping and messaging.

Notes

CHAPTER ELEVEN

Equipping Your Nominations Committee

A healthy simplified structure depends on a clear, spiritually grounded process for identifying, recruiting, equipping, and deploying ministry team leaders and Leadership Board members. The Committee on Nominations' work is not about filling slots. It is about calling and preparing disciples who can serve with accountability, clarity, and joy. When the church embraces this work with intention and consistency, leaders step into their roles with confidence, ministry teams flourish, and the congregation experiences a healthier leadership culture with greater Kingdom impact.

The Nominations Committee plays a vital role in a healthy model of simplified accountable structure. Because SAS creates a new leadership culture, the members of the Nominations Committee must understand this reality and how to discern and nominate leaders who will become part of this new, healthy leadership culture. If they don't, the leaders seated at the Leadership Board table will likely not be the leaders needed for a vital church future. The Nominations Committee is pivotal in launching and creating momentum for this shift in leadership culture.

What Are You Looking for in Leadership Board Members?

Acts Chapter 6 and Paul's letters to Timothy and Titus offer examples of qualifications for church leadership. Notice that the biblical qualifications focus on timeless qualities like "full of the Spirit and wisdom," experience in personal "household" management, being "above reproach," and practicing self-control in behaviors and relationships. Before anything else, church leaders need to be maturing disciples of Jesus Christ. Church Nominations Committees often try to build committees for reasons disconnected from fulfilling the mission of Christ, such as attempting to please different constituencies or to address concerns that a wealthy member does not feel excluded from decisions.

While we understand the political realities of leading a mostly "volunteer" institution, we know that every person included on the Leadership Board for non-missional reasons will distract your Leadership Board from doing God's business and from building a healthy leadership culture.

Even deeply devoted disciples may not be right for governance board work if they are unwilling to see beyond the ministry that they are personally leading. For instance, I (Blake) remember working with a passionate leader of a feeding ministry. The leader raised thousands of dollars each month in in-kind gifts from grocery stores for distribution and worked with nonprofits and churches throughout the city. But the leader was so passionate about her ministry that other ministries and groups, such as youth and children's ministries, were often pushed aside and their storage space "borrowed." This leader was so focused on one aspect of the church's ministry that the other areas were considered less important.

For this reason, we recommend that Leadership Board members *not* also be leaders of ministry teams. While we hope and pray that Leadership Board members will continue to be active participants in small groups, growing in their own discipleship, and active in missional ministries, this three-year season of churchwide leadership is a great opportunity for a person to hand off the ministry team leadership baton to another leader.

In coaching and business management, there is a metaphorical concept of leaving the frenetic activity of the dance floor and moving to the balcony where leaders can better see all the dynamics and gain a clearer perspective to figure things out.[15] So, instead of having a Leadership Board filled with representatives from different groups or ministries, many of whom may wish to prioritize their own ministry above others, your Nominations Committee is seeking to identify, recruit, equip, and deploy leaders who can see the church from this "balcony perspective."

Your Leadership Board members need to be completely dedicated to Jesus Christ, growing as disciples, and personally invested in the church's mission and vision. This is often a completely different process for identifying leadership than the practices we have inherited in church leadership. We can find experts in building, banking, and human

---

[15] See Ronald Heifetz and Marty Linsky's article "A Survival Guide for Leaders" in the June 2002 issue of the *Harvard Business Review*.

resources almost anywhere. But to lead a church, it is most important to have our most mature disciples at the table. I (Kay) once worked with a church that had a finance chair who did not attend worship, did not participate in a small group, did not serve in any ministry, and made absolutely no financial contribution to the church. I am still baffled how leadership decisions like this can (and do) occur.

Take some time to consider the type of leader the church needs at the table. Think through some of these questions and discuss them in your Nominations Committee meeting:

- What are the spiritual gifts, characteristics, and behaviors that would be beneficial for a Leadership Board member in the SAS model?
- What are the expectations of Leadership Board members related to regular worship attendance, participation in a small (discipleship) group, serving periodically, having a regular prayer life, and being a proportional giver (e.g., living and modeling their faith)?
- How will you ensure diversity amongst Leadership Board members? (*Including members from different racial, ethnic, and cultural backgrounds, with varying church tenures, age diversity, and socioeconomic backgrounds, will produce better conversations around the Leadership Board table and help the new Leadership Board avoid "groupthink."*)
- Would the potential Leadership Board member be available to attend most of the Leadership Board meetings?
- Has the potential Leadership Board member shown the capacity to check their personal agendas at the door?
- Has the potential Leadership Board member shown the capacity to maintain confidentiality?
- Would the Leadership Board member be able to openly support and authentically communicate the decision of the Leadership Board regardless of their personal feelings about the decision?
- How will the Nominations Committee gather recommendations and ideas about potential leaders as the nominations slate is created? How could your committee get the entire congregation involved in the nomination process? *(One method is to create an*

online recommendation form for congregants to submit candidate recommendations, along with rationales, for potential Leadership Board members. An "Interest Form" template is available in the SAS Resource Hub.)

- How will the Nominations Committee gather information to make faithful decisions? *(One recommended method is to interview—holy discernment conversation—potential leaders to better understand their hopes, dreams, and desires, along with their spiritual development and practices as disciples. A sampling of "Nominations Interview Questions" is available in the Pro+ SAS Resource Hub.)*

In addition to the people in your leadership development pathway, creating a new leadership structure is an excellent opportunity to invite leaders who have been sitting on the sidelines. For many high-capacity leaders, the cumbersome legacy committee structure seen in most churches is a repellent. High-capacity leaders want to be challenged and make a difference, but the common practice of endless reports from endless committees is not attractive. A simplified accountable leadership structure may be catnip to these high-capacity leaders. Therefore, expand your search beyond the usual suspects and have meaningful conversations with these potential leaders. Whatever appropriate characteristics, expectations, and behaviors are identified, potential leaders will discover them during the leadership development process. It is always best to be upfront with people rather than asking them to serve and then sharing the Leadership Board member expectations with them in arrears. *Set the standards and expectations upfront prior to inviting leadership commitments.*

Tools to Articulate Expectations

To articulate these leadership expectations, we recommend creating a job description for each ministry position. While job descriptions for paid staff positions are common, those for ministry positions are far less so. Unfortunately, without these job descriptions, much is left to personal and historical contextual interpretation and guesswork. To create a healthier and more robust leadership culture with higher engagement and greater impact, job descriptions are a critical component. Job descriptions provide clarity of purpose, authority, and responsibility.

They also indicate who to report to and who is responsible for equipping and answering questions. Effective church ministry job descriptions describe the required experience, skills, and giftedness as well as how the ministry ties back into the church's mission, vision, and core values.

The Implementing Phase includes a chapter that provides directions on creating a Leadership Covenant for the Leadership Board, a clarifying document that offers Leadership Board members guidance on expectations and relational boundaries. While we recommend that your Leadership Board draft a new covenant each year, the Leadership Board's existing covenant is a valuable tool for the Nominations Committee to identify potential future leaders and to share the expectations of Leadership Board members with future leaders. The Leadership Covenant can also be used as a model and template for ministry teams to create their own team covenant.

The Annual Nominations Process

So, it is time for the annual gathering of the Committee on Nominations and Leadership Development to gather and discern who should be nominated for which committees. Maybe your experience is different than ours, but most times, it goes something like this: "Okay, so where is the latest copy of the church pictorial directory? Let's look through the pictorial directory to see if it helps us identify some new people or those who haven't served recently. Who can we coerce to say yes? Who from the Nominations Committee should call so the nominee will most likely say yes?" This inherited process is more about filling spots with bodies and completing the required paperwork. It is time for a new day with a new process for a new outcome with greater Kingdom impact and a healthier leadership culture!

I (Blake) have spent a couple of decades attending Nominations Committee meetings. I quickly realized that there is a big difference between nominations meetings where we stare at the ceiling trying to conjure up a name versus nominations meetings where we have profiles of engaged disciple-leaders on the table in front of us. Our job is to strategically discern and manage the process of bringing leaders onto the elected committees, ensuring we have a variety of gifts and perspectives among our most mature disciples.

Holy Conversations with Leadership Board Candidates

We have seen several congregations flip the script on their nominations process. Instead of selecting leaders based on the Nominations Committee's best guesses and intentions, or even taking recommendations from the congregation, they discover that passionate disciples are actively seeking opportunities for servant leadership and shaping their process toward this goal. Usually, a process that takes a few years to fully enculturate, the Nominations Committee can seek out "applications" (a form used for those interested in leadership) and conduct "job interviews," or, better put, discernment conversations for the few precious Leadership Board and Nominations Committee positions every year. In this process, the Nominations Committee and the pastor can discover the right giftedness to build the teams needed for the upcoming season of ministry. The interview/holy conversation will not only focus on the skills and giftedness the person can bring to the leadership table but will also be used to share the purpose and responsibilities of the Leadership Board and expectations of its members. This time will also allow the potential leader to share about their faith journey and their practices as a disciple. Again, you can find these two resources in the Pro+ SAS Resource Hub.

Pro+SAS Resource Hub

An interest form and a holy discernment process are not without risks. Before a congregation considers it, the overall relational health of the church must be excellent, the mission and goals crystal clear, and an intentional leadership development pathway (the responsibility of the Committee on Nominations and Leadership Development) must be ongoing. Otherwise, the only people who "applied" might want to join the Leadership Board to bring their own agenda. For instance, when I (Blake) was serving as a local church pastor, I was always concerned when a member constantly asked to be put on the Staff/Pastor-Parish Relations Committee so "the church could start acting like a real business." I wasn't quite sure what that meant, but I could tell enough that his agenda had little to do with our congregation's stated mission, vision, and strategic plan. Some churches start using an application process ("Interest Form") a year or two into the new structure, once the Leadership Board's identity is established and the church's leadership development pathway is on track. Other churches choose to make this adaptive change upfront, clearly indicating there are changes in leadership discernment and expectations. Either way, this shift is critical and required to create a healthy, accountable leadership culture.

An Invitation to Lead

Your members have been burned before. A pastor or a Nominations Committee member has called them, sharing that "We need you on the committee. No one else will say 'yes,' so I need you to agree. Don't worry, it won't take up too much time. It's really just a committee on paper. There isn't any outside work to do, so all you will need to do is show up at the quarterly meetings." Well, we suppose some folks may jump at that incredibly compelling opportunity to serve Jesus, but perhaps a bit more thought and preparation is required! When we set low expectations for leaders, we get low-quality investments and commitment from them. While some faithful, gifted, and talented leaders may say "yes" to such an invitation, the committee will always be on their back burners. High-capacity leaders will instead channel their God-given talents to other pursuits (perhaps outside the church) where they feel valued, can bring value, and have impact.

Think back to when you received a compelling and a less-than-compelling invitation to serve. What made the difference? How did the invitation affect your willingness to serve?

With your change to a simplified accountable Leadership Board, you have the opportunity to invite high-capacity leaders to REALLY make a meaningful impact both inside and outside the church. This won't be a committee on paper that meets a few times a year to write a report. Your Leadership Board will be filled with agents of transformation, listening to the Holy Spirit, discerning God's vision, and guiding the congregation into the mission field in the name of Jesus Christ. So, make sure your invitation is personal by connecting the requirements and expectations for Leadership Board members to the gifts you see in the potential leader. Share last year's Leadership Board covenant so the expectations are crystal clear.

Before prospective Leadership Board members say "yes," they need to know that Leadership Board service will require work: preparation before meetings, task assignments between meetings, sharing responsibility for the board's spiritual formation and leadership development, difficult conversations about mission and accountability, strategic and generative work, the shouldering of risky ministry experiments, and bold leadership. They will actually be able to make decisions rather than simply make recommendations to yet another committee. They will receive encouragement and discover personal growth. Along the way, they will pray (A LOT). And, most of all, they will have the opportunity to serve Jesus Christ, our Risen Savior, by steering the congregation toward a trajectory of reaching new people and disciple-making. Now, THAT's a compelling invitation! And it is the start of transforming your church's leadership culture. This shift in leadership culture must start with a shifting approach in the Nominations Committee's work using interest forms, conducting holy conversations with potential leaders, setting expectations, and identifying key leadership and discipleship required.

Nominations and the Leadership Board Chair

Because of the Nominations Committee's expanding role in leadership development and the changes in the nominations process, we suggest, as a best practice, that the Committee on Nominations identify and nominate the Leadership Board chair for the charge conference election. Because of the holy conversations related to spiritual maturity, being called as a leader for this particular season, sharing faith stories, and the deep discernment the Nominations Committee is called to exercise, the Nominations Committee is therefore best qualified to identify and nominate the Leadership Board chair. We also recommend that in the first January meeting, the Leadership Board chair be elected by the Leadership Board to serve simultaneously as the chair (or president) of the Board of Trustees, in accordance with ¶ 2530 of *The Book of Discipline* and the laws in many states for the boards of directors of incorporated nonprofits. We believe in simplifying the structure, and having a different "Trustee chair" from the Leadership Board chair only invites confusion.

Leadership Development Is a Process, Not an Event

A healthy nomination process actually begins months before nominations start.

Notice, the official title of this committee is the Committee on Nominations **AND Leadership Development**. Churches must have an intentional process of developing leaders. When churches have a leadership development process, it feeds the nominations process and readies leaders to serve on ministry teams and in administrative leadership.

In the leadership development process, potential leaders are invited into several sessions over weeks or months to journey with other potential leaders. This will be a time of discernment, faith development, and gift assessment led by the pastor and members of the Nominations Committee. Remember, as the Nominations Committee, you are seeking to raise three to six leaders for the Leadership Board and Nominations Committee each year to fill vacancies as classes roll off. In order to have these leaders prepared and ready to commit, you will likely need eight to ten leaders in the leadership development pathway. Some leaders will discern that they are better suited to lead ministry teams than to serve as Leadership Board members (that's actually a pathway to SUCCESS!). Others might realize the timing for such a leadership commitment is not quite right. You may find that some who enter the process do not complete it, or that the Nominations Committee discerns they are not quite ready or equipped for leadership.

The leadership development process helps prepare leaders and sets expectations for leadership across the various areas. Being crystal clear regarding the expectations of Leadership Board members, Nominations Committee members, and ministry team leaders sets the foundation for helping both the Nominations Committee and the potential leader discern whether this is the right leadership role at the right time. Setting expectations raises the bar for leadership and prepares the Leadership Board, Nominations, and ministry teams for success. Nothing is worse than being invited to serve and then having the expectations clash with the realities of the position.

The following is a list of expectations to be identified in collaboration with the existing SAS Leadership Board, the pastor, and the Committee on Nominations for potential Leadership Board members.

- Identify the markers of discipleship expected of a Leadership Board member, such as worship attendance, discipleship formation, generosity, prayer, service, and faith-sharing.

- Share attendance expectations for Leadership Board meetings. Inform the potential leader of the meeting frequency, time, duration, and any stipulations for virtual attendance.

- Set expectations for reading *Mission Possible 4,* being formally trained in SAS, and participating in the onboarding process.
- Set expectations for being responsible and accountable for missional decisions—not having a seat at the Leadership Board table to advocate for personal preferences, a particular ministry, team, or special-interest group.
- Set expectations for additional gatherings and meetings, such as spiritual retreats, serving together as a Leadership Board, and participating in town hall meetings, etc.
- Set the expectation that each member of the Leadership Board will lead the Leadership Board in prayer, spiritual formation, and leadership development on a rotational basis.
- Share expectations concerning confidentiality.
- Share the changing relationship as a Leadership Board member with family, friends, and fellow disciples to eliminate triangulation and support the Leadership Board's work.
- Set the expectation of reviewing the Leadership Board packet prior to meetings to come prepared to discuss and make decisions.
- Set the expectation and importance of attending an annual strategic ministry planning retreat (identify the location, date, and time, if available).
- Share a sample of the current Leadership Board's Leadership Covenant to set the expectation that the new Leadership Board will be creating a similar covenant and hold one another accountable to the covenant.

When it comes to the question of using assessments in the leadership development process, there are a few schools of thought. On one hand, using assessments might shed light on someone's leadership style and strengths for the first time. Others may have already encountered this in their work life. I (Kay) like to use assessments such as DiSC, StrengthsFinder, and Enneagram. I find them to be great coaching tools. Self-awareness is critical in being an effective leader. If a person is not self-aware, an assessment can be a valuable tool for building awareness and identifying their leadership and teaming styles.

It might be helpful to use assessments as a springboard to help leaders understand how to work with other leaders with different leadership styles in a team or board setting. Learning how to work effectively together as a team that is trusting, accountable, vulnerable, and transparent can be challenging, but it can be very rewarding with fruitful results. Ensuring a variety of leadership, work styles, and personalities on the Leadership Board provides a well-rounded approach to leadership and decision making.

Assessments might be a great tool for leadership development, but don't use them as the sole tool for selecting people for leadership nominations. For example, you would not want to nominate only leaders who are a "D" (dominance) on the DiSC assessment for the Leadership Board. A mix of leadership styles on the Leadership Board—combined with skill, self-awareness about leadership style, and the ability to work well with others—leads to a much richer, more favorable leadership and missional outcome.

In addition to using self-awareness inventories to equip individual members, work must also be done to build healthy team processes. Creating and implementing building team processes for meetings and decision making encourages everyone to engage beyond fitting into preconceived inventory-based roles. Two examples favored by Blake for this type of group-equipping include Edward DeBono's old-but-relevant "Six Thinking Hats"[16] parallel thinking system and the *Harvard Business Review*'s question-based meeting agenda.[17]

You will find more resources and information on leadership development in Kay's book *Gear Up! Nine Essential Processes for the Optimized Church*[18] and in the book she coauthored with Phil Schroeder, *Launching Leaders: Taking Leadership Development to New Heights*.[19]

---

[16] Edward de Bono, *Six Thinking Hats* (Little, Brown, and Company, 1985). Blake has used *Six Thinking Hats* for years in church leadership settings and swears by it as a simple way to improve the quality of group thinking and decision making. The method gives teams a shared language for exploring ideas, brainstorming, testing assumptions, and reducing unproductive conflict without oversimplifying complex issues.

[17] Roger Schwarz, "How to Design an Agenda for an Effective Meeting," *Harvard Business Review*, March 2015.

[18] Kay Kotan, *Gear Up! Nine Essential Processes for the Optimized Church* (Abingdon Press, 2017).

[19] Kay Kotan and Phil Schroeder, *Launching Leaders: Helping Congregations Get Past First Base* (Abingdon Press, 2016).

Both books are outstanding resources for developing a leadership development process. *Launching Leaders* also offers a ready-to-go leadership development process you can start using right away until you develop one tailored to your context. Also, check out Kay and Blake's first book together, *IMPACT! Reclaiming the Call of Lay Ministry.*[20] Future Leadership Board members will need to understand that the goal of the Leadership Board is to lead the church in impacting the mission field, not simply to maintain the institution and keep their fellow Sunday school members happy.

Notes

---

[20] Kay Kotan and Blake Bradford, *IMPACT!*

CHAPTER TWELVE

Training Leadership Board Leaders

To gather the tools for this new leadership journey, we recommend that each new Leadership Board member receive a copy of this book and read it *before* attending their required Leadership Board training, or perhaps as part of their personal discernment of accepting a leadership nomination. In November, early December, or very early in January, each new Leadership Board member should attend an equipping workshop led by an Authorized SAS Coach. This training is also helpful for new members of the Nominations Committee. Typically five or six hours, the workshop provides a deep dive into the SAS model. If this training is not available in your area, we have on-demand training for Leadership Board members online at kaykotan.com/sas-2 for your convenience.

This equipping is critically important. Without proper training, a new leader will arrive at the leadership table on January 1, unprepared with the necessary tools and understanding. Churches set leaders up to fail when they are expected to serve without first equipping them with the proper training and tools. Each year, new members joining the team should have the same training expectations. We find that existing Leadership Board and Nominations Committee members also find the training helpful in their second and third years—especially in the first few years of implementing SAS and living into a new leadership culture. Additionally, if time allows, it is also helpful for the Authorized SAS Coach to lead a session with the new Leadership Board so members can get to know one another and create their Leadership Covenant together before January 1, after completion of their training. This applies only to the first Leadership Board, not to subsequent years. After the first time, this work will instead be completed at the fall strategic ministry planning retreat, which is covered in the Implementing Phase in Chapter 21.

Investment in the Equipping, Discerning, and Designing Phases early in the process will pay tremendous dividends later. This investment pertains to both the technical and adaptive changes the congregation and leaders experience, as well as the emotional reactions to a change in leadership structure. The church can't simply rely on a new organizational chart to address its leadership shifts and challenges. Setting expectations through Leadership Covenants, Guiding Principles, and regular investments in equipping opportunities creates a healthy culture of leadership, including expectations, accountability, and a commitment to investing in leaders. We can't overemphasize this point: **moving to a simplified accountable structure shifts the *entire leadership culture* of the church!**

One Hat for One Leadership Board

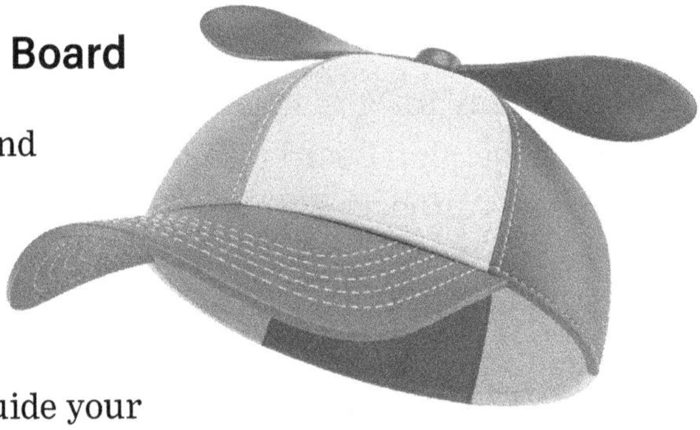

Before we introduce the tools and best practices of SAS: Leadership Covenants, executive session practices, standard agendas, Guiding Principles, or the annual planning cycle that will guide your Leadership Board throughout the year, we must begin with the most important shift of all. *A simplified accountable structure requires a new way of thinking about governance and leadership.* Everything that follows in this book builds on this foundation. If the Leadership Board understands the unified nature of its work, then the tools, meeting rhythms, and adaptive practices found later in this book will make sense and take root. If the Leadership Board does not understand this shift, the tools become no more than a list of disconnected techniques. *The Leadership Board must shift into a mindset of holistic governance grounded in accountable leadership.*

In the inherited multi-committee model, particularly in United Methodist congregations, churches operate with four separate administrative committees. Finance focuses on budgets. Staff/Pastor-Parish Relations handles personnel. Trustees oversee property and legal concerns. The Council or Administrative Board wrestles with vision and reporting from the different committees. Each group meets separately and considers its own lane of responsibility. This model produces silos, slow decision making, and frequent confusion about who has authority for what.

A simplified accountable structure works differently. There are no siloed committees. The Leadership Board *is* the Finance Committee, which *is* the Staff/Pastor-Parish Relations Committee, which *is* the Trustees, which *is* the Council. One board. One body. One unified approach to spiritual leadership and organizational governance.

In our equipping workshops, we describe how to start functioning as a Leadership Board by imagining four hats on the table. When the conversation shifts to the facility or property insurance, the Trustee hat goes on. When the agenda reaches personnel matters, the Leadership Board puts on its Staff/Pastor-Parish hat. When the subject is the budget, the Finance hat is worn. And when vision and mission are the focus, the Council hat sits proudly on everyone's head. Note that we don't have "specialists." We don't have Bob wearing the Finance hat while Susan is wearing the Trustee hat. No! The whole Leadership Board changes hats together because it functions as a whole.

Over time, we hope the Leadership Board becomes so experienced in this model that switching hats becomes second nature, and the Leadership Board begins to *approach issues with all four lenses (hats) at once, using a holistic approach* to opportunities and challenges. Nimble leadership in our modern age rarely requires only a staffing fix or only a facilities solution. One of the greatest benefits of SAS is that leadership becomes holistic rather than divided by committee silos. This holistic approach is also a gift when it comes to consultation with your district superintendent. Rather than consulting with the DS through only the S/PPRC lens, leaders can provide the DS with a much more comprehensive overview of the life of the congregation.

When Blake teaches this part of his SAS presentation, he brings out a brilliantly absurd, multicolored baseball cap with a spinning propeller on top. That single hat holds all four colors, each representing one of the former administrative committees. It is one hat symbolizing one Leadership Board. The propeller reminds leaders to rise above the weeds of daily management, gain some strategic "altitude," and view decisions from the 30,000-foot perspective of adaptive, accountable governance rather than slipping back into management tasks. The Leadership Board's job is to see the whole picture. The multicolor propeller hat helps everyone remember that governance is holistic, visionary, and always aligned with mission.

Caution: We have heard stories of churches that didn't do any training or coaching and took the "four hats" metaphor a bit too far. They were having individual meetings for Finance, Trustees, etc., and everyone was exhausted by the weekly meetings and the minutiae of management. Instead of a holistic SAS approach that values accountability and trust, they were doing the multi-committee legacy structure with just nine people!

This chapter begins with the hat metaphor because it is more than a teaching tool. It is an identity shift. It is a leadership culture shift. A simplified and accountable Leadership Board leads differently. It leads as one. The next sections will help you live into that identity through practical tools that support accountable, adaptive leadership. But before any of that will work, your Leadership Board must understand the posture and purpose of simplified accountable governance:

One hat. One board. One mission.

Onboarding Your New Leaders

At one church early in my ministry, I (Blake) thought I had embedded a fresh purpose and set of processes into a church leadership system. It was only after I was appointed elsewhere that I discovered they were embedded only in the small team, not the larger body—a regret I still carry to this day. Earlier in this book, we shared about congregational leaders who inherited a "sports-car style structure," but only the initial Leadership Board and the pastor (or perhaps only the pastor before she was moved) understood the intricacies of the system. So, as members of the Leadership Board rotated off and new leaders were added, fewer and fewer members understood SAS. Without intentional, ongoing leadership development, equipping, and onboarding, the modified structure fell apart and was deemed a "failure."

To enculture the changes, a host of new practices and commitments need to replace the "way things are done around here." Remember, the legacy committee structure and its associated practices have been around for *decades*. It will take time and intentionality to change this deeply rooted leadership model. Building in written tools will help your Leadership Board become a covenant group with clear roles, expectations, and boundaries.

In addition to equipping Leadership Board members, it is recommended to implement an onboarding process for them. The onboarding would include the following tools and information sharing:

- Provide the dates and locations for all the upcoming Leadership Board meetings, retreats, etc.
- Explain how to access the (historical, current, and future) digital Leadership Board files, including agendas, minutes, financial reports, packets, etc.
- Provide an overview of the appropriate interaction and areas of confidentiality with fellow congregants, friends, and family shifts when serving in a governance position.
- Provide an overview of a Leadership Board packet, what it contains, and how to review it before meetings.
- If a board member is not familiar with reading and understanding financial reports, spend time reviewing the reports to explain the content and what board members need to pay attention to.
- Provide a current copy or access to the church's Guiding Principles.
- Review the agenda and explain each element and how the Leadership Board acts upon each.
- Prepare the new member for what is expected and how to lead the spiritual formation and leadership development time. Share the dates for when the incoming member will be responsible for such.

Learning from Your First Year as a Leadership Board

During the first years of a simplified accountable structure, your Leadership Board will need to set new patterns, behaviors, expectations, rhythms, and methods of "doing business." Leaders must hold themselves accountable to one another to *actually* engage in new leadership practices within this new structure and shift the leadership culture. Otherwise, it will be the same old business in just a different configuration. Too often, I (Kay) find congregations that simply conduct business as usual with fewer people or slip back into old ruts too soon without the intentionality of new practices. Here are a few tips to consider for your first year (and beyond) in the new simplified accountable structure:

- Practice accountability from the beginning.
- Do not be afraid to ask questions. Others often have the same unasked question.
- Come to the Leadership Board table with curiosity and grace.
- Have team members sit at the table, and observers sit in chairs along the perimeter to clearly define who has a voice and voting rights.
- Configure your space to encourage meaningful conversations and allow eye contact among all members of the Leadership Board. We suggest seating board members at a round or oval table, with guests seated around the room's perimeter.
- The pandemic made many of us experts in online meetings. Your Leadership Board will need to carefully consider how many regular meetings or Leadership Board members can use this technology without negatively affecting the group's teamwork.
- Sometimes, your Leadership Board will need to take votes. Consensus is a fine goal, and it is great when the Leadership Board is all in agreement. However, consensus cannot be a requirement for your church to move forward. We have seen churches that utilize a unanimous consent requirement become immobilized by a minority of members who control the church's future. Remember, alignment with and responsibility to the mission and vision are the ultimate filters and outcomes required for faithful, missionally aligned decision making.
- Remember that Guiding Principles are a living, breathing document open to edits and additions, as needed, to provide a permission-giving culture within healthy boundaries. The traditional Church Council model is often the bottleneck in the decision-making process. The Guiding Principles are intended to empower ministries, not bring them to a screeching halt!

As leadership lives into this new structure, they will discover that they need to revise or adjust their Leadership Covenant (more on this in Chapter 17), Guiding Principles (more on this in Chapter 18), or standard practices. Each year, the Leadership Board is composed of one-third new people. For that reason and to support ongoing leadership growth, review the covenant each year and edit it as the Leadership Board and the Holy Spirit lead. Each Leadership Board member has a responsibility to hold both themselves and one another accountable to God and to each other.

Notes

CHAPTER THIRTEEN

Accountable Leadership Comes First

What Is Accountable Leadership?

Accountability is the marriage of responsibility and authority. In other words, accountable leadership is when a person is given both the responsibility and authority for a job, project, or ministry, and their supervisor holds them accountable for the intended and agreed-upon outcome. Accountability often gets a bum rap because it is often confused with blaming or disciplinary actions. Yet blaming is actually quite different from accountability. While accountability connects responsibility and authority, blaming usually occurs when someone has responsibility but lacks the actual authority or capacity to fulfill expectations. Accountable leadership is not centered on disciplinary action or punishment. Rather, accountability is about support, encouragement, collaboration, identifying needed resources, uncovering obstacles, and providing clarity in how to get back on track.

> *Being held accountable is an act of generosity and compassion.*
> *It is a gift that someone gives us to correct our wrongs, unlearn,*
> *and do better for the sake of our own growth.*
> *It might be uncomfortable, but it is worth the discomfort.*
>
> **Minaa B.**[21]

Accountable leadership is not only a list of things your Leadership Board *does*. It is also about what your Leadership Board *is*, and how, individually and collectively, each member shows up and leads inside and outside Leadership Board meetings. Accountable leadership entails the

---

[21] Minaa B., *Owning Our Struggles: A Path to Healing and Finding Community in a Broken World* (Broadleaf Books, 2023).

attitude and approach with which you and your fellow Leadership Board members engage in your leadership roles. We can't emphasize this point enough: adopting and implementing a leadership model of accountability is a transformation in leadership culture. Changing culture is hard work that requires persistence, practice, intentionality, and missional focus. Similarly, adaptive leadership never comes with a downloadable plan or a bullet-point list of things "to do" to be effective and fruitful in every situation. If we had that, we would not need adaptive leadership. Instead, adaptive leadership is about a willingness to journey, create, innovate, and experiment.

Accountable Leadership in the Church

Accountable leadership in a church is quite simple in concept, but much less readily or eagerly practiced. I (Blake) remember the most disheartening planning meeting of my ministry. It was the team's first meeting to set our plans for the year. A key leader brought preliminary copies for everyone. What we received was discouraging. We each received a single sheet of paper (with the date of three years ago printed at the top) and a listing of events for January through December. For each item/event, the printed dates from three years ago were marked out, and last year's date was handwritten beside each event. Additionally, last year's "preliminary" schedule was marked out, and instead, the current year was scribbled beside all the other years' updates. It was planning by photocopy!

In a church culture where we often do ministries *"just because ..."* (e.g., *just because* it sounds charitable, or *just because* Mrs. Matriarch wants to, or *just because* we've always done it that way), accountable leadership feels radical. Rarely do we create ministries with the desired transformational impact in mind and work backwards from that goal. However, both of your authors are formed by Wesleyan Christianity, and so *accountability* is part of our history and formation. The early Methodist societies always kept count of members, money, and ministry.

While we may think of a Methodist annual conference as a business meeting, revival, or equipping event, its origins were as an annual accountability tool: how many new class meetings and bands (small groups) were formed, how many souls were reached for Christ, and how well were our traveling preachers leading the expansion of the Church into new territory for new people? We can recover that meaningful, transformative accountability today—that is, if we are willing to start with our end in mind (impactful transformation) and then work backwards from our goal while creating systems of accountability under the stewardship of the new Leadership Board.

Here are some other important reasons to consider implementing accountable leadership into the life of your church, beginning with the Leadership Board:

1. It marries responsibility and authority with accountability.
2. It promotes church unity.
3. It functions on a high level of trust.
4. Decisions can be made quickly.
5. Mission/vision fulfillment is the driving force—not management (or maintenance).
6. Ministry goals and objectives can be adjusted as needed.
7. Missional focus and strategic alignment provide guideposts and goal posts for leaders.
8. High-capacity leaders are more likely to engage in this model of leadership.
9. It helps eliminate preference or personality-driven decisions and replaces them with missionally driven decisions.

I (Kay) have found the book *Winning on Purpose* by John Edmund Kaiser[22] to be an invaluable tool for applying accountability leadership to simplifying structure. In working with pastors and churches across the nation, it has become very apparent that most churches do not practice accountability—regardless of structure. In fact, some churches are

[22] John Edmund Kaiser, *Winning On Purpose.*

quite resistant to enacting accountability practices. In our work with churches, if they are unwilling to adapt to accountability practices, we do not recommend structure simplification. If accountable leadership is not put in place along with simplification, the result will simply not be conducive to operating as a healthy organization. In fact, it can quite possibly create the opposite. Accountability can be put into action without structure simplification, but simplification without accountability is **bad news**! Therefore, we offer this caution when training on the simplified accountable structure:

- ***Some** churches can move to a simplified accountable structure and be effective.*
- ***All** churches should practice accountable leadership.*
- **No** church should move to a simplified structure without accountable leadership practices.

Stay in Your Lane: Roles and Responsibilities

Church leadership can be incredibly difficult. Your church is your family. You walk alongside your fellow members through births, deaths, and challenging life moments. You disciple one another, encourage each other, gather to swing hammers at a Habitat for Humanity build, pray together, and kneel side-by-side to receive communion. Moving into church leadership can place enormous stress on these existing relationships.

Both of your authors believe strongly that mutual accountability is a Christian discipling value that has been underutilized and misunderstood in the modern iteration of Jesus' Church. However, accountability is even more important for those who willingly take on the mantle of a church leader. Using a football team metaphor, let's remind ourselves of the distinctive roles for the Leadership Board, Leadership Board chair, pastor, staff/ministry team leaders, and the congregation:

Position	Players	Functions	Metaphors
Ministry	Congregation	Serve in impactful ministry, disciples nurturing and developing disciples, reaching new people for Christ	Teammates, champions, athletes
Management	Staff/Team Leaders	Identify, recruit, equip, and deploy disciples for ministry. Coordinate resources, disciples and ministries.	Assistant coaches and specialists
Leadership	Lead Pastor	Spiritual leader and shepherd. Supervise and evaluate staff. Align ministries, staffing, and resources to the vision and goals.	Head coach, quarterback, captain
Governance	Board	Stewardship, Generative work, Strategy. Hold Lead Pastor (and ministries) accountable to the vision and goals.	Commissioner, umpire, scorekeeper & cheerleader

Chart is adapted from *Winning on Purpose: How to Organize Congregations to Succeed in Their Mission*, John Edmund Kaiser.

Before a Leadership Board can lead with clarity and confidence, every person involved must understand the distinct roles and responsibilities within accountable leadership. A simplified structure only works when the Leadership Board, the pastor, and the staff or ministry teams each stay in their lane and embrace the work that belongs to them. Confusion about roles is one of the quickest ways for an SAS Leadership Board to drift back into old habits of micromanagement, blurred authority, or silo decision making. This section outlines how accountable leadership functions when everyone understands their lane. The Leadership Board governs. The pastor leads and aligns. The staff and team leaders manage and coordinate, and the ministry teams carry out the strategies/ministries that advance the mission. When each group fulfills its role and stays out of lanes that aren't theirs, the church becomes healthier, more focused, and more effective in its Kingdom impact.

When I served as a district superintendent, I (Blake) found that most of the congregational conflicts I was called upon to address had their roots in a lack of clarity about roles, not in theological differences. Similarly, both of us (Kay and Blake) have seen countless opportunities to reach new disciples lost because the pastor, staff member, or ministry team leader was not given creative space to innovate due to unclear expectations about authority, responsibility, or accountability. This means when we apply the lessons of accountable and adaptive leadership, clarity matters.

Leadership Board's Role in Accountable Leadership

- Accountable to Jesus Christ for the Great Commission
- Fiduciary responsibility
- Generative work
- Strategic work
- Church governance—not management!
- Annual goals to forward the mission and vision
- Holding the senior pastor accountable to the vision and goals in partnership with the DS
- Creating and updating policies, procedures, and Guiding Principles
- Aligning resources to the mission, vision, goals, and strategies
- Examples of maturing spiritual leaders
- Adhering to the Leadership Covenant
- Annual strategic planning retreat
- Understanding the shift in role and responsibility from congregant to leader
- Blessing the congregationally discerned vision articulated by the pastor
- Communicating with the congregation

Pastor's Role in Accountable Leadership

- Spiritual leader/shepherd
- Keeper of the mission
- Communicator of the congregationally discerned vision
- Example of an evangelist
- Chief fundraiser
- Main recruiter
- Developing and equipping new and existing leaders
- Hiring, supervising, and evaluating (and, when necessary, terminating) both paid and unpaid staff as outlined in the Guiding Principles
- Holding staff (paid and unpaid) accountable for leading their ministry areas and fulfilling the church's mission and vision through goals and strategies
- Monitoring the accomplishment of church goals and making adjustments in associated strategies and staff as required to ensure achievement of those goals

Staff and Ministry Teams' Role in Accountable Leadership

- Coordinating with the pastor to create strategies to fulfill the church's goals identified by the Leadership Board
- Connecting congregants to the church's discipleship pathway through all ministries and helping them take their next faithful step
- Identifying, recruiting, equipping, and deploying ministry team members

- Coordinating ministry efforts
- Creating and updating job descriptions for ministry team members
- Following Guiding Principles
- Holding ministry team members accountable
- Helping ministry team members connect their ministry to their identified strategies and to the church's goals, vision, mission, and core values
- Evaluating all ministries and making appropriate shifts (e.g., purpose, intended outcome, missional effectiveness and alignment, and resource consumption)

Living Accountability as a Leadership Board Member

As a Leadership Board member, you are always "on duty" until your term of office ends. You are now responsible for holding the pastor accountable and ensuring the pastor holds ministry team leaders and staff accountable. Serving as a Leadership Board member may change the nature of some of the relationships with your family and fellow disciples. Sometimes that means initiating difficult conversations with your fellow church members. Sometimes it means deflecting or redirecting conversations to avoid a conflict of interest or triangulation. It means holding certain information about staff and clergy sacred and confidential—even from family! Serving in this capacity means fulfilling the fiduciary and legal responsibilities of a trustee and member of the nonprofit corporation's board of directors, even when it might be socially difficult. Gone are the days when you could gossip about the church (which wasn't in alignment with scripture anyway) or enjoy "roast the preacher (or staff member) for Sunday dinner" with friends or family. In Chapter 17, you'll find detailed information about the Leadership Covenant to address this.

Living Accountability as Staff and the Ministry Team Leader

We encourage every ministry team to practice and model the Accountable Leadership Cycle to encourage and support a culture of accountability to Christ's mission for the church. This cycle begins with the Leadership Board articulating the church's mission, vision, core values, and setting annual goals. This critical work guides the ministry teams in setting their objectives (ministries, events, programs). Each ministry uses the following Accountable Leadership Cycle to identify ministries, events, and programs to align with the church's mission, vision, goals, and core values. The intended purpose is identified upfront, along with the desired outcomes and vitality measurements. Planning is then completed accordingly. When the event or program concludes (or periodically for more ongoing ministries), the Accountable Leadership Cycle is used to aid the necessary evaluation and reflection. Using this tool, especially for evaluation, will allow you to depersonalize the experience and evaluate more objectively.

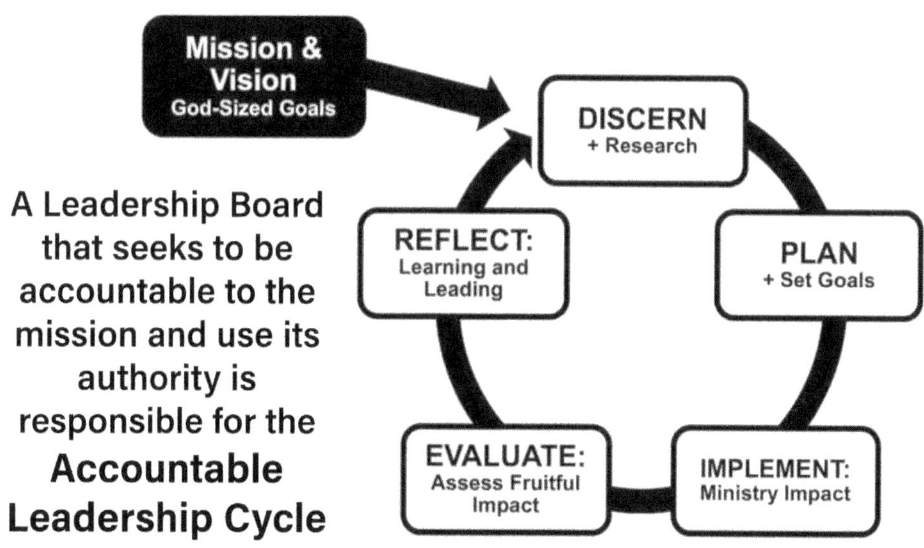

Accountable Leadership Cycle	
Mission, Vision, and Purpose (God-sized Goals)	Ministries should flow from your mission, vision, core values, and goals. Accountability is ultimately rooted in following Christ's mission for the congregation.
Discern + Research	The first step of the cycle is to discern ministry needs as rooted in the mission and vision. This takes prayerful conversation and research, such as demographic studies, neighborhood prayer walks, conversations with local leaders, such as the local school principal or mayor, and listening to unchurched neighbors.
Plan + Set Ministry Objectives	The ministry team and the ministry team leader should plan and set objectives for the proposed ministry, including trackable measurements. For example, a "bridge event" to connect with neighbors will need plans for members to greet and get to know guests, not just "run the event." Similarly, a strategy for such an event would be to provide appropriate follow-up with guests within twenty-four hours and meaningfully connect with one new family. Ministries without planned objectives for transformational impact become random "feel-good events." The ministry team should create clear objectives as part of their ministry planning.
Implement: Ministry Impact	The responsible ministry team is now ready to execute the plan using the predefined objectives. Ultimately, every serving disciple on the team (and the church) is accountable to the mission of the particular ministry and the congregation's larger overall mission and vision. Impactful ministries seek to make disciples and transform the world.
Evaluate: Assess Fruitful Impact	The ministry team should assess the ministry from proposal to event to follow-up and thank-you notes. What worked well? What needed work? What surprised the team? What was the Kingdom impact? Using the ministry's identified objectives, how did the ministry measure up? What did the team learn? Were there any Holy Spirit sightings during the ministry? This evaluation is a vital step in accountability.
Reflect: Learning and Leading	A solid evaluation enables the team leader and pastor to learn about the mission field and the congregation's capacity for ministry follow-through. This reflection time is different from an evaluation. While an evaluation is about doing things right, reflection is about doing the right things. Reflection is a skill and an intentional practice that invites the congregation's leaders back into the season of prayerful learning and discernment about the congregation's future.

CHAPTER FOURTEEN

Adaptive Leadership

You have your structure set. The initial set of Guiding Principles is complete. A Leadership Covenant has been created and signed. Now it's time to have a meeting, right? But wait! Don't fall into the trap of thinking a new structure will automatically create better or different conversations at the table. After all, even Moses had to deal with the "Back to Egypt Committee."[23] More than technical fixes are needed to lead the congregation into fulfillment of Christ's preferred future for your church (vision). Now is the time to deeply consider how adaptive leadership changes the very nature and culture of leadership.

Leadership in the Crucible of a Crisis

The 2020-2021 COVID pandemic demonstrated the inadequacy of technical fixes and "change by copy/paste." In his book *Strengthening Congregational Decision-Making and Governance Supporting New Expeditions*,[24] Blake writes:

> *In spring 2020, almost every church in America suddenly had to adapt, with a few days' notice, from ministries designed to gather people in intimate settings to online worshiping and discipling communities. I had to learn a new sentence: "Our primary worship service is online, but we are also offering several intimate, socially distant and safe in-person worship experiences throughout the week. Please bring your own mask." I did not learn that particular string of words in seminary. Very few of our preachers were trained to be televangelists, but adaptation was key, not only for institutional survival, but for missional fruitfulness. We all learned a powerful lesson—the inherited, months-long decision-making process would no longer work. To be fruitful during a pandemic, adaptive*

---

[23] Exodus 16:2-3.

[24] Blake Bradford, *Strengthening Congregational Decision-Making and Governance Supporting New Expeditions*, Market Square Publishing, 2022.

leadership in churches meant that congregations would either succumb to unsustainable pastoral authoritarianism or create simpler systems of lay leadership decision-making. Rapid cultural change is not going away.[25]

The strong executive leadership needed in the first couple of weeks of the crisis evolved into a few different patterns:

- Some congregations never moved out of crisis reaction mode, with clergy authoritarianism resulting in either an appreciative (but sidelined) congregation or an angry one that was exiled from decision making and congregational leadership. One pastor speaking to me (Blake) explained this binary by saying, "They were all behind me saying, 'We have your back,' then I looked back, and suddenly they were all carrying knives."

- Some congregations figured out a way to limp through the crisis by having their existing administrative committees make decisions—but with little alignment and stunted creativity. Existing ministries stalled, creativity became sluggish at best, and the rich interconnectedness of the congregation deteriorated.

- Some congregations simply folded under their own weight and inertia. While they might not yet be closed, the difficult future that seemed five or ten years away was now on their doorstep.

Some congregations thrived. Lay and clergy leadership structures were simple, adaptable, and connected enough to seek out information and make timely decisions with group support. Other groups and ministry teams were held accountable to the church's continuing mission and given the freedom and flexibility to adapt or shift their resources toward new ministries that enabled the gospel to be shared and the community to be served.

Adaptive Leadership in the Apostolic Age

While "adaptive leadership" may feel like a new term, leadership in a changing world is nothing new. It is part of our Bible-based DNA as Christians. The biblical narrative of the Jerusalem Council in Acts 15

---

25 Blake Bradford, *Strengthening Congregational Decision-Making and Governance Supporting New Expeditions* (Market Square Books, 2022).

shows us an example of ancient adaptive leadership. The fledgling Church had to consider a new way of being (the potential inclusion of Gentiles into the Church) while staying connected to their traditions and identity (including the rite of circumcision). There was deep disagreement, and because the issue was important, the disagreement was deeply felt. Acts 15:6-7 says, "The apostles and leaders called a special meeting to consider the matter. The arguments went on and on, back and forth, getting more and more heated" (MSG).

In seasons of change, when established systems and expectations are failing us, leaders must learn to understand and interpret the new reality, adapt the organization (in this case, the church) to respond to it, and remain true to the institution's foundational values and mission. It is not easy. If challenges were easy, we wouldn't call them *challenging.* In Acts 15, the apostle Peter attempted to reframe the issue based on his experience of what Jesus Christ, through the Holy Spirit, was doing amongst the Gentile believers.

> *Then Peter took the floor: "Friends, you well know that from early on God made it quite plain that he wanted the pagans to hear the Message of this good news and embrace it—and not in any secondhand or roundabout way, but firsthand, straight from my mouth. And God, who can't be fooled by any pretense on our part but always knows a person's thoughts, gave them the Holy Spirit exactly as he gave him to us. He treated the outsiders exactly as he treated us, beginning at the very center of who they were and working outward from that center, cleaning up their lives as they trusted and believed him. So why are you now trying to out-god God, loading these new believers down with rules that crushed our ancestors and crushed us, too? Don't we believe that we are saved because the Master Jesus amazingly and out of sheer generosity moved to save us just as he did those from beyond our nation? So, what are we arguing about?" There was dead silence. No one said a word. With the room quiet, Barnabas and Paul reported matter-of-factly on the miracles and wonders God had done among the other nations through their ministry. The silence deepened; you could hear a pin drop.*
>
> **Acts 15:7-13 (MSG)**

The leaders of the early church looked at the "presenting issue" and at the mission of the church as defined in the Great Commission and the

Great Commandment of love and figured out a pathway into an unknown future. It took the apostle James to "break the silence" and suggest a new set of guidelines that met the needs of the new reality while remaining consistent with the words of the prophets.

> *James broke the silence. "Friends, listen. Simeon has told us the story of how, at the very outset, God made sure that racial outsiders were included. This is in perfect agreement with the words of the prophets ... "God said it and now he's doing it. It's no afterthought; he's always known he would do this. So here is my decision: We're not going to unnecessarily burden non-Jewish people who turn to the Master. We'll write them a letter and tell them, 'Be careful to not get involved in activities connected with idols, to guard the morality of sex and marriage, to not serve food offensive to Jewish Christians – blood, for instance.' This is basic wisdom from Moses, preached and honored for centuries now in city after city as we have met and kept the Sabbath."*
>
> **Acts 15:13-15, 19-21 (MSG)**

After a process of discernment and consensus-building (Acts 15:22 says, "Everyone agreed: apostles, leaders, all the people"), the decision was then communicated to the larger church through representatives and an apostolic letter. This first Jerusalem Council shows us that adaptive leadership may be difficult. But creative, well-discerned, missional decisions at the meeting table can change the entire trajectory of the church and its ability to reach new disciples for Jesus Christ.

Changing the Conversation at the Table

When teaching a course on polity and administration, I (Blake) was assisting a new pastor in understanding the principles of the simplified structure model, and, of course, the concepts of accountable and adaptive leadership came up. The student pastor's assignment: write up a process to manage the divergent paths that members wanted to take in leadership. As we dug deeper, the matter of Robert's Rules of Order came up again and again. Apparently, the congregation had learned years ago that *correct parliamentary procedure* was the answer to all their problems. But now, the congregation was *stuck*. The difficulty now was that "doing business right" could not solve the complex problems their church was facing. The challenges the congregation faced couldn't be fixed by a technical change to parliamentary processes for motions and seconds. The church needed a "shock to the system." So we decided on a radical course of action: an entire season of talking about ministry—of discernment, discovery, and conversation—with no motions or voting allowed. Instead of everything being in "good order" and each "side" trying to "win" by having enough votes, the Leadership Board focused on being prayerfully dedicated to Christ's mission and vision for the congregation and experimented with different processes to come to decisions—adaptive leadership!

We are living in a complex culture very different from the one in which most of our congregations were founded. The solutions that worked so well for us in the past are now anchors pulling us underwater. There is a popular saying in the business world, "What got us *here* won't get us *there*." Technical changes alone won't get us into Christ's God-sized dream for your congregation. The technical changes of restructuring (simplification) and accountable leadership provide space for adaptive leadership (missional creativity).

There have been many books written about adaptive leadership, both secular and church-related. Tod Bolsinger has gifted the church with an excellent metaphor of "canoeing the mountains" by comparing adaptive leadership to the explorations of Lewis and Clark,[26] who literally created the map of the West for the young U.S. government. Lewis and Clark had expected to find a river that would flow all the way to the Pacific Ocean, but instead, they had to figure out a way to turn their canoeing tools and skills into mountaineering skills when they ran into the Rockies.

As part of his early consultation work with the Arkansas Conference in the late 2000s, former Alban Institute consultant Gil Rendle used a story about taking one step at a time to help our entire conference reimagine leadership and ministry for a new generation. Gil asked us to imagine a mother sending her son to lock up the barn doors at night. It was dark. The son couldn't see the barn, much less the doors. So his mother gives him a flashlight and sends him out again. The son comes back—the flashlight, while appreciated, is still too dim to help him find the barn. The mother sends him out a third time, saying, "You don't need

---

[26] Tod Bolsinger, *Canoeing the Mountains: Christian Leadership in Uncharted Territory* (InterVarsity Press, 2015).

to see the barn. You know the basic direction. *Just keep walking to the end of the light*." As the son walked forward, the path grew more illuminated with every step. Eventually, the barn was revealed. All he needed was the faith that the barn was in a certain direction, the flashlight as a tool to help him move forward, and a willingness to take each step (Gil, now retired from the Texas Methodist Foundation, later published this parable in *Doing the Math of Mission: Fruits, Faithfulness, and Metrics*[27]).

In rural Arkansas, this story had quite a resonance. Many of our lay and clergy annual conference members had grown up on farms or still lived on them. They knew the darkness of night outside the city limits. These metaphors and stories helped us see that part of adaptive leadership meant having some level of comfort with the unknown and the uncharted. We could set proximate goals, be clear about our direction, and start heading toward making an impact for Christ. We didn't need to know and plan for every step. In fact, we couldn't know every step of the journey. Our world and the soul of every person are simply too complex. We would have to monitor and adjust. We would have to be willing to *adapt*.

To take the concept of adaptive leadership to a whole other level, here are some words from Kotan taken from her book *Being the Church in the Post-Pandemic World*:

> *Allow me to offer a distinction between adapting and innovating:*
>
> ***Adapting** is taking something you already have, or is already known, and making it suitable for a new use or new conditions.*
>
> ***Innovation**, on the other hand, is introducing brand new methods, ideas or products.*
>
> *Adapting is more of a technical change. Innovation is adaptive change. A technical change is more mono-focused, having an easily determined fix. A technical change is less complex (often a single issue), takes a shorter time, and is easier to identify and enact a solution. An adaptive change is more complex, multi-layered, has*

---

[27] Gil Rendle, *Doing the Math of Mission: Fruits, Faithfulness, and Metrics* (Rowman & Littlefield Publishers, 2014).

longer term effects, has no easy answers, and often calls us to move outside our comfort zone of knowing, doing, and/or being.

Let's explore another important distinction the pandemic has presented for our consideration. When we look at the pandemic as an ***interruption****, we are seeing it as a delay. It is though we hit the pause button, and when the world returns to "normal" we will simply hit the play button again.*

On the contrary, ***disruption*** *is a major disturbance, something that changes your plans, interrupts some event or process, or a break in the action—especially an unplanned and confusing one. When the church sees the pandemic as a disruption, the leaders embrace the opportunity of knowing going back is no longer an option. A disruption allows a church the opportunity to be awakened for the need to change at a much deeper level.*[28]

We can take these learnings and distinctions from the pandemic context and apply them to the move toward a simplified accountable structure. Do leaders see the structural simplification and accountable leadership as a technical or adaptive change? Treating the new structure as a technical change now allows for the adoption of new methods, ideas, processes, and culture. Treating the new structure as an adaptive change, leaders see it as an opportunity to start fresh and view the mission and ministries through a new, innovative lens. Likewise, if leaders see the new structure and leadership styles as a simple interruption, most everything will remain the same or quickly return to what the church has always done. On the other hand, if moving to a simplified accountable structure is viewed as a disruption, there is a great opportunity to be awakened to lead and create impact at a much deeper level.

The legacy forms of leadership and structure we inherited are simply not built to adapt. These legacy forms of structure and the leadership styles they encourage are about fixing problems to get the church "back to business." Business, in this case, usually means back to focusing on membership (not Christ-centered disciple formation or evangelism)

---

[28] Kay Kotan, *Being the Church in the Post-Pandemic World* (Market Square Books, 2021).

and making folks feel comfortable (rather than transforming the world). The multiple committees and "checks and balances" built into our inherited structures are all about maintaining the status quo. But the "status ain't quo." The church is losing ground. Lives aren't being transformed. Disciples aren't being made. Your church needs to be able to adapt to uncharted territory and into a future we can't quite see—setting proximate goals, being brutally clear about the mission and vision you have discerned, and holding one another accountable to make an impact for Christ. By placing these adaptive leadership responsibilities onto your Leadership Board, you are enabling your church to move out of maintenance mode and into transformation mode.

Those churches that truly live into a new simplified structure with accountable, adaptive leadership have experienced a positive change in their trajectory. The changes do not occur overnight, and they aren't easy. The culture doesn't shift quickly, nor does it come naturally. But for those churches truly committed to leading a church on its mission and willing to make the shifts necessary to do so, the outcomes are remarkable.

- First, there is renewed health among the leaders.
- Second, there is a change in the nature and content of conversation around the leadership table.
- Third, there is renewed hope and energy within the life of the congregation.
- Fourth, there is renewed commitment and understanding of the mission to make disciples.
- Fifth, there is renewed focus—someone is piloting the ship. All the passengers know the itinerary. All the passengers realize they are on a working ship (like an aircraft carrier on a mission—not a cruise ship being entertained and served) and know their assigned task as part of the team.
- Sixth, there is an opportunity to create a shared, common language—first with the Leadership Board and continuing as the Leadership Board guides the larger congregation into uncharted waters.

Applying Both Adaptive and Technical Shifts to SAS

Simplified, Accountable Leadership is a *deep, adaptive* shift in *leadership culture.*

As the Leadership Board makes the technical changes of consolidating the four administrative teams, the opportunity for adaptive changes is now theirs. The technical change of having the people representing the collective functions of Trustees, Finance, Church Council, and S/PPRC in the room at the same time is now imaginable—most likely one of the factors motivating the move to this simplified structure. Now is the time for the adaptive changes to kick into gear. Remember, adaptive change is all about implementing changes we do not necessarily know how to implement. It is time for disruption and innovation! Be patient with yourself and one another but hold each other accountable for living into the adaptive changes.

The biggest shifts in adaptive change are modifications to the agenda, conversations, focus, and, hopefully, missional impact. The Leadership Board is to govern—not manage—the day-to-day operations of the church. To govern effectively, the Leadership Board must take a balcony view and adopt a new role. Most churches find it difficult to move from the typical ground view and work (management) to the balcony view and work (governance). Church leadership has historically not functioned at that level.

If the Leadership Board modifies the agenda as recommended, this adaptive shift can begin. If the new Leadership Board uses the traditional agenda (new business, old business, reports, etc.), it will typically only make the technical change of having fewer people around the board table, rather than the conversational shifts required for adaptive changes. Adaptive (innovative) changes take shifts in our values, beliefs, attitudes, and behaviors. As you can imagine, these types of changes are much more difficult to implement than changing the number of people sitting at the table or the number of meetings scheduled!

Remember, technical changes are solving known problems with known solutions. Adaptive changes result from addressing known or unknown problems with unknown solutions, often in unknown environments or situations. Adaptive change starts with adaptive thinking and adaptive learning. We must be willing to adopt new thoughts, understandings, and behaviors to achieve adaptive change. We can't expect adaptive change at the staff and ministry team levels if it is not modeled at the Leadership Board level.

Adaptive leadership means risk, both from external factors (experiments sometimes fail) and from internal factors, particularly sabotage from congregants concerned about all the changes. The more the Leadership Board focuses your congregation on the disciple-making mission, the more others with peripheral concerns or feelings of lost power will criticize the direction.

I (Blake) remember from Latin class that the word "decide" means "to cut off." As your Leadership Board makes decisions, folks will feel cut off or cut out. Gil Rendle writes about this experience in his book *Journey into the Wilderness*:

> *Adaptive work is not tidy. In his theory of change from a systems perspective that takes into consideration the insights of chaos theory, organizational consultant John Scherer notes that in order for change to be birthed, two "parents" must be present – pain and possibility. There must be a discomfort sufficiently strong to make the people want to be different and a possibility promising enough to support the people through change. Walter Brueggemann once commented that the central task of leadership is to manage the hopes and the fears of the people. Indeed, managing hopes and fears—pain and possibility—in a congregation, a conference, or a corporation is a spiritual task of great faithfulness. Scherer demonstrates that if the leader can surface the appropriate pain, hold clearly the*

possibility of what can be, and help people let go of old assumptions, then the people will enter a stage of chaos—the truly creative environment where change happens.

It may be helpful to recall that the wilderness is required. In Mark's gospel, as soon as John baptized Jesus in the Jordan and the voice from heaven proclaimed Jesus as God's son, we are told that the Spirit immediately drove Jesus into the wilderness (Mark 1:12). Wilderness, chaos, change is neither tidy nor comfortable, which underscores the true difficulty of adaptive leadership in a system designed for the comfort of problem-solving management.[29]

The wilderness is a difficult place. Like the explorations of Lewis and Clark, it is often uncharted, and like the story of the boy finding the barn, it can feel incredibly dark out there with your meager flashlight. The Leadership Board's job is to keep pointing toward the Promised Land of God's dream for your congregation while carefully and prayerfully dealing with the inevitable pushback and sabotage inherent with adaptive leadership. Moses had to deal with the "Back to Egypt Committee" of murmurers (Exodus 16), who were more comfortable with slavery than the unknown. Your Leadership Board will need to help one another—and the larger congregation—stay on track with the larger mission and vision that you have discerned. Keep casting the vision. Vision leaks!

A Word of Caution: Leading adaptive change is hard. As we've said, adaptive change calls for cultural shifts within the church. It takes time, persistence, and perseverance. Too often, when the new culture or approach is just about to break through, conflict, unrest, nervousness, or weariness erupts. This is a time when some leaders or Leadership Boards throw in the towel and retreat (head back to Egypt). Yet, this is often the time when one last push will get the adaptive change over the last hump or hurdle. It just takes that last little burst of persistence for the adaptive change to take hold. Often, when leaders are at a crossroads of change, anxious relationship systems default back to what is known and comfortable. Adaptive challenges are the true test of leadership.

Pay attention! If steady progress has been made, don't give up just before you cross the finish line because of some negative tension. Leaders

---

29 Gil Rendle, *Journey in the Wilderness: New Life for Mainline Churches* (Abingdon Press, 2019).

working on adaptive changes should expect some pushback. Don't ignore the opportunities to further equip, communicate, and reinforce along the way either. On the other hand, remember that sometimes the biggest obstacles (hurdles) occur right before the finish line comes into full view. Keep your eye on the finish line and don't give up.

Staying on Track

Part of adaptive change is holding your fellow Leadership Board members accountable not only to the Leadership Covenant but also to their governance roles. If one of your fellow Leadership Board members ventures into what we refer to as the "tall grass" of management, it is your responsibility as a fellow Leadership Board member to call the leader into accountability for their governing role and lane. We must do it—but, of course, this is done with love and grace! If we do not hold them accountable, we will soon find ourselves returning to our natural management tendencies, where, once again, no one is steering the missional ship! Keep in mind this is NOT the sole responsibility of the chair or the pastor. It is the responsibility of every member of the Leadership Board.

Some churches we have worked with have had a lot of fun helping everyone stay in the governing mode. Some have developed a few creative strategies, too. Some use vocal reminders such as "tall grass," "time out," or "management warning" to rein in the conversation. Other churches have developed hand signals, such as the time-out symbol or the well-known stop signal. Others have placed an object in the middle of the table to be picked up when the conversation veers off track. Use a method that fits your Leadership Board's personality and context. The method might even change from time to time. The important part is to have a method that helps a leader recognize when they're drifting out of their lane and get things back on track quickly and efficiently, without debilitating the Leadership Board.

Alignment

It is the responsibility of the Leadership Board, pastor, and staff to ensure missional alignment at all levels. There are four key areas of alignment: budget, facilities, calendar, and people (mainly staff and ministry team leaders).

The Leadership Board's responsibility is to ensure the budget aligns with the mission, vision, goals, and core values. For example, we would be kidding ourselves to say we value children if we have no children's ministry budget or if it's the first ministry area to be cut. Too many times, the budget drives the church. Instead, allow the mission to drive the budget. The budget should be built around identified needs, supporting objectives that accomplish the goals that make the vision a reality as the church lives out its purpose—the mission of making disciples. One telltale sign of church decline is when the budget/dollars (and perhaps even a culture of scarcity) drive all decisions.

The calendar reveals what we value and how we use our time and energy. It is derived from the objectives that flow from the goals, vision, mission, and core values. The objectives translate into the activities, events, and ministries that fill our calendar (time commitments) and require time, capacity, and energy. The calendar should reflect ministries and activities that align with the church's identified annual goals. If leaders simply copy the calendar from one year to the next, the church becomes calendar-driven rather than mission-driven. The pastor is accountable for the calendar alignment with the staff and ministry team leaders.

Paid staffing (clergy and laity) should typically represent about 50 percent of a stable church's budget. For a growing church, the percentage might reach 60 percent. Typically, when the paid staff budget exceeds these thresholds, congregations hire staff to do the ministry rather than equip disciples to engage in the ministry. Staff (whether paid or serving disciples who are like unpaid staff) need to be aligned with the goals and specifically the resulting objectives of their ministry area. We must ensure our staff is spending their time, energy, and budget on the areas the Leadership Board has deemed the focus (mission, vision, goals).

Strategic Ministry Planning in an SAS Leadership Board

Before you know it, it is the end of the year AGAIN. It just slips up and catches you off guard. We all have the best of intentions of making this upcoming year our best ever. Sometimes we even take initial steps. Other times, we have great intentions, but we just never quite put the plan into action to make it happen. Time and time again, we see councils/boards set some wonderful goals for the year. They are worded just so. Then they are packed away—until the end of the year. Then someone mentions them, and leaders pull them back out to review. Upon review, leaders find they failed to achieve their well-intentioned goals for the year. Unfortunately, too often board members simply do not keep these priorities on the front burner to direct the church's focus, time, resources, capacity, and energy. Leaders want and hope to achieve the goals to fulfill the mission and vision, but they lack the intentionality needed to guide the church toward accomplishing them.

So, we encourage you to plan your year in leadership, keep your goals in front of you the entire year, and be intentional about how you use your meeting time. There is more on planning an entire year of board meetings in Chapters 19 and 20, but let's take a few pages to review strategic planning as a church.

Strategic planning is an intricate part of what it takes to serve as accountable and adaptive leaders. Strategic ministry planning helps leaders claim that balcony space with the balcony view. We recommend that, in addition to regular checks on progress toward your God-sized goals and impact in your congregation and mission field, your Leadership Board take a strategic ministry planning retreat annually so you can spend adequate time together discerning and intentionally mapping your congregation's future.

Allow us to provide a quick overview of the five parts of strategic ministry planning:

1. **Mission:** The purpose of the church—why you exist. Every church exists to make disciples of Jesus Christ for the transformation of the world, as Matthew 28:19-20 indicates. It also happens to be the mission statement of The United Methodist Church, as indicated in ¶ 120 of *The Book of Discipline*:

   The Mission – The mission of the Church is to make disciples of Jesus Christ for the transformation of the world. Local churches and the Church's extension ministries are the primary arenas where disciple-making occurs.

Please do not waste any more time trying to discern or articulate your church's mission. It has been clearly laid out for us. Embrace it!

The Leadership Board is accountable to Jesus Christ for the church's faithfulness in making disciples for the transformation of the world.

2. **Vision:** A church's vision connects its purpose, its identity, and its narrative. This is the unique method your church uses to make disciples in your local context for this season. Every church has the same mission, but its unique method and future are articulated in the vision. Vision is God's preferred future for your church. Vision emerges from the sweet spot of your congregation's gifts, your leaders' passions, and a specific need, gap, opportunity, or problem in your community. In today's quick-paced culture, vision usually needs to be recast every couple of years. The pastor is accountable for articulating the congregationally discerned vision. In his book *Church Leadership,* Lovett Weems, the retired director of the Lewis Center for Church Leadership at Wesley Theological Seminary, shared that a key question for leaders is, "Are you willing to wear the vision the same way that people wear clothes?"[30] Vision provides the energy, momentum, focus, and enthusiasm for church vitality.

3. **Core Values:** Values exist in your church whether you have named them or not. Think of it as your DNA or your church culture. It is who you are. It is the personality of your congregation. They guide your decisions. Core values are usually fairly static unless there is intentionality in moving towards aspirational values. Even if there is intentionality in moving towards aspirational values, this shift is normally slow. If you have not identified your core values, now is the time to do it. There is a worksheet to get you started in *Strategy Matters.*[31] A comprehensive book we highly recommend on core values is *Identifying Core Values for the New Expedition* by Ken Willard.[32]

4. **God-sized Goals:** These are the activities or action steps to be taken in the upcoming year that will enable the church to live into your vision and mission. Usually, there are three to five big, overall God-sized goals named each year to focus your congregation's resources. One of your goals may be implemented over multiple years (planning and building a new facility) and needs to be updated based

---

30 Lovett H. Weems Jr., *Church Leadership* (Abingdon Press, 2010).

31 Kay Kotan and Ken Willard, *Strategy Matters: Your Roadmap for an Effective Ministry Planning Retreat* (Market Square Books, 2020).

32 Ken Willard, *Identifying Core Values for the New Expedition* (Market Square Books, 2021).

on your experience over the last year. Other goals may need to be adapted at some point in the year if context or circumstances shift. The Leadership Board holds the pastor accountable for goals and casting/articulating the congregational vision.

5. **Objectives:** This is where the rubber hits the road. Objectives are where the goals grow hands and feet. The staff (paid and unpaid—aka ministry team leaders) are responsible for creating and implementing the objectives (ministries, events, and programs) to make an impact in fulfilling the congregational goals. In the accountable leadership model, the pastor holds the staff and/or ministry team leaders responsible for meeting the objectives.

For a complete guide on strategic ministry planning retreat for planning, implementing, and the post-retreat follow-up steps, check out the resource guide created by Ken Willard and Kay Kotan, *Strategy Matters: Your Roadmap for an Effective Ministry Planning Retreat.*[33]

Notes

[33] Kotan and Willard, *Strategy Matters.*

CHAPTER FIFTEEN

Right-Sizing Your Equipping Process

Equipping leaders must always be right-sized to the congregation's staffing pattern, pastoral capacity, and ministry complexity. The goal is not uniformity across churches but faithfulness to the core principles of simplified accountable leadership. Equipping looks different in large, midsize, and small congregations, yet in every context, the aim is the same: to release people for ministry, clarify accountability, and align leadership energy with the church's mission.

Large and Multi-Staff Congregations

In large or multi-staff congregations, equipping is primarily about releasing staff time and energy for ministry impact rather than pulling staff deeper into governance. Permission-giving Guiding Principles become essential tools in this context. Clear Guiding Principles allow staff to make day-to-day decisions without seeking board approval for every action, which increases agility and trust while reducing unnecessary meetings and delays.

In these congregations, staff members do not attend Leadership Board meetings or submit written reports to the Leadership Board. The Leadership Board governs through vision, strategy, and accountability rather than operational oversight. This separation is critical. When staff regularly attend Leadership Board meetings, the Leadership Board is easily pulled into management work, and staff are subtly trained to govern upward rather than lead outward.

If an associate or executive pastor is responsible for supervising staff or overseeing major ministry areas, that individual may, within clear boundaries and expectations, attend Leadership Board meetings as a guest. In this case, their role is not to report on activity but to participate in strategic alignment and accountability conversations related to the Leadership Board's goals and priorities. We will have more to say in the

Implementing Phase section about executive pastors.

The lead pastor, or a clearly designated staff leader, holds staff and ministry team leaders accountable for objectives that flow directly from the Leadership Board's goals. Accountability is focused on outcomes and missional alignment rather than task completion. In large congregations, equipping leaders well means trusting the structure enough to let it do its work.

Midsize Congregations
(Full-Time Clergy with a Mix of Paid and Unpaid Staff)

In midsize congregations, equipping centers on the pastor's role as a developer and deployer of ministry leaders. The pastor identifies, recruits, equips, and deploys ministry team leaders rather than attempting to manage entire teams directly. This shift is essential for sustainability and growth.

Rather than meeting with full ministry teams, the pastor meets regularly with ministry team leaders. These leader-focused meetings clarify expectations, provide coaching, and reinforce alignment with the church's mission and strategic priorities by holding the leader accountable for the identified objectives. Ministry team leaders are then responsible for equipping and leading their teams.

The pastor holds ministry team leaders accountable for missional alignment and progress toward clearly defined objectives aligned with the church's goals set by the Leadership Board. Accountability is not punitive or micromanaging. It is relational, goal-oriented, and rooted in shared purpose. When equipping is right-sized in midsize congregations, pastors avoid burnout, leaders grow in confidence, and ministry becomes more focused and effective.

Small Churches
(Shared or Less Than Full-Time Pastor)

In small churches, equipping must be especially realistic and honest about the limited pastoral time available. When pastors serve part-time, bi-vocationally, or across multiple charges, additional leadership support is required to sustain ministry.

In these contexts, the Leadership Board chair or another Leadership Board member may serve as a liaison to one or more ministry team leaders. In some cases, Leadership Board members may need to function as ministry team leaders themselves. This is not a failure of structure. It is a necessary adaptation to context. It is also an opportunity to evaluate congregational capacity and impact for possible shifts in how congregational energy and time are used.

Notes

CHAPTER SIXTEEN

Common Challenges in the Equipping Phase

Nominations Challenges During the Equipping Phase

"But I'm always on a committee."

Back in the section explaining the Discerning Phase, I (Blake) describe my experience with a Trustees chair at a large church who had served in that position for thirty years, succeeding a fellow who had served as chair for multiple decades before him. The church was large enough (over 2,000 members) that there were plenty of high-capacity leaders who could have stepped into that important role. Pastors came and went, but the Trustees' membership was eternal. Over the decades, even the thought that he would rotate off became verboten—it was almost seen as treason. As your congregation seeks to create a simplified accountable leadership structure, challenges such as these will surface. In our *Greatest Expedition Series*, Blake wrote in the *Strengthening Decision-Making* volume:

> *This concept is difficult for a member whose identity—sometimes their sense of self—might be wrapped up in holding the same church office for decades or who doesn't feel particularly gifted in leading ministries and prefers the administration of the church (I would actually call that a spiritual issue). When churches hand out offices and roles to placate certain families or constituencies, it distracts from the difficult work of servant leadership. Bob is not on the Leadership Board to represent the choir. And Bob, along with every member of the board, is responsible first to the mission of Jesus Christ. The Leadership Board should represent the entire church as it seeks faithfulness and fruitfulness in this mission.*
>
> *While one could look at a simplified board and think that it shrinks the pool of involvement and leadership, actually the reverse is true. I believe that people (especially new disciples) today are not looking to fill a slot. Disciples are seeking to have meaning in their lives and*

> *make an impact in the world for Jesus Christ. Keeping a chair warm on an administrative committee which has no real responsibility or authority does not bring meaning into their life and neither does cumbersome decision-making processes. If it takes too long for a ministry idea to become a ministry reality, today's leaders will drop out. Twenty-first century disciples want to be able to see how their participation in ministry is actually growing new disciples or changing lives. Actually, this was always the case.*[34]

Not everyone currently on administrative committees will have a place on the new Leadership Board, but all will have a place to serve. Over time, mainline churches have elevated administrative committees as the place of "real power" and "where things really happen." We (Kay and Blake) have seen too many congregations that vet leaders for administrative committees but let anyone who passes a background check run the church's missions and ministries. Frankly, this approach is upside down, backwards, and wrong-side-out! We need creative, talented, spiritually gifted leaders who coordinate ministries, lead small groups, and form disciples! These are the church's highest-impact areas!

We hope (and recommend) that the Nominations Committee will look beyond the membership of the congregation's current administrative committees when recommending a new slate of leaders for the Leadership Board. Having all the former leaders from the traditional structure govern in a new Leadership Board will waste an opportunity to add new people with fresh eyes and innovative ways of leading. And frankly, we have witnessed that it is far easier for new leaders to implement a new leadership model than for most existing leaders within the inherited structure to make the necessary shifts to adopt it.

Rotate Your Leaders ("We Can't Lose Susan!")

One of the quickest ways a simplified structure begins to drift is when congregations, worried about losing the wisdom of their first class of leaders, stop practicing rotation. The fear sounds faithful: "We can't lose Susan," "Bill is our only financial mind," "No one knows the history of the facility like Sharon." But this fear is precisely what undermines

[34] Blake Bradford, *Strengthening Decision-Making and Governance Supporting New Expeditions.*

accountable leadership. Rotation is not a technical preference. It is a core design feature of the simplified accountable structure, and it protects the mission far more than any one individual can.

Rotation keeps leadership healthy by preventing the quiet consolidation of influence we saw so often in the traditional structure. Before SAS, long-serving members on multiple committees often became the informal centers of power. SAS (and compliance with the *Book of Discipline*) corrects this by limiting terms and creating rolling classes. When churches immediately reappoint leaders or extend terms because those leaders are "too important to lose," they unintentionally rebuild the very patterns SAS exists to transform. This is true even for the inaugural slate of Leadership Board members. Don't make the common mistake of arbitrarily selecting the first nine members of a new Leadership Board only from the pool of your church's existing elected administrative committee members. Healthy governance requires shared authority, regular infusions of new perspectives, and the expectation that *no one* becomes indispensable.

Rotation also protects the leaders themselves. Many faithful servants resist stepping off the Leadership Board because they love the work, feel responsible for keeping things afloat, or struggle to imagine someone else carrying the mantle. Yet, one of the most consistent patterns we have seen is that leaders who never rotate off eventually burn out. Rotation creates a holy pause. It gives leaders breathing room to rest, renew, and re-engage in ministry teams where their gifts may flourish in new ways. It allows people to serve without slipping into over-functioning or gatekeeping. By stepping off for a season, leaders rediscover joy rather than obligation.

A further benefit is how rotation strengthens the leadership pipeline. The Nominations Committee cannot do its work faithfully if the slate is already assumed year after year. Rotation creates openings, broadens responsibility, and invites new voices into the conversation. It also signals to the congregation that leadership is not a closed circle. When rotation is ignored, the Nominations Committee has little to discern and even less to develop. When rotation is practiced, the Nominations Committee becomes a spiritually attentive body that shapes the future of the church through its prayerful work.

And here is the good news. A rotated leader is not gone. They remain valuable, just not as voting members of the governance board. Many of your most gifted leaders make tremendous contributions to short-term work teams, helping complete assignments from the Leadership Board. They can offer historical insight during a facilities project, serve as mentors to new Leadership Board members, or provide expertise in finance, property, or personnel matters without holding authority that clouds lines of accountability. Their wisdom is still available but in healthier, more flexible ways that benefit the whole church. I (Blake) have seen this recently in my current congregation. After an excellent tenure as a key leader, a chairperson rotating off has discovered a new kind of joy in supporting and equipping the incoming chair. Their wisdom continues to be honored, while the new chair steps fully into the role with confidence and clarity, drawing freely on the former chair's deep technical and strategic knowledge. As the pastor, it has been deeply satisfying to watch that leader move from holding authority to offering mentorship, and to see how both leaders and the wider church are strengthened in the process. Leadership rotation, when practiced well, becomes a shared spiritual gift rather than a loss.

This is as true for small congregations as it is for large ones. Small churches often feel the strongest pressure to ignore rotation because "no one else will serve." But rotation is even more vital in these settings because the few leaders who carry the load need rest. Rotation keeps authority distributed and allows new leaders—often unexpected ones—to emerge. If numbers require it, a leader may rotate off for the minimum required time and then return to service later. The rhythm matters far more than the size of the pool.

Ultimately, rotation keeps accountability alive. It reminds leaders that they serve for a season, offer their best, and then make space for others. It keeps the Leadership Board from stagnating and the congregation from slipping back into old patterns. It models a deeply Wesleyan truth: we offer ourselves fully, we release the role when the season is complete, and we trust God to raise up the next faithful stewards of the mission.

In addition to these recommendations and practices, state laws often require that boards of directors of incorporated nonprofit entities (The Leadership Board in SAS and the Board of Trustees in the legacy multi-committee structure) serve for set terms. While terms can usually be renewed, the terms of office must be set and published.

Committee on Nominations AND Leadership Development

As your congregation lives more deeply and adaptively into SAS, here are a couple of other reminders.

First, remember that the Committee on Nominations and Leadership Development is also responsible for *leadership development.* With this in mind, potential leaders after the first year will have participated in a leadership development process. Following this intentional leadership development process, discernment will be required on both the part of the potential leader as well as the Nominations Committee members to determine whether this is the right season and the right person for church leadership, and for which role.

Second, I (Kay) highly recommend that part of the leadership development process include learning and resourcing Peter Scazzero's materials in *Emotionally Healthy Spirituality*[35] and *The Emotionally Healthy Leader.*[36]

Third, the Nominations Committee will want to create an ongoing intentional leadership development pathway. Check out *Launching Leaders*[37] by Kotan and Schroeder as a guide for creating a process, building leadership and spiritual habits, and starting a pathway for leadership development.

Passive-Aggressive Nominations

Please don't use the nominations process to address interpersonal issues. Blake often exhorts congregational leaders to avoid using *The Book of Discipline* or an SAS restructure to solve a Matthew 18 problem. Reading this book, we know that a few readers will have a particularly difficult person in mind and imagine using simplification to finally remove that annoying leader from office ("Sorry, Ralph, I suppose your position was just eliminated; oh, well"). Using the transition to simplified accountable structure for these purposes will poison the

---

35 Peter Scazzero, *Emotionally Healthy Spirituality: It's Impossible to Be Spiritually Mature While Remaining Emotionally Immature* (Zondervan, 2017).

36 Peter Scazzero, *The Emotionally Healthy Leader: How Transforming Your Inner Life Will Deeply Transform Your Church, Team, and the World* (Zondervan, 2015).

37 Kay Kotan and Phillip Schroeder, *Launching Leaders: Taking Leadership Development to New Heights.*

entire foundation of the process. Instead, follow Jesus' plan for disciples to engage other disciples with accountability and reconciliation as found in Matthew 18. Talk with your "Ralph" honestly and don't use the restructure as a tool for punishment or favoritism. Let's keep our eyes solidly on the Great Commission and Kingdom impact during this transition and leave all other agendas on the curb.

Honorary Leadership Board Members

A simplified accountable structure has no seats reserved for honorific positions. Every member of the Leadership Board is a working leader elected by the congregation for a term of service and held accountable to the mission, vision, and Guiding Principles of the church. Election matters. It is the congregation's way of entrusting spiritual authority and expecting spiritual accountability.

SAS does not create places for people to serve simply because they have always served or because they hold a certain status within the community. Sometimes churches feel internal pressure to give a Leadership Board seat to someone who has been a long-tenured leader, a faithful donor, or a respected figure in the church's history. This is the first type of honorific expectation. These individuals may be beloved, and their contributions may be significant, but SAS leadership is not a lifetime appointment or a courtesy position. It is *active governance.* Every person on the Leadership Board must engage in the work, share responsibility, and be evaluated in accordance with the church's mission. If someone is not able or willing to serve in this way, they should not be appointed or reappointed outside the nominations and charge conference elective process simply to preserve tradition or avoid relational discomfort.

A second kind of honorific pressure is more subtle. Some members are highly successful in business, influential in civic life, or carry a natural authority that others defer to. They may be generous, charismatic, or deeply respected. But those qualities alone do not qualify someone for accountable leadership. If a person is not a dedicated disciple of Jesus Christ, they are not yet ready for the vulnerability, humility, and covenantal responsibility that SAS requires. Accomplishment is not discipleship. Influence is not accountability. Spiritual readiness matters more than community reputation.

For these individuals, the healthier path is often relational rather than structural. Pastors and key leaders may feel pressure to "give them a seat" to keep peace or honor their status. But this only undermines the model's integrity. Instead, create space to value them without granting governance authority and responsibility. Have coffee with them. Invite their insight on a particular ministry or mission effort. Ask for their wisdom in an advisory, non-governing capacity. Recognize their gifts while making clear that SAS leadership is not a recognition of influence but a call to accountable service. Most people respond well when they feel heard and respected, even if they are not placed on the Leadership Board. In equipping leaders for donor development work, I (Blake) often quote the rapper Pitbull, "Ask for money, get advice. Ask for advice, get money twice."[38]

Honor belongs in relationships, gratitude, and shared ministry. It does not belong in governance seats. In SAS, leadership is elected and accountable. It is called simplified ACCOUNTABLE leadership, after all!

Work Lanes

Much like family backyard football games, smaller schools provide students with more opportunities to participate. In larger schools, students most often don't have the opportunity to play multiple sports. For example, those most gifted in basketball will likely not have the opportunity to also play tennis. Those gifted in track and field will likely not have the opportunity to also wrestle. Sometimes student populations in larger schools are so huge that even talented athletes don't get to play on a team, or they spend most of the games on the bench. Only elite athletes are given the opportunity to play. Yet, in schools with smaller class sizes, a student can participate in multiple sports.

The same is true for small churches. There are all kinds of opportunities to participate. Some may even say there are too many. With so many activities offered, the same few people run from one game to the

---

[38] Pitbull feat. Christina Aguilera, "Feel This Moment," track 3 on *Global Warming: Meltdown* (RCA Records, 2012).

next without knowing the final score—let alone discerning whether they even want to participate! There is just an expectation of participation.

In larger churches, we refer to "four lanes" of accountable leadership as distinct roles: governance, management, leadership, and ministry (see Chapter 13). Often, leaders struggle to stay in their respective lanes. Those elected to serve in the governance lanes often veer into management and become tempted to park there, while those called to serve in ministry find themselves stalled in management by excessive congestion. The ministry lane—the church's most critical pathway—is left deserted, and the mission of the church unrealized.

In healthy churches with over sixty (or so) engaged people, these four distinct lanes—operating with responsibility, authority, and accountability—all have different people. No matter the size of the church, the idea is to reserve as many disciples as possible to serve as teammates (for impactful ministry). Note that anyone leading a team (whether paid or unpaid) is in management and should be considered part of a staff team. Management is not hired to do the ministry. Those leading ministry teams are responsible for identifying the gifts, graces, and passions of disciples and recruiting them into areas of ministry that align with those gifts, graces, and passions. The leaders then equip the disciples for ministry and deploy them to impact, nurture, disciple, and reach new people for Christ to transform communities and the world.

In smaller churches, rather than assigning different people to different lanes of ministry, we have to think in terms of the different hats of work within the church. If no clear distinctions exist among the various types of work to be completed, the church leaders will likely not travel in all the lanes or recognize the distinctions and value of the different kinds of work. The default lane is management, regardless of the church's size. The most important lanes are ministry (locomotion) and governance (steering). Unfortunately, in most any size church, the governance lane almost always has grass growing up in the cracks of the asphalt because it is so seldom traveled. The ministry lane is greatly underutilized, as our denomination has placed a high value on committee work and meetings rather than releasing people for the highest Kingdom impact work—ministry!

POSITION	PLAYERS	FUNCTION
Ministry	Disciples	Serve in impactful ministry, nurture and develop disciples, reach new people for Christ
Management	Staff and Ministry Team Leaders	Identify, recruit, equip, and deploy disciples for ministry, coordinate resources, disciples, and ministries
Leadership	Lead Pastor	Spiritual leader and shepherd. Supervises and evaluates staff and ministry team leaders. Aligns ministries, staffing, and resources to the vision and goals.
Governance	Leadership Board	Responsible for Stewardship, Generative Work, Strategy, and holds the lead pastor accountable to the vision and goals.

Leadership Board Challenges During the Equipping Phase

The Equipping Phase helps shape the culture of the Leadership Board. It forms habits, clarifies expectations, and creates the structures that will guide the church for years to come. When equipping is strong, the Leadership Board grows in confidence and alignment. When equipping is neglected, the Leadership Board often drifts back into old patterns and loses the clarity that SAS is designed to create. The following challenges appear frequently in churches that struggle to implement the model. Naming them early helps your Leadership Board avoid them.

Year One: The Most Crucial Season

The first year sets the tone for everything that follows. Many congregations stumble here because they assume the new structure is simply a rearranged or stripped version of the old one. The most common mistake is automatically placing current administrative chairs or committee members on the new Leadership Board without discernment or training. These leaders may be capable, but SAS requires different work and different mindsets.

Another early challenge is confusion about the Trustees' role. Without clear Guiding Principles and focused equipping, Leadership Board members often revert to acting as a building maintenance team instead of a governing body. SAS expects Trustees to govern facility decisions and policy, not repair door hinges. The building maintenance team is a ministry team, not a governing committee.

Many first-year Leadership Boards also fail to equip every new Leadership Board member and the pastor with training on the model. Without shared training, alignment quickly breaks down. This is why using a neutral outside trainer, such as an Authorized SAS Coach, is so important and recommended. Authorized SAS Coaches bring experience, best practices, and distance from local dynamics. Time and time again, we have found that it is impossible for a pastor (even those equipped and practiced in SAS in other appointments) to effectively or neutrally "coach" their own church in SAS. It presents a conflict of interest and may even be interpreted as imposing the model onto the congregation. Therefore, we highly recommend using an Authorized SAS Coach instead.

Finally, the practice of using work teams must be started early and continued consistently. When the Leadership Board tries to handle detailed tasks collectively in its meetings, it wastes the team's time and loses focus on its governance role. Delaying the creation of Guiding Principles also keeps the Leadership Board stuck in management rather than moving into true governance.

Year Two: The Pipeline Problem

By the second year, a new set of challenges appears. Many Leadership Boards neglect to create an onboarding process for new members. Without it, new leaders are confused and often default to the old committee mindset. Training for new Leadership Board members is equally important. If only the first class of leaders has been trained, the model will not last, and a new leadership culture will certainly not develop.

Some congregations also experience a stalled leadership pipeline. If new leaders are not being identified, equipped, and invited into service, the Leadership Board becomes static. Likewise, when a new pastor or staff member arrives without SAS training, the system can quickly unravel. Consistent, ongoing training and coaching are essential for every new leader.

Year Three and Beyond: Drifting Without Training

The challenges of Year Two repeat every year that follows if equipping is not continuous and intentional. Leadership Boards without a consistent onboarding process and annual training drift. Leadership pipelines dry up. Pastors and staff arrive without clarity about their roles. Over time, the structure begins to resemble the traditional model it replaced.

SAS thrives when Leadership Boards are trained annually, leaders are replenished, and new voices are equipped for the work of accountable leadership. Equipping is not optional. It is the operating system that sustains the model.

Notes

SECTION FOUR

Implementing

When they got to Jerusalem, Paul and Barnabas were graciously received by the whole church, including the apostles and leaders. They reported on their recent journey and how God had used them to open things up to the outsiders. Some Pharisees stood up to say their piece. They had become believers, but continued to hold to the hard party line of the Pharisees. "You have to circumcise the pagan converts," they said. "You must make them keep the Law of Moses."

The apostles and leaders called a special meeting to consider the matter.

The arguments went on and on, back and forth, getting more and more heated.

Then Peter took the floor: "Friends, you well know that from early on God made it quite plain that he wanted the pagans to hear the Message of this good news and embrace it – and not in any secondhand or roundabout way, but firsthand, straight from my mouth. And God, who can't be fooled by any pretense on our part but always knows a person's thoughts, gave them the Holy Spirit exactly as he gave him to us. He treated the outsiders exactly as he treated us, beginning at the very center of who they were and working from that center outward, cleaning up their lives as they trusted and believed him.

"So why are you now trying to out-god God, loading these new believers down with rules that crushed our ancestors and crushed us, too? Don't we believe that we are saved because the Master Jesus amazingly and out of sheer generosity moved to save us just as he did those from beyond our nation?

So what are we arguing about?" There was dead silence. No one said a word.

With the room quiet, Barnabas and Paul reported matter-of-factly on the miracles and wonders God had done among the other nations through their ministry. The silence deepened; you could hear a pin drop.

Acts 15:4-13 (MSG)

Implementing Phase Introduction

The Implementing Phase is the fourth step in the simplified accountable structure process and marks the first full year of actually leading the church through this model. During this phase, the Leadership Board creates the initial Guiding Principles, Leadership Covenant, and policies and procedures (if not already completed). This phase includes the first strategic ministry planning retreat and living into both the technical and adaptive leadership cultural changes in this model. During this time, the Leadership Board begins growing into a leadership model of accountability, while the Nominations Committee journeys through creating a leadership development pathway and its first season of selecting three new leaders for the Leadership Board, who will roll off after the first year.

Who Is Involved in This Phase?

The primary participants in this phase are the elected Leadership Board members and the pastor, who together carry out the work of governance and mission alignment. The Nominations Committee remains involved but in a different capacity than in the previous phases. The Authorized SAS continues as a teacher, resource provider, and accountability partner, helping the church live into the model with health and confidence to shift the leadership culture of the church.

What Is the Timing of This Phase?

While the Implementing Phase refers to the first official year of the new structure, most congregations discover that it takes time to fully inhabit the culture of accountable, adaptive leadership. Most churches need more than one year to internalize the habits and mindset of SAS and shift the leadership culture of the church. This is especially true when a new pastor or staff member arrives without prior experience in the model. They will require focused equipping and coaching during their first year to keep the system aligned and thriving.

Understanding the Implementing Phase

Everything up to this point has been preparation. You have moved through Discerning, Designing, and Equipping. In the Implementing Phase, you are no longer deciding whether simplified accountable structure is right for your congregation, nor are you simply preparing leaders to understand it. You are preparing to live into it.

In this moment, clarity meets practice, and well-designed structures begin to encounter real people, real habits, and real context. No congregation implements SAS perfectly—and that is not failure! It is a reality of faithful growth, because implementing is as much about relationships as it is about the technical steps and tools.

Implementing is a journey, not an event. The model will stretch, adapt, and mature as leaders learn to use it together in your unique context. What matters most in this season is not perfection but faithfulness, humility, and an openness to learning. The sections that follow are designed to help real leaders grow into healthier patterns of accountability, trust, and shared missional focus over time.

The Implementing Phase is the season when the Leadership Board starts to shape the church's emerging leadership culture. As the Leadership Board practices accountable governance week by week, patterns settle in. Some long-standing habits from the old structure will naturally surface, and the Leadership Board will need to address them with openness and grace. At the same time, new rhythms of trust, alignment, and mission-focused decision making begin to take root. This first year, the congregation starts to feel the difference between committee-based leadership and accountable, unified leadership and governance.

Alongside this work, the Nominations Committee enters its first cycle of selecting three new Leadership Board members who will join once the original class rotates off at the end of the year. This is also when the Nominations Committee begins building an intentional leadership development plan to continually identify, recruit, equip, and deploy new leaders into ministry.

The Implementing Phase is the year (and beyond) when leadership takes shape, culture shifts, and the church begins to experience the clarity, efficiency, and freedom that comes from leading with one board, one mission, and one shared commitment to accountable discipleship.

Notes

CHAPTER SEVENTEEN

Leadership Covenant

Leadership covenants exist because the work we share is sacred, and the stakes are high. Decisions made by a Leadership Board shape the spiritual health, vitality, direction, and witness of the congregation. A Leadership Board will *do* many things. A covenant names *how* we will be with one another while we do that work. It creates a shared understanding of expectations, boundaries, and behaviors before conflict arises, not after. Covenants are not rules meant to control people; they are commitments freely made that help leaders practice trust, honesty, and accountability together. In a simplified *accountable* structure where fewer people carry greater responsibility, a covenant protects both the church's mission and the relationships of those who lead it. It reminds us that *how* we lead matters just as much as *what* we decide.

A Leadership Covenant begins by naming the posture we bring to the table. Mutual accountability must be practiced from the very beginning. Leaders are accountable first to Jesus Christ and to God's mission for the church. Accountability does not flow upward or downward alone; it is shared. If the Leadership Board does not model accountability, then accountability will not exist anywhere else in the congregation. As leaders of the church, the Leadership Board and the pastor must be the first to model and practice accountable leadership to begin the shift in the whole church's leadership culture. Leaders can't expect change from others if they are not first willing to practice individually and collectively as a board.

A spirit of curiosity and grace sustains that accountability. Leaders are encouraged to attend meetings ready to ask honest questions and listen carefully to one another. Questions are not interruptions to the work; they are often the pathway to clarity and shared understanding for the whole board. A covenant helps create a space where curiosity is welcomed rather than feared.

A covenant also asks leaders to leave outside agendas at the door. Personal issues, individual priorities and preferences, and unresolved conflicts cannot drive the work of the Leadership Board. Leadership Board meetings are not private or personal time; they are God's time. When leaders honor that truth together, the Leadership Board becomes a place of trust, discernment, and faithful decision making, leading to missional effectiveness.

Each year, as a few members roll off the Leadership Board and a few new ones come on, a new Leadership Covenant is created for their work ahead. The covenant is completed at the fall strategic ministry planning retreat if all new members who will be coming onto the Leadership Board are present. If not all are present, the Leadership Covenant must be completed at the first meeting of the new Leadership Board at the beginning of the year.

A covenant is a sacred agreement with God and fellow Leadership Board members, written and signed to detail leadership expectations and a shared code of conduct to which each member commits. It speaks to how Leadership Board members will work together, conduct themselves individually and collectively, collaborate as a team, and foster a leadership culture of respect with a missional focus. Without a covenant, Leadership Boards are more likely to struggle with ambiguity, unmet expectations, and misunderstandings.

A healthy team covenants together, and expectations are known and agreed upon before the work begins. In Kay's consulting, she always suggests that the covenant creation be started from scratch each year. The previous Leadership Board would not want to impose last year's covenant on the current Leadership Board, which is composed of one-third new members. Of course, it can be used as a template, but copying last year's covenant over to this year takes away from its sacredness, the opportunity for new leaders to weigh in on its content, and the exercise of a fresh start and perspective each year. Once the covenant is agreed upon and put into writing, have each board member sign (individually with a pen—not digitally) the covenant. This is a sacred time and practice, so approach it as such.

I (Kay) am often asked for a copy or sample of a Leadership Covenant. I hesitate to offer one because when I do, church leaders often fail to engage in the sacred and needed process of developing their own covenant in their own words. Leaders often skip the critical conversations needed to articulate and discuss the expectations they have for one another and to build a mutual understanding of how they will work together. Instead, leaders copy a template covenant, call it good, and happily mark it off their "to-do list," missing the *importance of the process* in creating the covenant. The discernment process of creating an agreement that leaders "own" and articulate in their own words is vitally important and binds Leadership Board members in their critically important leadership and missional work together.

However, with those concerns stated and, in the spirit of collaboration and connection, the following is a resource your authors created to get you started. This example of a simple Leadership Board covenant, titled "The Rules of the Road,"[39] found on the following page, can be adapted for your context.

[39] Kay Kotan and Blake Bradford, *Mission Possible for the Small Church: Simplifying Leadership, Structure & Ministries in the Church* (Market Square Books, 2023).

Rules of the Road

A Leadership Board Covenant

Decisions Are Made by the Leadership Board Members Who Show Up:

A. The charge conference elects the Leadership Board and Committee on Nominations and Leadership Development in accordance with *The Book of Discipline of the United Methodist Church.*

B. Except for official Trustee legal business (which requires a majority of members to be present for a quorum), *The Discipline* defines a quorum as the members of a committee who are present.

C. Leadership Board members are expected to attend all Leadership Board meetings, unless they are ill or out of town. If needed, members can join meetings via speakerphones or video chat. If Leadership Board members miss three or more meetings per year, the Leadership Board chair will speak with the Leadership Board member to ascertain if the member's seat needs to be vacated and filled by someone who can be more active and engaged.

D. Teleconference or online meeting participation is okay if allowed by the group, but the United Methodist Church does not authorize voting "proxies."

E. The Leadership Board will move from an open meeting into a confidential "executive session" whenever the Leadership Board is conducting Staff/Pastor-Parish Relations (S/PPRC) business. Only official S/PPRC members (aka the Leadership Board in SAS) can be present for this component of the meeting, so all guests will be invited to leave. The minutes of the executive session should be kept separate from the rest of the Leadership Board's minutes, and all the appropriate S/PPRC restrictions of *The Book of Discipline* apply, including voting restrictions and strict confidentiality.

F. Leadership Board members will review the meeting packet, sent by the Leadership Board chair one week in advance, before each meeting and come fully prepared to participate.

G. During a duly called and advertised meeting, we don't delay Leadership Board business because someone is missing unless there are extenuating circumstances, such as foul weather.

Leadership Board Members Are Disciples of Jesus and Fiduciary Officers:

A. Leadership Board members carry, support, and promote the church's mission and vision at all times.

B. Leadership Board members are role models for the congregation. Therefore, members will model mature discipleship by being present in worship at least three times per month, giving proportionally, having an active prayer life, serving in mission a minimum of three times per year, being active on a ministry team, being in a consistent faith formation group, and openly sharing their faith with others in the secular world.

C. Leadership Board members will encourage and support their pastor and fellow Leadership Board members.

D. Leadership Board members will hold themselves, the pastor, and other Leadership Board members accountable for their leadership roles and responsibilities. This includes allowing others to hold the board members collectively and individually accountable.

E. Leadership Board members shall recuse themselves from any situation that could be construed as a conflict of interest.

F. Leadership Board members have no special or unique personal authority or ability to demand time or actions from the pastor, staff, or ministry team leaders outside that work assigned by the Leadership Board.

G. Staff and ministry team leaders report directly to the pastor, or supervisor designee—not to individual Leadership Board members. Leadership Board members will not supervise staff, give staff direction, or carry messages between staff, the pastor, and other leaders. To avoid triangulation, concerns will be addressed through the appropriate and agreed-upon channels.

H. Leadership Board members will act in good faith, serving out of loyalty to the church's mission, obedience to *The Book of Discipline of the United Methodist Church,* and to the policies set forth by the charge conference and annual conference, and in faithfulness to their duties as Leadership Board members.

I. Leadership Board members hold one another, the congregation, and the people in the mission field in daily prayer.

We Will Speak the Truth in Love (Ephesians 4:15)

A. Communication will be respectful, open, and honest. As a Leadership Board, we will address disagreements with transparency and maintain our missional focus on making disciples of Jesus Christ. Leadership Board members will not participate in "parking lot conversations" related to their roles as Leadership Board members.

B. Conflict and disagreement are a natural part of life together in the church. When concerns arise, we will follow the guidance of Jesus in Matthew 18 and address them at the appropriate level. Leadership Board members do not receive or carry complaints as individuals. When concerns are shared with us, we will listen respectfully but will not take ownership of a concern that does not belong to us or act as mediators or advocates outside the work of the Leadership Board acting together. We will help ensure concerns are directed appropriately: Concerns about staff will be addressed first with the staff member and then directed to the pastor. We will encourage individuals with concerns to first go directly to the staff member or pastor. If concerns persist, others may be invited into the conversation (the pastor in situations involving staff, and the board in cases of concern about the pastor). The board would receive these concerns in their role as the Staff/Pastor-Parish Relations Committee. Concerns about Leadership Board decisions or actions will be addressed first with the chair and then with the Leadership Board as a whole.

C. In accordance with *The Discipline of the United Methodist Church,* the pastor will be present in all meetings unless the pastor is voluntarily absent. At no time will we support or participate in secret meetings that undermine the integrity or authority of the pastor or the Leadership Board.

D. Individual Leadership Board members are representatives of the Leadership Board throughout their leadership terms. Leadership Board members have a fiduciary duty to the Leadership Board and the church to uphold the highest standards of integrity in their relationships and to support the mission of the congregation, including publicly supporting other congregational leaders, staff, ministry leaders, and clergy.

E. Leadership Board members will hold each other accountable as disciples of Jesus and as church leaders through our prayers, presence, gifts, service, and witness. The Leadership Board (in its role of S/PPRC) will hold the pastor accountable in collaboration with the bishop and district superintendent.

We Will Balance Transparency and Confidentiality

A. The Leadership Board, in its role and responsibility as the Staff/Pastor-Parish Relations Committee, is held to a high standard of confidentiality in personnel and clergy appointment matters.

B. Leadership Board members understand that, as leaders, derogatory comments or conversations about personnel (especially the pastor) are inappropriate and should be avoided. Concerns will be processed only with the collective Leadership Board and the district superintendent.

C. The United Methodist Church supports open meetings (BOD ¶ 722) at all levels of the church. Exceptions are Staff/Pastor-Parish Relations Committee work and some legal work of the Trustees, such as property negotiations. In those cases, guests will be excused, and the minutes will reflect the transition into and out of executive session. A separate set of minutes for the executive session shall be kept, noting that those not on the Leadership Board were excused from the meeting.

D. No secret meetings are allowed, and when the Leadership Board is doing the business of the Staff/Pastor-Parish Relations Committee, the pastor (or DS) shall be present (see BOD ¶ 258.2 for particulars).

We Are a Leadership Board with a Unified Voice

A. Leadership Board members are encouraged to invest in Leadership Board conversations and decisions with vigor and passion. However, once the Leadership Board has reached a decision, each board member will publicly and individually support the decision without exception, whether or not they personally agree with it. A unified voice and message from the Leadership Board are essential.

B. Leadership Board members will not call out or undermine the collective decisions of the Leadership Board.

Pro+SAS Resource Hub

Note: You'll find a copy of this Leadership Covenant in the Pro+ SAS Resource Hub, along with a second sample.

Notes

CHAPTER EIGHTEEN

Guiding Principles

Guiding Principles are the church's way of painting clear lines on the field so ministry can flourish. Think of a soccer field (Blake's kids both played soccer). The lines on the ground do not play the game. They do not score goals or block shots. They simply make it clear where the ball is in bounds, where it is out, and what counts as fair play. These boundary lines create clarity and freedom. They keep players from stopping the game every five seconds to ask the referee what to do next. The boundary lines allow the team to play with confidence.

Guiding Principles serve the same purpose in the life of the church. They are operational policies, guidelines, and procedures that set healthy boundaries for day-to-day ministry. They keep the Leadership Board focused on governance instead of management and prevent pastors and staff from slipping into micromanagement. Guiding Principles create clarity, granting permission and helping ministry leaders make decisions within well-marked limits. They enable more effective, efficient decision making by making macro-decisions once rather than micro-decisions continuously. When the lines are clear, the game flows. They also free up the bottlenecks created by older committee structures. Instead of waiting for the Leadership Board to make every ruling, pastors, staff, and ministry leaders can act confidently and responsibly within the field the Leadership Board has marked.

When used well, Guiding Principles reduce the number of decisions the Leadership Board needs to make in its meetings.

Allow us to offer a suggestion filter for your Leadership Board's consideration regarding the Guiding Principles. Every time the Leadership Board makes a decision, ask whether it should become a church policy or a new guiding principle. In other words, could a guiding principle be established or modified that would allow a decision to be made earlier or a ministry to proceed faster by the pastor, staff, or ministry team leader without the Leadership Board's intervention? Developing a guiding principle or policy is a best practice as it ensures that ministry and operational flow are not disrupted while waiting for the board to meet and make a decision. We are not suggesting that there needs to be a guiding principle for everything. However, in many cases, a guiding principle would allow for a more natural and timely flow of ministry and day-to-day operations if the Leadership Board could grant greater permission within acceptable parameters. Creating a culture that grants permission to staff, the pastor, and ministry team leaders fosters a healthier environment for people to engage in their ministries when accountability is coupled with it (and have some fun along the way!).

Most churches start with a blank piece of paper when creating their initial Guiding Principles. While we have the United Methodist Church's *Book of Discipline* to guide and direct us, there is certainly a need for local operational policies and procedures. Guiding Principles complement the BOD—not replace it—and may further clarify it in the local context. A church's Guiding Principles are a documented operational guide.

The clarity created by Guiding Principles is especially important in small church settings, where decisions are often granted verbally or by tradition. Unwritten rules rarely survive pastoral transitions or leadership turnover. What one pastor informally blesses, the next may unknowingly block. Documenting these operating procedures is more efficient and effective, saving time and reducing confusion. The new person doesn't feel they have to ask the "family" for permission or directions every time they try something new. The information is recorded and accessible to everyone.

Just like with the Leadership Covenant, I (Kay) am often asked for a sample of Guiding Principles. Again, we hesitate to offer a sample because so many will simply adopt the sample and be done. If our sample were simply adopted, the whole spirit and purpose of the exercise would be missed. Each church operates uniquely, and therefore, a cut-and-paste approach will likely not be thorough or contextual for your specific church. Also, this approach does not align with the intention of Guiding Principles—being a fluid document that shifts easily and frequently as needed.

However, once again, in the spirit of collaboration and resource-sharing, we offer the following as possible Guiding Principles. Consider them as a "catalog of possibilities" that will hopefully help your Leadership Board think creatively about how you manage the decision-making process in a way that fits your church context and culture.

Note that some of these sample guiding principles conflict with one another. This is intentional to provide a sampling of different approaches and decisions for the same topic. Each Leadership Board must determine how they wish to balance the responsibilities and authority of the Leadership Board, the pastor, and the staff/ministry team leaders. You will find an editable version of this "catalog" of examples and a list of topics to consider addressing in your Guiding Principles in the online Pro+ SAS Resource Hub.

Pro+SAS
Resource Hub

Guiding Principles Catalog

The ____________ Church's mission, vision, and core values serve as the foundation for its Guiding Principles and operational decisions, subject to the *Book of Discipline of The United Methodist Church* and all policies and actions approved by the charge conference and the ____________ Annual Conference of the United Methodist Church. The Leadership Board shall review the church's mission, vision, and core values annually and shall ensure that ministry, financial, and structural decisions are aligned with them.

(The Guiding Principles shall begin by clearly listing the church's mission, vision, and core values.)

Structure:

- Anytown United Methodist Church operates under the governance structure prescribed by *The Book of Discipline of The United Methodist Church*. Under the church's simplified accountable structure, all *Book of Discipline* and congregational policy references to the Church Council, Board of Trustees, Staff/Pastor-Parish Relations Committee, Endowment Committee, and Finance Committee shall be understood to refer to the unified Leadership

Board. The Leadership Board assumes all responsibilities, qualifications, limitations, authority, and expectations assigned to these committees in *The Book of Discipline* (BOD) and carries them out as one integrated governing body.

- The Leadership Board functions as the governing body of the church, responsible for mission, vision, fiduciary oversight, clergy accountability, and strategic guidance. Day-to-day management, ministry supervision, and operational decision making are delegated to the pastor, church staff, and ministry team leaders. Leadership Board members will refrain from engaging in management tasks or directing staff outside established supervisory channels. The Leadership Board will ensure that the church maintains an up-to-date organizational chart reflecting the current decision-making process, supervisory relationships, and chain of command and communication. This chart will be reviewed annually and included in this Guiding Principles document.

- The Anytown UMC charge conference includes the members of the Leadership Board, the Nominations Committee, pastors appointed to the congregation, the treasurer (if not a paid staff member), and all active and retired clergy who have designated our congregation as their home charge conference.

- The Leadership Board serves as the incorporated institution's board of directors and serves as the executive committee of the charge conference.

- To encourage broader participation by members of the church, the Anytown UMC requests that the annual charge conference be convened as a church conference to extend the vote to all professing members of the congregation (2024 BOD ¶ 248).

- Because the Leadership Board serves as the congregation's Staff/Pastor-Parish Relations Committee, Leadership Board members may serve only one additional consecutive three-year term. All Leadership Board members shall be professing (or associate) members of the Anytown UMC congregation. No staff member or immediate family member of a pastor or staff member may serve on the Leadership Board. Only one person from an immediate family residing in the same household shall serve on the Leadership Board. Immediate family members are listed in ¶ 258.2.b of the BOD.

- Because the Leadership Board serves as the congregation's Board of Trustees, only Leadership Board members who are at least 18 years of age may vote on Trustee responsibilities. These actions require a simple majority of a quorum composed of the nine lay members eligible to vote. The pastor, as required by *The Book of Discipline*, participates in discussion but does not vote on Trustee actions. For this structure, Trustee responsibilities refer to all duties related to property, incorporation, legal issues, contracts, insurance, investments, and any other responsibilities assigned to Trustees under ¶ 2525–2551 of the United Methodist *Book of Discipline*. All Trustee actions shall be recorded in the minutes and clearly identified as decisions made while the Leadership Board was seated as Trustees.

- Leadership Board members are nominated by a separate and independent Committee on Nominations and Leadership Development, chaired by the pastor, and elected by the charge conference as described in the BOD. The Nominations Committee will be responsible for developing new leaders and equipping them for future Leadership Board positions, as well as members for the Nominations Committee and ministry team leaders.

Leadership Board Operations and Meetings

- All meetings of the Leadership Board shall be open to the public, except for any meeting or portion of a meeting in which a personnel matter or a matter of legal negotiations is considered. In those cases, the Leadership Board will transition into executive session. Minutes of executive session agenda items concerning personnel matters will be kept separately as part of the "S/PPRC" files.

- The Leadership Board may meet and conduct official business through in-person, online, or hybrid formats. Online or hybrid meetings may be held through Zoom or other comparable virtual platforms. Under ______________ state law, properly convened electronic meetings are considered as valid as in-person meetings, provided that all participants can hear one another and fully engage in discussion and decision making (*check your state laws!*). Attendance, quorum, motions, and votes taken in online or hybrid meetings carry the same authority and effect as those conducted entirely in person. The meeting format will be recorded in the minutes.

- The Leadership Board may conduct official votes by email or other approved electronic means when time-sensitive decisions are required between regular meetings. Each Leadership Board member will be asked to respond within twenty-four hours of the email's sent time unless a different response window is stated. Leadership Board members may concur, not concur, or request that the matter be brought to an online or in-person meeting as soon as practical. If no response is received within the stated response window, the member's vote will be recorded as concurrence for the decision. The results of all electronic votes will be documented in the minutes of the next regular Leadership Board meeting.

- The Leadership Board will communicate transparently with the congregation regarding missional progress, resource alignment, and significant decisions. The Leadership Board will offer regular congregational town hall sessions that include opportunities for two-way communication (minimum of twice a year).

- Guiding Principles may be amended by a simple majority vote of the Leadership Board at any regular meeting, provided that the proposed change is included in the meeting packet at least seventy-two hours in advance. All revisions will be dated and published in the digital Guiding Principles archive.

- Consent Calendar: Items may be removed from the consent calendar at the request of any Leadership Board member, with agreement of a minimum of three (*or two or one—depending on your approach*) additional Leadership Board members. Removed items will be transferred to the discussion agenda for fuller consideration.

  OR

- Consent Calendar: Items may be removed from the consent calendar at the request of any Leadership Board member. Removed items will be transferred to the discussion agenda for fuller consideration. Leadership Board members are encouraged to remove items from the consent calendar when clarification, discernment, or discussion would strengthen the board's work.

- All Leadership Board actions, including actions taken in its capacity as the Board of Trustees or as the Staff/Pastor-Parish Relations Committee, will be recorded in official minutes. Executive session minutes concerning personnel or legal issues will be kept in secure, restricted-access files.

- Individual Leadership Board members shall not issue instructions, requests, or assignments directly to paid staff unless specifically authorized by Leadership Board action. All staff direction flows through the pastor or designated supervisor.

Financial Matters

- Once the budget is approved, those responsible for the various ministry areas (e.g., staff, ministry team leaders, and members) have the authority to spend their assigned budgets in alignment with the objectives for their ministry areas, as approved by the pastor. No further approval is needed to access the budget in their area of responsibility. However, the treasurer must be consulted regarding any single purchase or expenditure over $_______ for purposes of cash flow. The treasurer does not approve or deny purchases; rather, they confirm that large purchases will not create cash-flow issues.

- The pastor is responsible for reviewing financial line items in the ministry areas with the appropriate staff or team leaders to ensure staff accountability to the Leadership Board.

- Any member of the Building Maintenance Team has the authority to purchase supplies for building maintenance, repair, and improvement up to $_______ without approval. The Building Maintenance Team leader can authorize purchases for building maintenance and improvement up to $_______. Purchases up to $_______ can be approved by the pastor (executive pastor or business manager). Any purchases over $_______ need Leadership Board approval unless the expenditure is already identified in a capital expenditure line item in the approved budget.

- Director-level staff can authorize budgeted purchases up to $_______. Purchases up to $_______ can be approved by the pastor (executive pastor or business manager). Any purchases over $_______ need Leadership Board approval unless the expenditure is already identified in a capital expenditure line item in the approved budget.

- Any expenditure over $_______ will require three bids. Preference will be given to hiring or contracting with local companies that offer competitive bids within $_____% of other bids. If the expenditure is already approved in the budget and meets the previous criteria, no further approval is needed. The ministry team leader or staff member responsible for the purchase will provide the Leadership Board (or the pastor or business manager) with documentation of the bids.

Facility Use

- The church administrator, under the supervision of the lead pastor, is delegated the authority to approve events and short-term uses of church facilities (up to three months) by third-party nonprofit groups when the requested use is consistent with the congregation's ministry objectives, the Social Principles of the United Methodist Church, and ecumenical objectives as outlined in ¶ 2533.3 of *The Book of Discipline*. If the church administrator has concerns about whether a request meets these criteria, the pastor is authorized to review and approve or deny the request. If the pastor has concerns or determines that the request warrants broader discernment, the matter may be brought to the Leadership Board for consideration. This guiding principle is explicitly subordinate to the authority granted to the pastor in *The Book of Discipline*. Nothing in this policy shall prevent, limit, or interfere with the pastor's right to use any church property for religious services or any other proper meetings or purposes recognized by the law, usages, and customs of The United Methodist Church, as stated in ¶ 2533 and related paragraphs, and confirmed in Judicial Council decisions.

- The church administrator, under the supervision of the lead pastor, has been delegated full authority and responsibility to make decisions about facility usage as outlined in the Anytown UMC Facility Usage Policy. Requests that do not align with the Facility Usage Policy may be reviewed by the pastor or the Leadership Board for an exception (with a reason) upon the requester's petition.

- The facilities of Anytown United Methodist Church will continue to be under the authority of the Leadership Board (legal Board of Directors/Trustees) and the charge conference of Anytown United Methodist Church, as detailed in the current edition of *The Book of Discipline of the United Methodist Church* (BOD 2020/2024). The Trust Clause, as outlined in ¶ 2501ff, and all other property requirements of the current edition of the BOD, remain in effect for all property and facilities and shall not be subordinated by any Lease Agreement. Usage of church property must be consistent with the Social Principles and ecumenical objectives (¶

2533.3), as found in the current edition of the BOD. Any properly approved lease agreement or facility use agreement event shall not encumber or obligate the ________ Annual Conference of the United Methodist Church or its Districts as outlined in ¶ 2510 of the 2020/2024 BOD. Approval for lease agreements shall follow the process defined by the current BOD, and require the approval of the DS and the District Board of Church Location and Building.

Personnel

- The pastor has the authority to hire and terminate employees in accordance with the church's employee policies and procedures outlined in the Anytown UMC Employee Handbook. When terminating an employee, the pastor will invite a Leadership Board member to sit in on the exit conversation for purposes of liability protection. The pastor has the responsibility to supervise, discipline, and evaluate staff performance as outlined in the Anytown UMC Employee Handbook and the accompanying policies and procedures for supervising and evaluating employees. The Leadership Board will hold the pastor accountable for adhering to said policies, procedures, and handbooks.

  OR

- The authority to hire and terminate employees of the church shall be vested in the Leadership Board. The pastor (or designee) shall have the authority to interview and recommend candidates to fill open staff positions. The Leadership Board shall have the sole authority to determine the number of staff positions, approve job descriptions for each staff member, and set the salary paid to each staff member. The Leadership Board delegates to the pastor (and the pastor's designees) the authority and responsibility to supervise, discipline, and manage paid staff.

  OR

- The authority to hire and terminate employees of the church shall be vested in the Leadership Board. The Leadership Board delegates to the pastor (or the pastor's designated supervisor) the authority to hire and terminate lay staff below the director (or executive director) level, in accordance with the church's employee policies and procedures outlined in the Anytown UMC Employee Handbook. The pastor has the responsibility to supervise, discipline, and evaluate staff performance as outlined in the

Anytown UMC Employee Handbook and the accompanying policies and procedures for supervising and evaluating employees. The Leadership Board will hold the pastor accountable for adhering to these policies, procedures, and handbooks.

- The pastor (or designee) will review all paid staff annually using the approved evaluation process in the employee manual dated ________. Paid staff will review unpaid staff/team leaders annually using a similar evaluation process.

Weekday Childcare Tuition-Based Ministry

- The Weekday Childcare Advisory Team/Board (BOD ¶ 256.2.c) is fully amenable and accountable to the Leadership Board and shall submit an annual budget and recommended policy changes to the Leadership Board for review and approval.

  OR

- As a separately incorporated affiliate nonprofit, the Anytown UMC Weekday School shall maintain all appropriate licensures and is responsible for obtaining and maintaining the required licensure(s) to operate a childcare facility in the state of __________. This includes licensing requirements from the __________ Department of Human Services, documentation as a nonprofit 501(c)(3) organization, and local zoning and business permits. Anytown UMC Weekday School shall maintain appropriate liability insurance. The Anytown UMC Weekday School shall maintain copies of all current licensure(s) and proof of insurance with the business administrator of Anytown UMC. The Anytown UMC Weekday School shall maintain a master service agreement with the Leadership Board (legal Board of Directors/Trustees).

- Anytown UMC Weekday School shall submit an annual budget and monthly financial reports to the church office. The director of weekday ministries is hired, supervised, and evaluated by the pastor. The employees of the weekday ministries are hired, supervised, and evaluated by the director of the weekday ministries.

- All weekday ministry policies, procedures, parent handbooks, employee handbooks, and financial practices will be reviewed and approved by the Leadership Board.

Current Policies

The Leadership Board recognizes and approves the following:

- Governance and Staff Organizational Charts, effective _______
- Building & Equipment Usage Policies, effective _______
- Building Security and Key (or access card) Policies, effective _______
- Financial Controls Policies, effective _______
- Church Credit Card Policy, effective _______
- Personnel Policy Handbook, effective _______
- Safe Sanctuary/Safe Gatherings Policy, effective _______
- Stock and Gift Acceptance Policy, effective _______
- Clergy Accountable Reimbursement Policy, effective _______
- Parsonage Covenant, effective _______
- Church Internet and Technology Use Policy, effective _______

Additional Areas of Work that May Support Guiding Principles

The following topics were identified as valuable guiding principle areas but are not expressed as sample principles above or already covered in your main sample principles. They may be developed into additional principles as needed in your context:

Financial Roles:

- Authority and responsibility of the treasurer (and their relationship to the Leadership Board)
- Role and function of the financial secretary

Leadership Development:

- Relationship of Nominations and Lay Leadership Development to the Leadership Board

Childcare Governance:

- Clarifying the relationship between daycare/preschool and the church, including supervision, finances, and accountability, especially when a childcare ministry is separately incorporated

Building Safety:

- Policies related to alarms, fire suppression, lighting, evacuation procedures, inspections, and on-site safety
- Use and access of cameras, alarms, door keys, access cards, etc.

Technology and Data Security:

- Password protocols and backups
- Permissions for credit card usage and receipt requirements or reimbursement procedures
- Permission for local merchant account usage (e.g., charge account at the local hardware or business supply store)
- Access, passwords, and usernames for the church's merchant account for online giving
- Cloud backup, access, and data (e.g., financial, database, employee, and corporation minutes) retention requirements
- Appropriate firewalls and policies for safe internet access for children, youth, and employees
- Approved hardware, software, and app usage for employees

Counting of the Offering:

- Documented procedures for counting offerings and maintaining appropriate internal controls

Parliamentary Procedure:

  - o Defining the method (Robert's Rules, consensus, modified consensus)

CHAPTER NINETEEN

The Meeting Packet and the Agenda

The Leadership Board Packet as an Instrument of Stewardship

We have attended too many meetings that require attendees to pick up a dozen handouts before taking their seats. As we transition from one agenda item to the next, we're navigating a flood of new information and budget figures without sufficient time to process them. Then, as we move from one agenda item to another, we are all fumbling with new information and budget numbers we haven't had time to review. This approach produces inefficient meetings and undermines the Leadership Board's leadership capacity because members spend their time decoding information rather than discerning direction. Sending a Leadership Board packet ahead of time, along with consent calendar items, is an act of stewardship. It honors everyone's time and prepares Leadership Board members to do the work only they can do: deliberate, discern, and lead.

To adequately prepare for a Leadership Board meeting, a digital packet should be made available to each Leadership Board member by or in coordination with the Leadership Board chair for review a week or so before the meeting. This prepares the leaders for what Robert's Rules of Order calls the *consent calendar* section of the agenda. Other common words used for this section of the agenda include consent agenda, unified agenda items, general consent items, block approval items, and standard approval items.

Sending the packet out ahead of time with consent items keeps the Leadership Board from having to spend time in the meeting reading reports or listening to long (and often unprepared) oral reports. This also allows plenty of time to fully review the information, prepare questions, comments, or concerns, and participate fully in conversations and decisions. For instance, the minutes of the previous meeting need only be edited or approved, since the Leadership Board members covenant to review them before arrival. The financial report requires no approval unless there are changes to the previously approved budget or a cash-flow question is raised. A single covering motion can address any "approval" items identified as part of the consent calendar in the packet, including the minutes. If something needs to be removed from the consent items (be sure to have a guiding principle to identify the process for removing a consent calendar item), you can do so and shift the item later in the agenda.

Preferably, a staff member in an administrative role, such as an operations manager or church administrator, prepares the routine items for the Leadership Board packet. The Leadership Board chair and the pastor will co-create the agenda (more on this later in the chapter) and review the packet before it is distributed, and the administrator will often need to send reminders to contributors (i.e., treasurer or business manager) of packet materials. The pastor holds this person accountable (as a staff member who reports to the pastor or designee) for the timeliness, accuracy, and thoroughness of the packet. Many United Methodist conferences now offer free access to cloud platforms like Google Workspace or Microsoft Teams, and even when they do not, most providers offer free or deeply discounted nonprofit accounts for churches.

In my own ministry, I (Blake) have been using our church's Google Workspace Drive to create a dedicated folder for each meeting. Every document is placed in the folder, along with the previous minutes and an agenda that contains hyperlinks to each item. We recommend this kind of shared file structure because it keeps agendas, documents, and handouts readily accessible and easy to update when new information arrives. Cloud storage also allows all leaders to have consistent viewing access, search past meeting materials, and the ability to grant limited viewing or commenting access rather than editing rights. It even enables the Leadership Board to maintain live meeting minutes with clarity and ease. It also provides an easy way to add access for new Leadership Board members and remove access for those who are rolling off.

The packet's purpose and contents are to provide Leadership Board members with information to keep them abreast of the church's current status and to give each member time to review and prepare ahead of the meeting. The packet is provided as both a resource for communication and a tool of preparation. Members of the Leadership Board should read the packet before the meeting and come prepared to either vote to approve the items or move them to the discussion phase of the agenda.

Under simplified accountable structure, this kind of preparation is not optional. It is part of accountable leadership. Leadership Board members cannot govern wisely if they are encountering information for the first time during the meeting. The packet gives every leader equal access, equal preparation time, and equal footing for conversation. It also prevents meetings from drifting into staff-level management and keeps the Leadership Board focused on mission, vision, and outcomes. In SAS, stewardship includes stewarding time, clarity, and attention so the Leadership Board can offer its best discernment to the church.

Recommended Contents for the Leadership Board Meeting Packet

✓ Agenda

See the agenda section in this chapter for more information.

✓ Itemized list of consent calendar items

See details above. Include all the meeting minutes and all consent calendar documents listed. Blake likes to put these consent calendar documents in a separate folder within the meeting packet folder for easy distribution.

✓ Covenant

The signed Leadership Covenant is an ongoing reminder.

✓ Missional Accountability

This is based on how your Leadership Board intends to measure outcomes, establish metrics, trajectories, and goals, and present reports or graphs to aid in determining missional viability and effectiveness. This may be new information to capture and track.

Leadership Boards will need to decide which metrics they will track to assess the church's missional effectiveness. These metrics provide a dashboard of the latest information, metrics, and trends that are essential for leaders to understand. United Methodist Church denominational leaders require the tracking of metrics they refer to as "vital signs," which include worship attendance, professions of faith, small group participation, service participation, and financial giving. While these metrics may serve the purpose of the Leadership Board's missional accountability, most churches are finding that different metrics provide better insight for navigating the postmodern cultural context.

In *Becoming the Church People Choose: Charting a New Church Course for Relationships, Discipleship, and Leadership*, which Kay coauthored with Kelly Collins, they write:

> *Do we value what we measure, or do we measure what we value? What is simple to measure and what we're asked to measure often ends up being what we value most. We frequently equate value with measurability—especially when it's something we're required to measure. Take the time to ask these two questions: What is of true value, and for whom is it valuable? Then, measure that. Because Jesus defined every church's mission—to make disciples who transform their community and world—measuring missional effectiveness is essential. While many churches find this challenging, the difficulty does not mean churches get a pass. An organization can't stay afloat and accomplish its mission without continuously analyzing its effectiveness and making the necessary adjustments.*[40]

More insights and alternative missional metrics for consideration and discernment are offered in Chapter 8, "New Orbital Port Vitality Measurements" of their book. The first step is for the Leadership Board to determine what metrics need to be measured. The second step is to create a method for tracking the desired metrics. The third step is to track and monitor the metrics in their monthly meetings. The fourth step is to make the necessary shifts in missional strategies to improve effectiveness in the missional metrics.

✓ Describables

Not all fruits of ministry will appear in the metrics for missional effectiveness and accountability mentioned above. Those fruits are what we refer to as the describables or the stories of vital ministries. What lives are being touched by the ministries of the church? How are people growing in their faith? How is the church impacting the community in the name of Christ? The pastor will provide any pertinent describables in the

---

[40] Kay Kotan and Kelly Collins, *Becoming the Church People Choose: Charting New Church Courses for Relationships, Discipleship & Leadership*, (Market Square Books, 2026).

packet for the Leadership Board for information purposes, but likely not for discussion. Note: This is not required for each meeting, but it provides information on how to handle such a situation should it arise.

✓ Minutes

This refers to the minutes of the previous Leadership Board meeting as submitted by the acting recording secretary. Note: Minutes need to be taken, approved, and kept on file for future reference. Remember, the Leadership Board has the role and responsibility (among others) as the board of directors of the nonprofit corporation (the church's legal entity) and therefore requires these minutes.

✓ Financials

These reports should include the current year's budget-versus-actual report for each category or ministry area (not each line item), a cash summary, and a comprehensive balance sheet. There may be a note from the treasurer attached if there is something out of the ordinary or noteworthy for the Leadership Board to know or understand. For example, some Leadership Board members might panic at the summer slump in generosity numbers. The treasurer might include an income statement from the previous year, showing that the trend is expected and that the church is on track to match or exceed last year's giving numbers. During a stewardship campaign, the current and next year's anticipated number of giving units, dollars, and average giving amount could be included.

✓ Pastoral Accountability

The pastor will provide a written update or a dashboard (recommended to keep the board focused on governance and not management) on goal progress during the pastoral accountability time. These are the church goals set by the pastor and the Leadership Board at the annual strategic ministry planning retreat. While the written report or dashboard provides the Leadership Board with a more thorough and perhaps more time-efficient glimpse of progress toward the goals, the time on the agenda is also for questions and statements of accountability, support, encouragement, and celebration. This is often where a deep shift is required for Leadership Board members to have this type of conversation with their pastor. Therefore, due to the lack of experience and perhaps discomfort with such a conversation, accountability is sometimes not practiced. Having these accountability conversations is an extremely important part of the Leadership Board's accountable leadership responsibilities. Don't step over your responsibility! Note: View the complimentary "SAS Accountability" video in the SAS Resource Hub for demonstrated accountability conversations and tips.

✓ Reports

While we do not suggest or recommend requiring the inclusion of reports (particularly ministry team reports), there may be a group that just feels strongly compelled to share information with the Leadership Board. A group can write a report to include in the packet with the permission of the Leadership Board chair and the pastor. If a church must have reports, one suggestion is to use a standard report form with simple questions that clearly ask at the beginning whether the special report is an update or if some sort of Leadership Board action is required/requested. This may keep reporting ministry teams on mission and clear about why they are reporting. It might also help them identify that their request does not even need to go to the Leadership Board. Keeping ministry reports out of the packet and off the agenda reinforces the governance lane of the Leadership Board and places the authority and responsibility for such in the leadership lane of the pastor and their designees. If action is required for ministry teams, it is likely due to a gap in the Guiding Principles.

✓ Special Reports

From time to time, additional documents may need to be added to the packet. An example of such a document might be the three bids collected for a capital expenditure for either information only or for approval, depending on your Guiding Principles. Another example might be a report or information from a work group assignment in the "strategic work" section of the agenda for discussion and a decision on next steps. Perhaps the Leadership Board will study the demographics of the mission field and include a recent MissionInsite Report for discussion during the "generative work" section of the agenda to gain a greater understanding of the people in the church's mission field. Annually, the Leadership Board will usually need to process a consultation or assessment form for the bishop and DS, so the template could be included to help board members prayerfully contemplate and prepare their responses for the meeting.

The Meeting Agenda

When serving as a local church pastor, I (Blake) have had the joy of serving alongside so many excellent lay leaders in congregations. While we certainly took our mission seriously, we tried to fulfill our responsibilities with a bit of fun. After a series of multiple back-to-back meetings, one of my mischievous lay leaders presented me with a blue "participation award" ribbon emblazoned with an image of a coffee mug and a statement of deep and abiding truth written in gold foil: "I survived another meeting that should have been an email." Fair enough—I certainly deserved it!

When the purpose of a meeting is misunderstood, preparatory work is inadequate, or the agenda is disorganized, you and your fellow leaders will miss a leadership opportunity. Bad meetings create a lack of ownership in the group's processes and actions, encourage apathy, and degrade your team's and organization's leadership capacity.

Changing the number of people around the table is never enough. *You will also need to change the conversation at the table.* If you move toward a simplified accountable leadership structure but continue to use the legacy Robert's Rules of Order style of agenda (old business, then new business, and filled with endless oral reports), your new Leadership Board will never be able to operate, much less *lead* in a new and more effective way. It is time to create an agenda that reflects your missional focus, uses time efficiently, and assumes that Leadership Board members will come prepared to lead (as agreed in the Leadership Covenant). As the Leadership Board chair and pastor plan the meetings for the simplified accountable structure, great care will need to be taken to ensure they are fruitful.

The agenda is a guide for the most effective and efficient use of time and resources of the Leadership Board members. It is a plan of action. Working the plan allows us to be good stewards of our time and resources. Agendas are crucial and a necessary tool for effective, efficient leadership. Without an agenda, conversations will drift off topic, and we might not tend to the top priorities.

With the new model of leadership, a new agenda will be required. The new agenda serves multiple purposes:

- Keeps Leadership Boards in the governance lane and out of the management lane
- Allows the shaping of a new leadership culture
- Provides allotted times for critical conversations and decision making to move the mission forward
- Lays out the optimal format to prioritize the focus and work of the Leadership Board
- Highlights reminders of the most important work of the Leadership Board

In the beginning, the Leadership Board may not be as efficient as they will become over time as they practice the accountable leadership model using a new agenda. You will likely reach a point where the Leadership Board can finish its meeting in about ninety minutes. Of course, there will be times when longer meetings are needed, but most will be able to work within the ninety-minute format. This is especially true when Guiding Principles are in place, Leadership Board members review the packet ahead of time, stay in the governance lane in their work together, and maintain a missional focus in their decision making.

The agenda consists of three major portions that can be divided into about thirty-minute segments:

- Invest one-third of your time in spiritual formation and leadership development.
- Spend one-third of your time on the Leadership Board and pastoral accountability, approval of the consent calendar, and miscellaneous operational/administrative work.
- Invest the remaining one-third of your time on strategic and generative work.

When the majority of the Leadership Board's time and focus are on the strategic and generative work, they have lived into the governance model of leadership and missional focus. Try to minimize the time spent on maintenance, operations, and administration. If your Leadership Board is spending too much time on topics of maintenance, operations, or administration, the Leadership Board is likely still managing and/or lacking Guiding Principles.

We suggest creating a "docket" format that includes a running time for each agenda item so Leadership Board members can appropriately budget their discussion time. This practice of allocating time to each item requires the Leadership Board chair to be realistic with the time available and to calculate how much time can be allotted for each item. With a nine-person Leadership Board and the pastor, if everyone is expected to speak for a minute to share their opinion, ten minutes will be spent on each item. If you give an item five minutes, you expect no comments, unless folks are satisfied with each having thirty seconds to speak, not including any time to introduce the matter, vote, or reach consensus.

When you have an agenda with printed times, board members can adjust their comments to fit the allotted time. They can suggest that the item be picked up in a future meeting or that a work team prepare a proposal or do more groundwork for the entire Leadership Board to act upon. Having used a time docket for years, I (Blake) have found that this helps the Leadership Board chair set expectations for the Leadership Board. Of course, the group can always adjust as needed, but without any printed time allocation, team members can quickly get frustrated or feel like the Leadership Board chair is railroading the meeting. By setting up clear expectations, the Leadership Board chair can actually rely on the Leadership Board members to self-regulate.

The agenda is prepared by the Leadership Board chair in collaboration with the pastor. Here is a quick checklist for agenda preparation from the "SAS Board Chair Guidebook," available at kaykotan.com/sas2.[41]

[41] "The Ultimate Guidebook: The 2026 SAS Board Chair Guidebook," pdf, kaykotan.com.

Monthly Board Meeting

CHECKLIST

Below is a common checklist to use in preparing the Agenda for the monthly Leadership Board meeting.

✓ MONTHLY BOARD PREPARATION

- ☐ Gather documents for the preview packet including minutes, financial reports, and agenda-related items
- ☐ Create the agenda in collaboration with your pastor
- ☐ Refer to the Annual Rhythm Reference Chart for reminders of periodic areas of focus to place on the agenda
- ☐ Prepare the preview packet and post documents in the appropriate folders noting which documents are consent calendar, FYI, executive session, and regular agenda items
- ☐ Note the person responsible for leading the various agenda items and the time allotted on the final agenda draft
- ☐ Check the total allotted times for all agenda items and set a goal for 90-minute meetings
- ☐ Continue challenging the Board to move towards a greater time allotment for generative and strategic conversations
- ☐ Consider including the Leadership Board Covenant as part of the monthly packet to remind members of their commitment and responsibilities to one another and their work together
- ☐ Commit to having the packet and agenda to members at least seven days before board meetings

In preparing the agenda, the Leadership Board chair can (optionally, and not necessarily recommended) send a notice to Leadership Board members asking whether any items need to be discussed. We say "might" because not every request needs to be on a Leadership Board agenda. Some matters need to be held off-line or by a work team or other group before they are ripe for inclusion in the Leadership Board's agenda. Some items are simply not the work of the Leadership Board. If the matter is properly before the Leadership Board, then the Leadership Board chair should do some organizational preparation:

1. First, clarify the purpose and what category it belongs in (e.g., is it about making a decision, answering a question, or simply sharing information? And, is it for the consent calendar, or is it administrative, strategic, or generative work).

2. Second, estimate the time required (e.g., a few minutes for a discussion).

3. Third, prepare a proposed process for addressing the matter (e.g., a vote or proposing a new guiding principle to handle similar matters in the future).

Be sure the pastor and the Leadership Board chair are co-leading the agenda preparation. Neither of these two people should ever be surprised by a topic at a meeting!

The Leadership Board will meet monthly in the beginning. In a year or two, you *may* be able to move to bi-monthly meetings. Kay has worked with churches that have used the simplified accountable structure for years and have quarterly meetings. But in the beginning, as it establishes policies, procedures, and Guiding Principles, and lays the groundwork for a new leadership culture of accountability and adaptive leadership, the Leadership Board will need to meet monthly. Note that even if your Leadership Board has created a tradition of less frequent meetings, when you receive a new pastor, the Leadership Board will need to switch back to monthly (or even more frequent) meetings for several months to a year.

On each and every agenda for the Leadership Board (including all other church agendas), print the mission (Making disciples ...), vision, and core values of the church. This is a great reminder of the foundation and focus of the Leadership Board's conversations and decisions. One church I (Kay) worked with displayed large posters printed with its mission, vision, and core values in the board's meeting room. Not only was this a great reminder for the Leadership Board members, but every person who used that same room was reminded as well.

In this chapter, you will find an agenda template along with a sample agenda and an annotated explanation of each agenda item. This basic format can be used for each meeting, with the understanding that some meetings, such as the annual pastoral assessment, may require adjustments in the schedule, timing, and agenda flow. Notice the order of the agenda. It might appear that the agenda is reversed with familiar items missing from your typical Leadership Board agenda. **This is very intentional!** The most important items are at the top. If the first few items were placed at the bottom of the agenda as additions, Leadership Boards would never have time for spiritual formation and leadership development!

Also, notice that there are no oral reports from ministry teams or committees on this agenda. This is absolutely intentional and not an oversight. The purpose of the Leadership Board is not to hear reports. The purpose is to govern, guide, and set policies by serving as the congregation's lead body for stewardship, strategy, generative work, and accountability. The day-to-day ministries that comprise the church's activities should always reflect the congregational goals articulated by the Leadership Board. Those objectives established by staff and/or ministry team leaders relate to the goals and are all rolled up into the goal (accountability) report from the pastor to the Leadership Board. If the Leadership Board spends time hearing about each and every ministry detail, they are in management mode on the dance floor. The job of the Leadership Board is to be in the balcony with a missional focus, overseeing the entire "dance floor" of vital ministry and the congregation's relationship with the community.

Template Agenda for Simplified Accountable Leadership

On the following page is an agenda template for your review. An agenda template can also be found in the Pro+ SAS Resource Hub. Following the sample agenda template, you will find a sample agenda and an explanation of each agenda item.

MEETING AGENDA TEMPLATE

Day, Month, Date, 2026

Mission & Vision

(Mission & Vision Statements go here)

Leadership Formation . . . . 15 minutes
Opening Prayer & Spiritual Formation — Name

Development . . . . 15 Minutes
Leadership Development — Name

Leadership Board Accountability . . . . .5 Minutes
Review of Missional Accountability Measures — Chair

Pastoral Accountability . . . . 5-15 Minutes
Review & Progress of Annual Church Goals — Pastor

Consent Calendar . . . . .5 Minutes
Vote to approve consent calendar items presented in preview packet — Chair

Balcony and Mission Field-Focused Work . . . . 30-40 Minutes
Generative and/or Strategic Work — Name

Maintenance, Operations, & Administrative Work . . . . 5-30 Minutes
Pressing Issues and Problem Solving — Name

Communication . . . . 5-10 Minutes
What, Who, How, When, & Messaging — Chair

Closing . . . . .5 Minutes
Closing Prayer — Name

Explanation and Responsibility of Agenda Items

Prayer

Each person on the Leadership Board takes turns offering the opening and closing prayer. As servant leaders and disciples, leaders need to become comfortable praying in a group, and this expectation needs to be covered during the nominations process. This may also be a time to ask fellow Leadership Board members for personal prayer requests. I (Kay) have found it convenient and efficient for the Leadership Board chair to ask the Leadership Board member leading spiritual formation to offer the opening prayer, and for the Leadership Board member facilitating the leadership development to offer the closing prayer.

Spiritual Formation

You will quickly notice that every Leadership Board agenda begins with time for spiritual formation and leadership development. That choice is intentional. It is not filler, and it is not optional.

I (Blake) once worked with a church that believed those components were unnecessary—and it showed. During one meeting, a leader said to the pastor, "We already did church today. Just say a prayer, preacher, and let's move on." No! If we lose Jesus Christ as the foundation of our life and work together, and if we lose the Great Commission as our shared mission, we will eventually stop being the disciples God is calling us to be. Leadership in the church is not simply organizational work. It is spiritual work.

When we rush past formation and prayer to get to the "real business," we quietly shift our center of gravity. Without grounding ourselves in scripture, prayer, and the guidance of the Holy Spirit, leaders begin to rely on personal preferences, individual opinions, and competing agendas. Over time, the mission suffers, relationships fray, and the Leadership Board becomes no different from any other nonprofit governing body.

Starting every meeting with spiritual formation and leadership development reminds us who we are, whose we are, and why we are here. It recenters the Leadership Board on Christ, invites the Holy Spirit into our conversations, and prepares leaders to make decisions shaped by faith rather than impulse and preferences. This practice does not slow the board's work. It strengthens it.

Again, take turns allowing each member to share. Relate the spiritual formation to the leadership development topic or something on the agenda, if possible. Better yet, identify the relevant and necessary topics for these critical spiritual and leadership components during the strategic ministry planning retreat. A single topic may be desired or needed that spans multiple Leadership Board meetings.

This might be a time to challenge leaders to share where they have seen God at work in their own lives over the past week. This faith development time helps prepare them to share their faith in their day-to-day life. (See *Get Their Name*[42] by Farr, Kotan, and Anderson for more information on sharing your faith in small groups.) This is a time to dive deep and help our leaders mature in their faith and grow in their Christlikeness and knowledge. Do not glaze over this important time in the faith development of the Leadership Board, both collectively and for each member's individual spiritual journey. Bring topics that challenge the members and promote engagement and dialogue. Move beyond just reading a devotion during this time of spiritual formation together. Set expectations for conversation, sharing, processing questions together, and being vulnerable about our spirituality with one another. Remember, the leadership is modeling spiritual formation for other groups and the church as a whole. Refer back to the suggested list of topics created at the previous fall strategic planning retreat. Allow about fifteen minutes for spiritual formation.

Kay has created an annually published tool to help Leadership Board members dive into this rhythm titled, *Reflection Journal: Spiritual Formation and Leadership Development Resources for Leadership Boards*. This 70-page resource provides **an entire year's worth** of spiritual formation and leadership development content designed for the monthly Leadership Board agenda. Starting in January, each month you'll find a spiritual formation topic with reflective questions to help leaders develop more deeply as disciples and spiritual leaders and grow more comfortable sharing in their discipleship journey. For each month, you will also find a page to record spiritual formation notes, reflections, and insights. This resource can be found at kaykotan.com/sas-2 or as part of the comprehensive SAS Resource Hub Pro+ annual access pass.

---

42 Bob Farr, Kay Kotan, and Doug Anderson, *Get Their Name: Growing Your Church by Building Relationships* (Abingdon Press, 2013).

Leadership Development

Yep, you guessed it. Leadership development is a shared responsibility, too. Rather than choosing a random subject, be intentional in brainstorming leadership equipping and development topics and resources identified at the strategic ministry planning retreat. Leadership Board members can then choose a topic from the list that the group collectively decided to dive into, which the person leading the teaching time is passionate about. This approach provides ample preparation time as well. A topic may be covered in a single Leadership Board meeting or across multiple meetings, depending on the subject and the desired depth.

Make this an interactive time for the Leadership Board. Invoke conversation, in-depth sharing, and stimulating questions to help Leadership Board members grow in their leadership capacity, understanding, and implementation. Do not shy away from challenging subjects or from diving deep into them. Remember, this time is to develop and grow our leaders who are modeling servant leadership for the congregation. Allow about fifteen minutes.

As noted above, the *Reflection Journal: Spiritual Formation and Leadership Development Resources for Leadership Boards* includes spiritual formation materials as well as leadership development resources that help form and challenge leaders. Reflective questions are included to help the group process the information and challenge their thinking. Each month, there is a page for leadership development notes, takeaways, and action steps. Each *Reflection Journal* also includes a calendar, instructions for using the *Reflection Journal*, and additional pages for notes.

Leadership Board's Missional Accountability

In our earlier SAS agenda templates, we referred to this as the "new people" portion of the agenda. While the intent of the agenda item remains the same, a title change is required. This change is intended to help Leadership Board members gain a deeper understanding of the purpose and intended outcome of this agenda item. Take another look at the organizational chart for simplified accountable structure. In each example, the Leadership Board is accountable to Christ for leading the church in its mission to reach new disciples and form disciple-making disciples who transform the world. This agenda item calls the

Leadership Board to hold itself accountable for leading the church in fulfilling this Great Commission. While the previous "new people" reference was an attempt to provoke the missional accountability, monitoring, analysis, and conversation, it failed to do so. Instead, the outcome of the "new people" portion of the agenda became another meaningless statistic and a Sunday-centric measurement rather than a missional analysis.

The Leadership Board must first discern how it defines missional effectiveness in the life of the church. Once that is decided, the Leadership Board will next decide how to measure this missional effectiveness indicator. In other words, what lead and/or lag measures will the Leadership Board monitor each month to confirm that the ministries, resources, staff, teams, facilities, dollars, energy, and capacity are being deployed and leveraged to accomplish the mission of forming disciple-making disciples? If the church is missionally effective, how is the Leadership Board and the congregation celebrating, expanding, and sharing this great news? If not effective, how is the Leadership Board assessing and making decisions to course-correct and get back on track? There may be a measurement or two (not five or ten) that the Leadership Board determines are the best indicators of missional effectiveness. You'll find a great deal more on this topic in Chapter 8, "Orbital Port Vitality Measurements" of Kotan's book with coauthor Kelly Collins, *Becoming the Church People Choose: Charting New Church Courses for Relationships, Discipleship & Leadership.*[43]

Pastoral Accountability

Remember those annual goals set at the strategic ministry planning retreat? The pastor will provide an update on the progress of each goal. We suggest a dashboard-type report be included in the leadership packet. This will be fairly easy to provide—especially if the goals are SMART. Movement or progress in the dashboard results from activities, ministries, events, and programs conducted since the last dashboard update. What is occurring in the life of the church should be encouraging progress towards missional effectiveness and living into God's preferred future for the church (the vision). Analyzing missional

[43] Kay Kotan and Kelly Collins, *Becoming the Church People Choose.*

effectiveness from a dashboard rather than individual ministries keeps the Leadership Board and pastor on the balcony and off the dance floor.

This is where accountability will most likely need to kick in through adaptive change. Leadership Board members are unlikely to be experienced (or comfortable) with holding their pastor accountable. If progress is lacking, ask about it. Talk about it! How can the Leadership Board be encouraging? What support is needed? What obstacles are blocking progress? Are there gaps in training or resources for either the pastor or staff? Is the pastor having trouble holding staff and leaders accountable? If the goal progress is not on track, what progress is expected by the next meeting? Be specific in setting up expectations. Be sure to also acknowledge and celebrate progress and accomplishments!

Consent Calendar

The consent calendar time in the meeting is when items from the (electronic) packet sent out the week before the meeting are reviewed and/or discussed. Most of the leadership packet is typically handled through the consent calendar. As referenced earlier in this chapter, the consent calendar methodology should include all the agenda items that a Leadership Board needs to receive for archival reasons or to vote on for legal or *Book of Discipline* purposes. The most common consent calendar items are the minutes of the last meeting and current financial reports (budget vs. actual expenses and a balance sheet). Other items could include the signing of a contract that has already been approved, regular shifting of funds between accounts, or final approval of a guiding principle discussed at the prior meeting. The Leadership Board chair will ask for a motion to approve the consent calendar items. There is typically a motion and a second for such. Next, the Leadership Board chair will call for a vote to approve the consent calendar items. If approved, no further action is needed or taken beyond recording the vote in the minutes.

If a Leadership Board member requests the removal of any item on the consent calendar for further discussion or examination, follow the approved procedure identified in the Guiding Principles for such action. Items removed from the consent calendar in the packet for corrections or further discussion will be considered under the "Maintenance, Operations, and Administrative Work" on the agenda, under "Generative and Strategic Work," a future meeting, or by common agreement to adjust the agenda.

A covering motion for approval will be called for and seconded for all items that remain on the consent calendar. A vote to approve will then be taken. While this vote is more of a formality than anything else, it is important to maintain an accurate historical record of the Leadership Board's governing decisions. For some items, especially financial matters and statistical data, a short oral description may prove very helpful. This also addresses the complexity of learning and processing styles among Leadership Board members. The focus of any (infrequent) oral report should be to frame a fruitful, effective discussion that facilitates movement towards approval of the consent calendar items or towards the approved process for removing an item from the consent calendar for further discussion elsewhere on the agenda. Beware, though: it is easy to get off track and start long discussions about items on the consent calendar, which voids its purpose and distracts the Leadership Board from the more difficult—and more meaningful—generative and strategic work.

One further note on consent calendar items. In the packet and on the agenda, be sure to identify the items to be considered for the consent calendar. Too often, I (Kay) have witnessed packets full of information with no indication or identifying markers for how this information will be addressed on the agenda. Votes are taken without clearly indicating what is included in the consent calendar vote. Some Leadership Boards even include a separate digital file each month to clearly identify consent calendar items in their digital consent packet. Since my time on the appointive cabinet, where we juggled dozens of documents in each meeting, I (Blake) have made it a practice to go one step further by including hyperlinks for each document directly on the agenda, placed next to the relevant agenda item. This approach makes it immediately clear which documents are part of the consent calendar and which items will be addressed later in the meeting. Board members can click through the documents at home to prepare and then easily access the same materials on a digital device in the conference room, allowing the meeting to move efficiently from item to item without the need to print packets.

Balcony and Mission Field-Focused Work: Generative and Strategic Work

While the previous two agenda sections focused on formation and development, accountability for mission and goals, and on understanding the church's health and missional fruitfulness, this agenda time is used to help the Leadership Board remain outwardly focused, missionally attuned, and accountable to the mission field. This is, by and large, the most adaptive leadership work for the Leadership Board. The focus of these two agenda items is often foreign to Leadership Boards and pastors alike. Yet this work will likely prove the most fruitful and effective, helping change the trajectory of a church's vitality. When coaching Leadership Boards, I (Kay) often share that when this portion of the agenda becomes the focus and largest time consumption of Leadership Board meetings, the Leadership Board is truly in its governance lane and doing the mission-field focused (balcony) work that likely hasn't been done for years, decades, or perhaps ever.

The generative and strategic work of accountable leadership may be new, or at least not formally identified, as the rhythm of the church to become or remain contextually relevant for vital ministry to occur. This is also likely the work that has not previously received the necessary attention or was off the radar of the former Church Council in the traditional model.

After the following more detailed descriptions of both strategic and generative work, you'll find specific examples to help leaders begin to home in on particular types of this work and to focus on this most important duty.

Strategic Work

Strategic work is the act of analyzing the use of church resources towards missional focus, effectiveness, and alignment. The Leadership Board spends time ensuring that all resources are leveraged in the best possible way for vital ministries and the greatest Kingdom impact. This includes ensuring the facility and grounds (typically the church's largest asset) are leveraged for maximum missional effectiveness. Are the congregational and staff resources (capacity, time, energy, gifts, knowledge, and experiences) being utilized and leveraged to their capacity for missional vitality and impact? The budget and spending are analyzed to ensure alignment with the mission, vision, and goals that support effective, impactful ministries. What spending needs to cease, increase, or be reallocated? What resources should be allocated to achieve maximum missional effectiveness and alignment?

Generative Work

Generative work is exactly what it states: generating work for the Leadership Board. While this concept may sound strange, shifting into this critically important mode of governance is the most adaptive and accountable leadership move most Leadership Boards need to make—but it is also one of the absolute hardest. Why? First, the traditional Church Council models typically drove in the management lane. They dug into the weeds of day-to-day ministries and operations, avoiding the governance lane completely. When a Leadership Board shifts lanes from management to governance, the new lane may feel foreign, uncomfortable, and untraveled.

Generative work requires climbing even higher on the governance balcony to not only view the congregational dance floor but the community (mission field) dance floor, too. Generative work helps the Leadership Board better know, understand, and relate to the very people God is calling the church to reach, and helps board members become better informed and more culturally competent in bridging the gaps between the church and the community. This is true governance work as the Leadership Board and pastor adjust the sails, direction, or even GPS of the church to remain or become missionally effective with Kingdom impact.

What goals may need to be added, adapted, or changed to meet the changing ministry landscape and the needs of the mission field? What is shifting or changing in our context that we need to note, make adjustments, and make necessary adaptations? What is changing in our culture that will require the church to adapt to remain relevant to the people in our community we are trying to reach?

Below are examples of generative and strategic work. Note: This is not a list of suggestions but a set of idea sparks to help leaders understand the meaning and purpose of this critically important generative and strategic work.

BALCONY & MISSION FIELD FOCUSED WORK EXAMPLES

☑ GENERATIVE WORK

Hear from the Developer of a new residential or business community to learn about new neighbors.

Hear from the Economic Development Corporation officer from your community.

Meet with the local school superintendent or principal to hear about the trends they are seeing, needs they may have, and future plans they are making.

Take a deep dive into demographics to understand the top mosaic segment and their seven preferences, how it compares to your congregation, & what shifts would you want to consider.

Meet with a local apartment community manager/owner to understand who her community is, what they might need, how to connect with them, how to be a good neighbor.

Invite a local nonprofit organization leader who has common mission/vision with the church to explore ways to partner for deeper kingdom impact.

☑ STRATEGIC WORK

Analyze if all the resources (time, energy, passions, facilities, dollars) of the church are aligned with our mission.

Are our resources (time, people, dollars, facilities, energy) being leveraged in a way that is propelling our church into God's preferred future (our vision)?

Is our budget specifically aligned to our annual goals (which are this year's steps to living into our vision)?

What do we need to stop doing (celebrate its life and give it a funeral) that is no longer effective? (or liquidate or change)

Maintenance, Operations, and Administrative Work

Chapter 20 offers a January-through-December flow of work for Leadership Boards. Many items of focus in the annual calendar fit into this agenda item, including budget preparation, oversight of the annual stewardship campaign, removing operational bottlenecks, approving unplanned capital expenditures, organizing the strategic ministry planning retreat, and fulfilling fiduciary responsibilities, such as receiving the annual audit and ensuring the facility is properly insured. This type of work allows the Leadership Board to be proactive rather than reactive. This portion of the agenda was previously titled "Pressing Issues and Problem Solving" and "Fiduciary Work" in previous editions of *Mission Possible.*

While this work is important and necessary, it is primarily administrative; therefore, don't spend too much time here. Traditional Church Councils typically devote the majority of time and attention to this more familiar, comfortable work, making it easy to spend excessive time discussing these issues. When too much focus is placed on this area, the Leadership Board risks prioritizing administration over strategic and generative work.

This is an area in which work teams can be highly effective. Items pulled from the consent calendar may require discussion during this portion of the agenda. In addition, matters may arise that necessitate establishing a new guiding principle to allow ministry to flow without the Leadership Board's approval or intervention. At times, a new policy or manual may be under development and require review and approval by the Leadership Board. In other cases, an issue may be appropriate for a guiding principle that has not yet been created, or it may fall just outside a guiding principle and require handling as an exception.

This portion of the agenda provides space and time for the Leadership Board to address any matters that are stuck and need to be worked through. It can be used when individual team members have questions, comments, or concerns that need to be addressed for the overall good of the congregation, as it pertains to church governance, and the time for Leadership Board members to seek help from other Leadership Board members if they are stuck on individual or work-team assignments from the Leadership Board, such as the annual budget.

Make sure this time in the agenda does not become a catch-all for miscellaneous discussion with no structure or plan. Take time to gather feedback from Leadership Board members so issues and questions can be placed on the agenda before your meeting, and the board's time is used efficiently. Remember, comprehensive investments in developing annual leadership rhythms, policies, procedures, and Guiding Principles will enable the Leadership Board to minimize the time required to complete this work and enable them to instead focus on the vital strategic and generative work.

Communication

While a few items, such as personnel issues, require that the Leadership Board go into executive session and the minutes be preserved as confidential, the overwhelming majority of your Leadership Board's business is designed to be open and shared. Leadership Boards often get so wrapped up in their discussion that they forget to take the important step of communicating their actions and strategic work to the larger congregation, making needed assignments, and creating next steps. Therefore, every meeting should end with a time to discuss your communication plan.

The Communication Question for Each Decision Made	Purpose for the Communication Question
What decisions were made?	Recap of decisions to ensure all leaders are unified in understanding.
What needs to be communicated about the decision?	Helps identify the key components of the decision.
Who needs to know about the decision?	Identifies the person, group(s), or if the entire congregation needs to know about the decision.
What is the shared message about the decision?	Creates a common language and understanding for shared articulation of the decision.
Who is responsible for delivering the message?	Clearly identifies the person responsible for sharing the decision. This eliminates the risk that the decision will not be communicated.
How will the message be delivered?	Identifies the best method for delivery of the decision, such as text, email, newsletter, bulletin, USPS mail, video, worship slide, and/or verbal communication.
When will the message be shared?	Pinpoints the expected timing to share the message.

Here is an example of a communication plan:

> *The decision needs to be communicated in an email blast to the entire congregation within the next three days. The Leadership Board chair will write and send the email to announce that the Leadership Board will host a town hall meeting on (date/time) to present next year's budget and goals.*

By closing each meeting with a communications agenda item, you ensure that the Leadership Board's work is clear, captured in the minutes, and appropriately transparent and that it doesn't become detached from the life of the congregation.

Clarity about what should be communicated keeps the Leadership Board on task, places the work during the meeting in context, and connects the Leadership Board to the larger congregation. See Chapter 22, "Communications," for a broader perspective on connecting the Leadership Board's work to the larger church and community.

One More Thing: Executive Session as a Leadership Posture, Not Just an Agenda Item

The work of the Staff/Pastor-Parish Relations Committee (S/PPRC) must be kept confidential, according to the United Methodist *Book of Discipline*. Personnel work in a church is no different from personnel work in any professional setting. It involves private information, honest feedback, and sensitive conversations. Under the simplified accountable structure, this responsibility falls to the Leadership Board, which functions as the S/PPRC for pastoral support, evaluation, supervision, and concerns. Because of the sacred trust involved, confidentiality is essential. The importance of confidentiality should be covered in the Leadership Board Covenant and strictly enforced.

When the Leadership Board shifts into its S/PPRC role, the board enters an executive session. In an executive session, all guests and observers are excused. Only the lead pastor and duly elected Leadership Board members remain. Minutes from this portion of the meeting are recorded separately and kept in confidential S/PPRC files. This separation honors both legal and Disciplinary requirements and the pastoral covenant of trust.

During an executive session, the Leadership Board and pastor commit to speaking truthfully, respectfully, and in the spirit of Christian love. Polite silence is not helpful. Voices are meant to be heard. However, an executive session is neither a gripe session nor an open forum for unfiltered grievances. It is a space for collaboration, clarity, celebration, course correction, and shared accountability. The Leadership Board and the pastor are one team, entrusted with stewarding the church's mission together. In addition to this essential relational work, the executive session is also the appropriate space for sensitive personnel matters and denominational responsibilities specific to the S/PPRC, including annual consultation documents, supervision conversations, and confidential evaluations.

In earlier editions of *Mission Possible*, we recommended that Leadership Board agendas include executive sessions as a separate item toward the end. In this current edition of *Mission Possible 4*, we are refining that guidance. Executive session is less of an agenda item and more of a "floating status" that the Leadership Board enters when the nature of the conversation requires appropriate and necessary confidentiality. It is a state of mind and a shared covenantal understanding of trust, not simply a scheduled slot on the agenda.

This shift reflects what we have learned over the years of practice. Leadership Board conversations do not always move neatly from nonconfidential to confidential categories. Topics may surface organically during the meeting that require the Leadership Board to move into executive session. At other times, an entire called meeting may be convened as an executive session, such as when the Leadership Board is fully wearing its S/PPRC hat to complete annual consultation materials for the bishop and cabinet, meet with the district superintendent, or to address a sensitive staffing matter.

Even so, regular *relational* S/PPRC work should not be left to chance. It remains a healthy practice for Leadership Board meetings to include intentional time for the pastor and Leadership Board to engage in relational check-ins, support, encouragement, and mutual accountability. This time does not need to be long. Some months, it may be a simple five- or ten-minute check-in following communications and task assignments. Other months may require more extended conversation or a separately scheduled session. The keys are consistency and intentionality, not length of time.

During my (Blake's) season on the conference staff and as a district superintendent, our conference explicitly required new pastors and S/PPRCs (or SAS Leadership Boards) to meet monthly for their S/PPRC work during the first year of an appointment and then regularly thereafter. It was about relationship-building between the pastor and the committee and about supporting a healthy culture of accountability. Along the way, two consistent lessons emerged:

- First, one of my cabinet colleagues noticed a pattern. Whenever a midyear intervention was needed, the superintendent would ask the chairperson and the pastor, "Have you been meeting regularly with your S/PPRC?" In *every* case, the answer was "no." Communication breakdowns rarely happen all at once. They develop slowly when scheduled conversations are skipped. Healthy relationships are maintained through rhythm and intention, not reaction. Again, your monthly executive session doesn't have to be long, but it needs to be intentional and treasured.
- Second, when a Leadership Board moves into executive session ONLY when there is a problem, it creates unnecessary tension. Leadership Board members stiffen when the phrase "executive session" is uttered. Guests who are being excused feel uneasy. Pastors assume something is wrong. Regular executive session time normalizes the sacred work. It reinforces that relational and supervisory conversations are essential and routine, not exceptional.

Practically speaking, many Leadership Boards find it helpful to establish a clear rhythm for executive sessions. During the first year of a pastoral appointment, this often means setting aside a brief executive session at the end of each meeting. Placing it consistently after communications and task assignments signals that relational supervision and pastoral support are normal, expected parts of the Leadership Board's work rather than emergency responses. Later in a pastor's tenure, quarterly may be sufficient. At the same time, executive sessions should never be treated as a box to check. The Leadership Board must remain willing to shift into executive session at any point in a meeting when the nature of the conversation requires confidentiality in service of the church's mission. Whether scheduled briefly, entered fluidly, or convened as a fully called meeting-long executive session, this executive session status exists to protect trust, strengthen leadership relationships, and ensure that sensitive conversations are handled faithfully, confidentially, and in support of the congregation's shared calling.

More guidance about the expectations and practices that shape this relationship can be placed in the Leadership Board Covenant. Together, the covenant and the regular, intentional use of executive sessions safeguard the relational and spiritual health of the church's leadership system. They ensure that accountability is practiced faithfully and consistently, rather than sporadically or only in moments of crisis.

The Leadership Board at the Meeting Table

Configure Your Space for Meaningful Conversation

When meeting, gather in a circle so you can see each other. We recommend that Leadership Board members sit at the table and observers sit in chairs at the room's perimeter to clearly define who has a voice and voting rights. Perhaps light a candle in the center to represent Jesus at the table. I (Blake) once attended an administrative council meeting at a church I was coaching, where all the board members were seated up front in a single row, and the "audience" sat in rows facing them. It reminded me of a city council or school board meeting where constituents could go up to the microphone to argue their point to the board. Meanwhile, the board members couldn't even see each other. The space and configuration dictated an "us/them" approach to everything that the board did.

How the Board Makes Decisions

A Leadership Board should be very clear on how decisions will be made. While this could be included in the Leadership Board Covenant, we recommend that the Leadership Board remain flexible and use the process that best fits the subject at hand. There will be times when the Leadership Board must take formal action, including votes recorded in the minutes.

I (Blake) still remember a classroom exercise during a leadership course in seminary. My classmates and I were each assigned roles and told that our imaginary church had just received a significant financial gift. Our task was simple on paper: decide how to use it. What followed was anything but simple. Some people wanted to call for a vote. The assigned chairperson insisted that we could not move forward without full agreement, a process that she called "unified consent," a rule she declared on the spot without consulting the group. Even with a room full of seminarians and imaginary money, we spent more than an hour stuck in frustration, confusion, and bruised feelings, with no decision to show for it. Since that classroom exercise, I have seen real churches become immobilized by similar processes and unclear expectations.

While consensus is a worthy hope, it cannot become a requirement for the church to move forward. It is a gift when leaders reach broad agreement, but insisting on unanimity often leads to paralysis rather than faithfulness. When unanimous consent is required, a small minority can unintentionally hold the future of the church hostage. Over time, that dynamic erodes trust and drains energy from the mission.

One of the most helpful practices a Leadership Board can adopt is agreeing in advance on how each agenda item will be handled. Leadership Boards often assume everyone shares the same understanding of the decision-making process, but that is rarely the case. In good faith, different members approach the conversation from different angles. Some are still trying to understand the problem. Others are questioning why the topic is even on the agenda. Still others have already jumped ahead to solutions and are ready to evaluate options. When those approaches collide, meetings become inefficient and tense. Therefore, to be clear, for a given agenda item, the Leadership Board chair might say something like this:

> *Here is how I propose we handle this conversation. First, we will spend time making sure we have the relevant information in front of us. Next, we will name any assumptions we are making and check whether we share them. Then, we will clarify what matters most and what outcomes we are trying to achieve. Finally, we will work toward a decision that reflects those priorities and supports our mission. Does this process work for everyone, or do we need to adjust it?*[44]

Notice that this approach does not require the Leadership Board chair to use the same method every time. Different decisions call for different tools. Early in my ministry, I (Blake) was trained to use Edward de

[44] Adapted from Roger Schwarz, "How to Design an Agenda for an Effective Meeting," *Harvard Business Review,* March 2015.

Bono's *Six Thinking Hats*[45] approach when creativity and innovation were needed. In other settings, especially when tension was high or trust was fragile, I relied on structured listening processes to ensure people felt heard. During particularly conflicted moments in my work as a judicatory officer, I occasionally returned to Robert's Rules of Order because the troubled group simply needed an incredibly precise and clear structure to function.

The goal is not to champion one decision-making system over another. The goal is clarity. When board members agree on the process before they debate the substance, they are far more likely to make wise decisions and preserve relationships along the way.

Notes

---

[45] Edward de Bono, *Six Thinking Hats*.

CHAPTER TWENTY

Annual Leadership Rhythms

Leadership Rhythm

There is a natural rhythm to sound leadership. When a natural rhythm is discovered and practiced by the Leadership Board, the pastors, lay leaders, and congregation are usually much more comfortable with a simplified accountable leadership structure. A natural rhythm provides much-desired transparency and missional clarification. Sound rhythm helps manage healthy expectations, establish effective communication, and set a clear direction for the congregation. An intentional leadership rhythm keeps important matters from slipping through the cracks and eliminates rushed decisions on routine but less frequent work that could be missed. Rhythm promotes growth in leadership and spiritual maturity—vitally important, since a congregational Leadership Board partners with the pastor as the church's spiritual leaders.

The stewardship, strategic, generative, and accountability functions of board governance are themselves a rhythm. As you look at the monthly flow of meeting topics in this chapter, notice how these four beats show up month after month as the Leadership Board focuses on stewardship work (care and management of resources), planning and alignment (strategic work), creatively assessing its work toward fulfilling God's vision (generative work), and taking responsibility for leading the congregation in its mission of making disciples (accountability). For reminders on these four key functions, refer back to Chapter 13.

There is also a natural rhythm of the regular "church stuff" (e.g., pastoral review, budget preparation, employee evaluations, goal setting) we do annually at specific times of the year. A new natural rhythm develops when we can artfully combine the new work of the simplified accountable leadership (stewardship, strategic, generative, and accountability) with the regular governance business of congregational life.

Has your church found its rhythm? Please allow us to offer some insights on the rhythm of accountable leadership in the life of a church. We have found this rhythm to work with most churches, but feel free to adapt it to meet your needs and context. For instance, since your Leadership Board includes the duties and responsibilities of the Staff/ Pastor-Parish Relations Committee, your annual conference may have specific due dates for the pastoral assessment and consultation paperwork. Once the Leadership Board has found its rhythm, worship planning and ministry objectives will more likely be able to find their rhythm to sync with the Leadership Board.

At Your First Meeting of the Leadership Board Term:

- Create and join in a **Leadership Covenant**. A covenant is a sacred agreement with God and other board members. This covenant is a written agreement of the expectations and a code of conduct that should be agreed upon by the entire Leadership Board. Without a covenant, there will most likely be ambiguity (see Chapter 17).

- Explain and discuss your **model agenda** for healthy board meetings (see Chapter 19).

- Elect a **chair of Trustees** from the board's membership (annual requirement in *The Book of Discipline* and many state rules for nonprofit corporations). We recommend that the Leadership Board chair be elected by the board to also serve as Trustee chair.

- Spend quality time working on topics for the **Guiding Principles**. Create a work team or process to collaboratively work on the Guiding Principles outside board meetings. It will pay dividends for years to come! Be sure to orient the Leadership Board to the Guiding Principles each year (see Chapter 18).

- Call attention to the rhythm of the Leadership Board's areas of responsibility to remind members of the larger scope of work (see Chapter 20).

- Share and discuss the **Accountable Leadership Cycle** (see Chapter 13).

- Schedule the **monthly board meetings** for the year and set the date for the fall strategic ministry planning retreat.

January

Start the year with an intentional and well-organized orientation and formational time for new Leadership Board members. This will also help the continuing Leadership Board members "reset" and be reminded about the congregation's vision, the principles of accountable leadership, and the mutual expectations of Leadership Board members. There is a lot of organizational work to complete at this first meeting.

This is a time to review the expectations of leadership and the Leadership Board's practices for new people. See the following "Checklist for New Leadership Board Members." Finalize and have each Leadership Board member sign the Leadership Covenant (if this was not completed at the strategic ministry planning retreat).

- Set the board's calendar of meetings, town hall meetings, and annual strategic ministry planning retreat for the year, if you haven't done this already.

- As this is the first time newly elected board members are joining you at a regularly scheduled meeting, make sure they feel welcome and have received the appropriate training, onboarding, and resources.

- At the first gathering of the new Leadership Board—and each subsequent year—the board will need to elect the "chair of Trustees" as required by *The Book of Discipline*. It is recommended that the Leadership Board chair serve as the "chair of the Trustees" for legal and Disciplinary requirements. (In most states, the board of trustees is considered the board of directors for purposes of incorporation with your Secretary of State.)

- A person (recording secretary) will need to be named, or a rotation will need to be set up to take minutes at each meeting.

- Each Leadership Board member could be assigned a month to communicate to the congregation through newsletters, social media, and/or worship. Use the opportunity to share about the Leadership Board's general work, offer spiritual equipping from a lay leader's perspective, and keep the Leadership Board relationally and emotionally connected to the larger congregation. This practice also builds on the spirit of transparency.

- This is also a great time to assign responsibility and topics for spiritual and leadership development times in the upcoming months of Leadership Board meetings, if this was not done at the strategic planning retreat.
- Finalize the rotation and assignment of leading the spiritual formation, leadership development, opening prayer, and closing prayer for each month. Again, we suggest that the opening prayer be led by the same person as the spiritual formation time and the closing prayer be led by the same person who is facilitating the leadership development time. These roles are filled by two different people at each meeting, and every board member serves in at least one rotation each year.

As you begin your new year, be sure to have a commissioning of service for the Leadership Board in congregational worship, if it was not done in December. The congregation needs to be able to see their leaders, and this commissioning also serves as an opportunity to teach them about the responsibilities of spiritual leadership. Remember to also acknowledge and thank the Leadership Board members and Nominations Committee members who have just rolled off. You'll find eight ways to celebrate and show appreciation in Kay's blog post "Start the New Year Off With a Bang – Show Appreciation for Your Servant Leaders."[46]

---

[46] Kay Kotan, "Start the New Year Off with a Bang—Show Appreciation for Your Servant Leaders," January 7, 2025, https://kaykotan.com/blog/c/church-leadership/b/start-the-new-year-off-with-a-bang---show-appreciation-for-your-servant-leaders.

Onboarding Checklist for New Leadership Board Members

✓ Make sure Nominations has covered all expectations, including meeting dates & times, date and time of strategic ministry planning retreat, preparation for meetings, confidentiality, leadership covenant, etc.

✓ Provide a copy of the Leadership Board Covenant and the guiding principles so they can familiarize themselves with both.

✓ Add new Leadership Board Members to the board member email list (and remove members rolling off) and provide them with access to digital files.

✓ Assure each new Leadership Board Member is fully equipped for their new leadership role, including receiving a copy of *Mission Possible 4,* viewing the equipping on-demand webinar, or attending a live training workshop for a simplified accountable structure, and reviewing how to read and comprehend financial reports.

✓ Invite the new Leadership Board Members to shadow board meetings before they are officially seated to become more familiar with agenda flow and accountability conversations. After attending those meetings, meet with them and ask them what questions or comments they might have about their experience.

✓ Don't forget to invite new Leadership Board Members to the Strategic Ministry Planning Retreat in the fall, prior to them being seated in January. This is a great time for them to get to know fellow board members. They will also have a voice and role in the strategic ministry planning that they will be held accountable for once they take their seat at the Leadership Board table.

February

Easter is coming! This would be a perfect time to ask your pastor accountability questions about expectations for first-time and returning guests during the upcoming Lenten season. You also need to ensure the spiritual health of your Leadership Board members. It is easy to focus on the business of doing church while forgetting that our real business is our relationship with Jesus Christ. So, perhaps plan a spiritual retreat for the pastor and the Leadership Board to kick off the Lenten season. The spiritual retreat is a time for fasting, prayer, relationship-building, and spiritual discernment.

At the end of January, your congregation submitted statistical end-of-year information on membership, ministry, and financial health. Your February meeting is a great opportunity to compare trend lines over multiple years. Your district or conference office can provide you with charts that track annual statistics over a decade. What is growing? What is shrinking? Where are the gaps?

Note: Those trending reports are also available on umdata.org/churches. Simply fill in your church name, city, state, and conference. Once a list of churches appears, select your church. You'll then be taken to a screen detailing the church's current statistics and information. Click on the button titled "Healthy Church Initiative Download." This will download a spreadsheet detailing a 20-year trend of statistical information. No username or password is needed to access this information.

If you run a January-December financial year, you should have closed your books by the February meeting. Take the opportunity to review the rhythm of giving and expenses over the year, and be sure to fulfill your fiduciary responsibilities regarding church finances, taxes, audits, and related matters.

To get ahead of work schedules, midwinter is usually the best time to begin preparing for any needed facility improvements that are likely to be completed during the spring or summer months.

March

It is a good idea to have two to three annual gatherings (town hall meetings) with the congregation to keep lines of communication open and demonstrate transparent, accountable leadership. March might be a good time to schedule a congregational town hall meeting, perhaps connected to your Lenten theme. Leadership Board members should share about the state of the church, pray together for the church's neighborhood mission field, celebrate wins, and provide a progress report on the church goals. Take some time for feedback, which could include intentional "table talk" (imagine several round tables with a different Leadership Board member at each, asking a set of questions and practicing intentional listening) or other methods that have proved fruitful in your context. The purpose of these town halls is to inform, encourage, receive feedback, and build trust.

April

With first-quarter financial numbers now in, your Leadership Board should assess the congregation's finances in greater detail. Is the church on stable footing as you begin to head into the summer months, when giving is traditionally lower? What will the stewardship or generosity campaign be for this fall? Who will lead the campaign? What preparations need to be made? Is a temporary work team needed to help prepare with the pastor?

Consider a time for the Leadership Board to serve together in the community as an act of missional leadership and team-building.

May

Review policies and procedures. Are all job descriptions complete? Do any need to be updated or revised? Are there any updates needed in the employee manual? Are Guiding Principles in place (see Chapter 18)? Do any of these need to be revised or updated? Are the building usage policies updated? Are there any missing policies or procedures that would make everyday church life work more efficiently or effectively?

June

We are now halfway through the year. A more in-depth review of goals might be helpful.

Are we on track to meet all goals? Where are the gaps? What shifts need to be made? Are more resources needed? Do we have the right personnel (paid and unpaid) in the right place to accomplish the goals? How can the Leadership Board be encouraging and supportive while practicing accountability?

July

July is the usual time that new pastoral appointments begin in the United Methodist Church. In our book *IMPACT! Reclaiming the Call of*

Lay Ministry,[47] we devote an entire chapter to the significant evangelism and visionary opportunities of receiving a new pastor and offer tips for leadership teams to be "co-owners" of the pastor transition process alongside the new pastor. If you are receiving a new pastor, the June meeting will probably be about supervising the work of various teams assigned particular tasks:

- Prepare a welcome celebration for the new pastor and their family, if applicable.
- Share the pastoral transition with the wider community and local media as an evangelism and relationship-building opportunity.
- Organize a process of intentional relationship-building and orientation through cottage meetings or listening sessions with congregation members in July, August, and September.
- Schedule a series of appointments and make introductions for the new pastor to meet with community leaders and strategic church members.
- Work with the current and incoming pastor to share information, congregational metrics, and community demographics.
- As the Nominations Committee begins to meet, what gifts would be helpful for the Leadership Board members to have in the next season of the church's life? Notify the Nominations Committee of requests the Leadership Board might have. What would a potential new Leadership Board member need to know about the commitment and expectations of being a Leadership Board member before accepting the nomination?

This is a great time to ask the lead pastor accountability questions about plans to reach new people during the Back-to-School and Advent seasons.

July might be the time for another town hall meeting. While not usually a "high attendance" month in many churches, July could provide a time for your Leadership Board to connect with your deeply engaged members and leaders.

Use this time to gather information, such as community opportunities

---

[47] Kay Kotan and Blake Bradford, *Impact!*

to reach new people, ideas for launching or growing ministries, and to gauge which areas might bring excitement or passion. Use the information collected in your fall strategic ministry planning retreat to set your upcoming goals and priorities.

If you have received a new pastor, use the July meeting to help them understand how your church uses the simplified accountable leadership structure. It is one thing to see the simplified structure on paper; it is quite another to experience it in practice. The enculturation of a new pastor to the church's mission and vision, the congregation's Guiding Principles, the concepts of accountable leadership, and the board's template agenda are all squarely the responsibility of the governing board in its capacity as both the Church Council and the Staff/Pastor-Parish Relations Committee. If the new pastor has no prior experience in SAS, seriously consider engaging an Authorized SAS Coach to work with the pastor and the Leadership Board chair to ensure a healthy and thorough introduction and implementation.

August

This is a very important month! The Leadership Board will make final preparations for the strategic ministry planning retreat and conduct it in August or September. Are staff evaluations complete? Have any compensation change requests been received from the pastor for budgetary considerations?

If you have received a new pastor, the listening sessions or cottage meetings should be in full swing. What has your new pastor learned about the congregation? Your community? How are Leadership Board members introducing the pastor and facilitating new relationships with the pastor and community leaders? Also, district superintendents will often check in with the Leadership Board chair (if it is also the S/PPRC contact, as highly recommended) to inquire how the first few weeks of the new appointment are going. How is the Leadership Board helping your new pastor connect to the congregation, to community leaders, and to the larger mission field?

September

The strategic ministry planning retreat will be conducted (Note: Budget accordingly). We recommend that a neutral third party lead the retreat so the chair, pastor, and other Leadership Board members can fully participate without being unintentionally swayed by an internal retreat leader. There will be time to review and analyze the current year and plan for the upcoming one. The "work product" of a strategic ministry planning retreat is so much more than just getting plans on paper. The retreat is a time for team-building. It is also a time of play and fun. Do not forget to begin work on the new Leadership Covenant for the upcoming year, as well as your leadership development and spiritual formation topics (if the new incoming board members are present as recommended). Your Leadership Board has learned a lot over the past several months about how to be healthy, accountable leaders of your faith community. Take some time to make sure your learnings are incorporated into the Leadership Covenant and identify how best to invest in the leadership.

If possible, it is a best practice to include the new Leadership Board members who will be joining the board in the coming year in the strategic ministry planning retreat. This helps build relationships and also helps incoming board members develop a deeper understanding and commitment to the goals established for the upcoming year, during which they will have leadership responsibility. Having incoming board members present also allows time to complete the new Leadership Covenant for the upcoming year and to identify and assign spiritual formation and leadership development topics.

For a comprehensive resource on planning, implementing, and following up for a strategic ministry planning retreat, be sure to check out *Strategy Matters: Your Roadmap for an Effective Ministry Planning Retreat* by Kotan and Willard.[48] You will find it an invaluable resource for tying accountable leadership to the leadership rhythm offered here as well as for details on creating a strategic ministry planning retreat that leaders actually want to attend.

At many annual conferences, you begin work on your charge conference documents in early fall. Work teams may need to be deployed to work on different aspects of the report. That means you may assign a Leadership Board member to pull together a work team to get assistance from church members or staff with expertise outside the Leadership Board to complete different portions of the report, such as the facilities

[48] Kay Kotan and Ken Willard, *Strategy Matters.*

and finance reports. Eventually, your entire Leadership Board will need to approve and recommend the charge conference packet to the charge conference.

The Leadership Board will also need to coordinate with the independent Committee on Nominations and Leadership Development on preparing the slate of new Leadership Board members for approval at the charge conference. On-demand training for the Nominations Committee in an SAS model is available at kaykotan.com/sas-2. Chapter 11 offers tips to help your Nominating Committee fulfill this important task. The current Leadership Board will want to offer a copy of the current Leadership Covenant to the Nominations Committee so potential new leaders will have an idea of the leadership expectations. Also, be sure to provide the date of the strategic ministry planning retreat so the incoming leaders can also participate. If the Leadership Board is bumping up against some deeply ingrained leadership culture from the past, the Leadership Board chair may want to share this with the Nominations Committee so it can be covered in depth during the interview process and hopefully eliminate future issues.

October

Depending on your annual conference calendar, this may be the time of year when the pastor's evaluation by the Leadership Board is submitted to the district superintendent. Since the goal evaluation was completed the month prior at the strategic ministry planning retreat, the Leadership Board is now fully prepared for the evaluation. The Leadership Board has evaluative information rather than personal preferences and experiences as the basis of the evaluation.

After the upcoming year's God-sized goals are set at the Leadership Board's strategic ministry planning retreat, the pastor will work with staff and ministry teams on the objectives. This work most often takes place during an off-site staff retreat (Note: budget accordingly.) Once the objectives are set, budget requests can be made available to the Leadership Board for consideration via the pastor.

The second Sunday in October is Clergy Appreciation Day. How will the Leadership Board acknowledge and celebrate its clergy? How are the staff, ministry leaders, and other servant leaders celebrated?

November

The upcoming year's budget needs to be in its final revisions based on the stewardship campaign and the staff/ministry team leaders' budgetary requests. How is your budget aligning with the mission, vision, and strategic goals of the church? If you are not funding your God-sized goals, then it will be very hard to hold your pastor accountable for the results.

This may be the charge conference month if you did not already have one in October.

For the newly elected Leadership Board members, ensure you provide onboarding and thorough training to help them get off to a solid start. This includes supplying them with the latest copy of *Mission Possible* and attendance at an equipping workshop on SAS. Make sure this is not merely a one-hour overview session. Get your leaders to the deep-dive workshop, which is usually around five hours. If your district or conference is not providing this training, reach out to us at kay@kaykotan.com, and we will find training options for your leaders. We (Blake and Kay) also recorded an on-demand Leadership Board-equipping webinar. You can access this webinar at kaykotan.com/sas-2. You'll also find the "My Job" equipping webinar for Leadership Board members, which dives deeply into the technical BOD roles and responsibilities for Trustees, Finance, S/PPRC, and Church Council.

December

Early December is a great time to hold a "state of the church" gathering with the congregation. This is a time to review the year and share goals for the upcoming one. Celebrate the fruitful ministries and accomplishments of the year!

In December or January, your Leadership Board will likely need to complete consultation documents for the bishop and cabinet regarding the pastor's appointment. This work is both sacred and confidential. Only elected Leadership Board members (identified as Staff/Pastor-Parish Relations Committee members) should be present in discussions and the eventual vote recommending that your pastor return or move.

Annual Rhythm Reference Chart for the Leadership Board

Month	Focus
January	Elect "Trustee" chair, covenant, roles/responsibilities, commissioning service for outgoing and incoming Leadership Board and Nominations Committee members during worship
February	Easter plans, statistical trends, and facility improvement plans
March	Town hall meetings with feedback
April	Deep financial dive, stewardship campaign planning, serve together
May	Review to ensure policies, procedures, and Guiding Principles are up to date
June	Deep dive into goals to identify any needed shifts
July	Possible new pastor arrival, town hall meeting
August	Final retreat preparations, staff evaluations completed by the pastor, and feedback from cottage meetings, if a new pastor has been appointed
September	Strategic ministry planning retreat conducted, Nominations Committee is working on discerning new leadership for the upcoming year
October	Clergy evaluation, staff retreat, staff budget requests, clergy appreciation
November	Finalize budget, charge conference, and new leader training
December	"State of the church" town hall, clergy consultation

Notes

CHAPTER TWENTY-ONE

Year Two and Beyond

The first year of simplified accountable structure is about learning. Year two and beyond are about living into this new leadership model and culture.

Most churches experience meaningful change in the first year. Meetings are shorter. Roles are clearer. Decisions are made with greater confidence. But the deeper adaptive work of SAS does not happen quickly. It unfolds over time as leaders grow into new habits, shared expectations, and a common culture of accountability and trust. The second year is so important because it is the season when a Leadership Board pauses long enough to ask not just "Are we doing SAS?" but, "How well are we really practicing it?"

Honest Evaluation and Intentional Growth

One of the healthiest practices a Leadership Board can adopt in year two is honest self-evaluation. We encourage boards to assess how deeply they have adopted the core practices of simplified accountable structure, without defensiveness. A simple way to begin is by asking leaders to grade the board's work honestly. Not to judge or shame, but to clarify reality.

Are there areas where the board would give itself a solid "C"? If so, what would it take to move to a "B" this year? Or even an "A minus"? Growth does not require perfection. It requires intention.

Areas for evaluation might include:

- **Leadership Covenant:** Begin by evaluating how faithfully the Leadership Board is living into its covenant. Are leaders attending meetings consistently and coming prepared? Are they staying in their proper governance lane and maintaining a missional focus? Are they willing to engage in difficult but necessary conversations when the moment calls for it? Confidentiality is especially important. Is upholding confidentiality a topic that needs to be discussed? Once a decision is made, does the board speak with a unified voice, even when individual leaders may have disagreed during the process or even with the final decision?

- **Guiding Principles:** Guiding Principles should be revisited regularly to ensure they remain active and useful. Are they still clear and relevant, or have they faded into the background? Are they consistently applied to decision making, or are they referenced only when convenient? Guiding Principles lose their power when they exist on paper but not in practice. Identify and close any gaps in the Guiding Principles that require the Leadership Board to spend too much time on administrative work or stalls in ministries waiting on Leadership Board decisions.
- **SAS Agenda and Meeting Focus:** The SAS agenda itself deserves careful review. Leadership Boards should examine how well meetings align with the model's priorities. Is there a consistent time for spiritual formation and leadership development? Is there meaningful accountability for pastoral goals and the board's missional responsibilities? Are conversations primarily missional, strategic, and generative, or have meetings gradually drifted back toward operational detail and reporting?
- **Use of Time and Meeting Preparation:** Leadership Boards should also review how meeting time is allocated. What percentage of each meeting is focused on the care and attention for those already in the congregation versus reaching those not yet gathered? Are consent calendars being used appropriately to handle routine matters efficiently? Are packets, reports, and background materials sent to leaders at least seven days in advance so meeting time can be spent on discernment and decision making rather than on information sharing?
- **Accountability Practices:** Accountability is one of the most challenging and most important aspects of simplified accountable structure. By year two, boards should ask whether leaders are truly holding one another accountable. Are people gently but clearly called back into their proper lanes when boundaries are crossed? Is missional focus protected when conversations drift? Is accountability practiced as a shared commitment rooted in trust rather than as a top-down correction? What specific evidence is present that a new accountable leadership culture is emerging?

- **Policies and Procedures:** Finally, Leadership Boards should review the church's policies and procedures. Are they current, clear, and actually being used? Outdated or ignored policies undermine accountability and create confusion. Clear, well-maintained policies support healthy leadership and free the board to focus on mission rather than crisis management.

Many churches find our "SAS Church Inventory" to be a helpful tool during this phase. Used thoughtfully, it can surface patterns, strengths, and growth areas that are easy to miss in the day-to-day work of leadership. The "SAS Church Inventory" is available in the SAS Resource Hub.

SAS Resource Hub

Strengthening Financial and Strategic Capacity

By year two, Leadership Boards should also demonstrate a growing fluency in financial leadership that goes beyond approving budgets and monitoring balances. Leaders should understand how to read and interpret financial reports, recognize trends in giving, track the number of giving units, and notice changes in average giving. Leadership Boards should be able to discern when financial items belong on a consent calendar and when they require deeper conversation.

Strategic ministry planning should be a regular, scheduled practice, not an occasional event. Leadership Boards should ask whether strategic planning has a place on the calendar, who participates, and what outcomes it produces. Goals should be clear, measurable, and aligned with the mission. Pastoral goals and congregational goals should align and reinforce one another rather than compete.

Following strategic planning, churches find it helpful to hold a separate ministry planning retreat led by the pastor. This retreat allows ministry leaders to translate strategy into action (church goals into ministry objectives) and ensures that vision does not stall at the Leadership Board level.

Developing Leaders and Teams

Year two is also the time to notice shifts in how leaders are identified and developed. Has the work of the Committee on Nominations and

Leadership Development changed? Are different kinds of leaders being invited into service? Is there a clear process for leadership development rather than a scramble to fill slots?

Leadership development is not limited to the Nominations Committee. Leadership Boards should assess how well they understand and use work teams. Are teams empowered with clear purpose, defined authority, and appropriate support? Or are they underutilized, overmanaged, or pulled back into board-level work unnecessarily? Healthy use of work teams is one of the clearest signs that simplified accountable structure is functioning as intended.

Onboarding matters as well. Leadership Boards should be able to articulate how new leaders are oriented, trained, and supported. A strong onboarding process sets expectations early, reinforces the Leadership Board Covenant, and helps new leaders understand both the authority and accountability entrusted to them. When onboarding is intentional, leaders are formed rather than merely informed.

Coaching continues to belong alongside leadership development in year two and beyond. Churches that continue to grow into SAS often do so because they intentionally invite outside perspectives and neutral assistance. Authorized SAS Coaching provides a trusted partner who understands the model, United Methodist polity, and congregational systems. Coaching helps leaders reflect on patterns, strengthen accountability, and deepen their practice of shared leadership. Rather than being reserved for moments of crisis, coaching is most effective when used proactively as an investment in healthy leadership and long-term sustainability.

Listening to the Congregation

Leadership maturity includes listening. Leadership Boards should be willing to ask the congregation how they rate them on transparency, trustworthiness, and clarity of communication. How does the Leadership Board know? What feedback mechanisms exist, both formal and informal? What practices could strengthen trust and reduce confusion?

Public recognition also plays a role. January is an ideal time to thank those rotating off the Leadership Board and to commission those beginning service, along with leaders in key ministry areas. These moments reinforce shared leadership, gratitude, and accountability in the life of the church.

Growing into the Model

Simplified accountable structure is not something a church ever "finishes." It is something a church *practices*. As we all know, repeated practice helps us grow in skill, understanding, and more effective implementation. Year two and beyond are about deepening that practice, refining habits, and growing confidence. With intentional leadership development, thoughtful use of coaching, honest listening, and ongoing formation, SAS becomes less about structure and more about a shared way of leading faithfully for the sake of God's mission.

Notes

CHAPTER TWENTY-TWO

Communications

"Our church needs better communication!" Have you ever heard this? It is rare to do any sort of consulting work in a church without us hearing this from at least a few. Some may roll their eyes when they hear this because their perception is that people do not pay attention to what is said or printed. Yes, communication is indeed a two-way street. Yet the burden of providing clear, distinct, and timely communication lies with the church (Leadership Board, pastor, staff/ministry team leaders). Effective communication builds trust and fosters transparency. Trust and transparency are key to transitioning to a simplified structure and to modeling accountable leadership.

Transparency Is Required

One challenge of a simplified accountable leadership structure is that it significantly reduces the number of people who are formally "in the know." When a church moves from four or five administrative committees to a single Leadership Board, far fewer leaders are sitting in decision-making rooms. That reality makes communication more important, not less.

If we can all agree that congregations already need to do more to communicate well, it is important to consider the impact on communication when multiple committees are consolidated into one board. Many churches have depended, often without realizing it, on committee members to share the "business of the church" through informal and casual conversations. When those voices are no longer in the room, that informal communication network disappears. As a result, churches often need to communicate four times as much just to stay even with their previous level of shared understanding, which is often the level they already felt was inadequate.

There is also a natural team-building dynamic that develops within a Leadership Board. This can be a gift. Shared spiritual formation, leadership development, and discernment can deepen trust and clarity among board members. At the same time, it carries risk. If communication is not tended carefully, the Leadership Board can unintentionally become isolated from the wider congregation. The board may begin operating in its own reality, disconnected from the questions, concerns, and hopes being voiced elsewhere in the church.

Clear, consistent communication is therefore not optional. It is a core responsibility of accountable leadership.

Supreme Court Justice Louis Brandeis famously wrote that "sunlight is said to be the best of disinfectants." That insight applies directly to church leadership. The work of the Leadership Board needs sunlight, both for accountability to God's mission and for maintaining the trust required of spiritual leaders. For that reason (and in accordance with the requirements of *The Book of Discipline*), every Leadership Board meeting should be treated as an open meeting, except in clearly defined situations such as staffing matters or legal negotiations.

Relentless transparency in most areas of leadership builds credibility. When a congregation can see how decisions are made, understand the rationale behind them, and hear consistent communication from its leaders, trust grows. And when confidentiality is genuinely required, the congregation is far more likely to respect it. Transparency, practiced faithfully, strengthens both accountability and unity in the life of the church.

Commissioning of Leadership Communicates Values

One of the most powerful ways a church communicates its values is by what it chooses to name and celebrate publicly. Lay leadership, especially lay governance, should be lifted up and affirmed as a genuine form of ministry. In addition to the informational communication we recommend later in this chapter, commissioning leaders during Sunday worship is another important way to communicate with the congregation.

A commissioning service provides a visible, public expression of the trust placed in the Leadership Board. This may take place just before or just after the new Leadership Board is seated each year. Bringing the members of the Leadership Board forward during worship allows the congregation to know who is leading the church and reminds the congregation that leadership is both a responsibility and a calling.

Commissioning also creates space for blessing and gratitude. It offers an opportunity to pray for those beginning service and to sincerely thank those who are rotating off the Leadership Board. This moment does not need to be long to be meaningful. Its power lies in clearly defining the Leadership Board's role and the expectations that accompany it.

The act of commissioning communicates accountability as well as affirmation. When leaders are named and blessed before the congregation, their work is no longer hidden. It becomes part of the church's shared life. And do not forget the Nominations and Leadership Development Committee. Their work in identifying, equipping, and supporting leaders is essential and deserves recognition as well!

Commissioning is, at its heart, both an act of worshipful celebration and a communication strategy. It tells the story of shared leadership, affirms lay ministry, and reinforces the connections between worship, governance, and mission before the church ever reads a report or opens a newsletter.

Here are a couple of Kay's blog posts on commissioning and celebrating leaders that can be found in the SAS Resource Hub:

- "Valuable Ways to Appreciate and Celebrate Lay Servant Leaders"
- "Celebrate Servants"

SAS Resource Hub

Five Leadership Board Communication Strategies

Communication must come from several different levels of the organization: all Leadership Board members, the pastor, staff, and ministry team leaders. We believe part of the common communication concerns come when the burden of communication is placed on only one or two levels. Certainly, there needs to be a communication hub (perhaps a communication coordinator or office administrator), but information needs to come in and go out at all levels.

Because this resource is intended for Leadership Boards moving to simplified accountable leadership, we will concentrate on the communication responsibilities of the Leadership Board. There are five communication strategies we ask you to consider:

- Board conversations
- Congregational conversations
- Newsletter articles
- Digital communications
- Individual conversations

Board Conversations

In our sample agenda for every Leadership Board meeting, we suggest that the last agenda item be "communication." A simplified structure immediately becomes less accountable when others inside the congregation perceive the Leadership Board to be a secret group of insiders or the "pastor's buddies." As stated in Chapter 19, every Leadership Board meeting must include time to discuss which Leadership Board actions or discussions should be shared with the larger congregation and how best to share this message.

First, you may wish to make the leadership packet and minutes public for every member to read (except for executive session items, such as personnel matters or bids from competing vendors). But beyond sharing minutes, how might the Leadership Board help shape the congregation's Christ-centered purpose, its identity as an impactful faith community, and its ongoing narrative of faithfulness and fruitfulness before God? This chapter includes several suggestions, but we first recommend that Leadership Boards follow the recovery community's slogan: "Take the cotton out of your ears and put it in your mouth." In other words, take time to listen—listen to God, listen to your fellow congregation members that God is also working through, and listen to the needs of the community.

Congregational Conversations

Sometimes we refer to congregational conversations as a "town hall meeting," "quarterly conference," or "State of the Church Address." Choose a name that is appropriate and appealing in your context. The important thing here is not the title of the gathering but its practice. We suggest you hold these gatherings quarterly as you transition into the simplified accountable structure. As time goes by and the congregation becomes more comfortable with the model, the conversation frequency may need to be only a couple of times per year. The gathering is led by the Leadership Board chair and/or other Leadership Board designee(s). The pastor is in attendance but does not lead the conversation. The purpose of the conversation is to build trust, continuously cast the vision, offer information to the congregation, receive feedback, and answer questions. Most of the other communication strategies are one-way. Town halls and other congregational feedback opportunities offer the opportunity for two-way conversations.

The format for this gathering is based on the Leadership Board's governing focus. This means the Leadership Board will be presenting information on mission, vision, goals, and core values. The Leadership Board might offer information on the alignment of the church around these and/or present the budget or perhaps a financial overview of the church.

As you consider the rhythm of your town hall gatherings, understand that these congregational gatherings are not meant to be places for people to air their frustrations or dirty laundry. Therefore, create a focused environment by having an agenda and a stated time limit. When opening the meeting for questions, ask for questions around the specific topic at hand. For example, "What questions might you have about the goals set for this upcoming year?" If someone tries to hijack the meeting, goes off topic, or speaks disrespectfully, politely tell them you will have a private conversation with them immediately after the meeting. As a recommended alternative for open, large-group conversations, we suggest the use of other tools, such as table talks, where Leadership Board members each facilitate a table discussion from the same list of strategic questions to increase two-way communication and hear from a greater number of people while reducing the chance of one member attempting to "hijack" the conversation of the whole group.

Newsletter Articles

We often leave the newsletter creation up to one person, who writes articles, lays out the newsletter, adds graphics, and distributes it. One central person being responsible for the layout and distribution makes great sense. Yet, the newsletter needs to reflect multiple thoughts, perspectives, ideas, styles, and information from various areas and voices of the church.

The newsletter is a great medium for the Leadership Board to participate in the overall communication and transparency of the church. Assign a different member of the Leadership Board to contribute articles or information to the newsletter each month. Share what the Leadership Board is working on and the progress made. Share general financial information. Share the celebrations of the church. Please do not rely solely on the pastor or the Leadership Board chair for this leadership perspective. The newsletter is a great place to communicate the Leadership Board's missional focus and responsibility.

Digital Communication

In today's world, we must offer multiple ways to engage with social media and other digital communication. This might include texts, YouTube videos, Zoom, podcasts, X, Facebook, email, Instagram, and other forms. Find ways to engage the congregation through social media that align with both your congregation's context and the new people you are trying to reach. Sometimes we limit our communication to the preferences of only our members, missing opportunities to reach new people through more modern methods.

Again, do not limit this responsibility to only one person. The Leadership Board must employ new and creative digital communication strategies to engage the congregation. This might include newsy information, but it is also an opportunity to share a quote from a time of spiritual formation or leadership development during the Leadership Board meeting. You could add an occasional "leadership update," special episode to the pastor's weekly "Behind the Sermon" podcast, or host Zoom Q&A and brainstorming sessions with the congregation. If you have a daily devotional and shared scripture distributed on email and social media, intentionally include the Leadership Board members in the devotional-writing rotation. Using digital communication might also be as simple as a short post about the record-breaking attendance at the Christmas Eve service(s) that everyone can celebrate. Include the Leadership Board members on the church's website, along with their bios, so the congregation and potential guests can get to know the current leadership better. Be creative! Engage with your congregation!

Individual Conversations

As a member of the church's Leadership Board, you represent the church when having conversations with fellow congregants (including family and friends). You also represent the church in your community. Make sure you uphold a missional focus and the unified voice of the entire Leadership Board in these conversations. You play an important role as both a church and Christian ambassador. People look to you as a role model for the church. This does mean you will need to set aside your personal agendas and allegiances to your Sunday school class or favorite ministry and be willing to invest as a holistic church leader. You are one of the representatives of the *entire church*, both inwardly to other congregation members and outwardly to the community. Conversations about the church need to keep Christ's mission and vision for the congregation in the forefront.

Notes

CHAPTER TWENTY-THREE

Right-Sizing Your Implementation

Just as congregations must right-size their Discerning, Designing, and Equipping work, they must also right-size their approach to the Implementing Phase. The first year of SAS implementation looks different depending on the congregation's size, staff configuration, and inherited leadership culture. The structure is the same, yet the practical expressions vary. Right-sizing allows each congregation to honor its context while staying faithful to the core principles of accountable leadership. The goal is not uniformity. The goal is clarity, alignment, and a shared understanding of how governance works in your particular ministry setting.

In every context, right-sizing during the Implementing Phase allows the congregation to *live the model* rather than merely adopt its shape. Each church carries its own gifts and challenges into the SAS transition. By clarifying roles, reinforcing lanes, and honoring the unique rhythm and context of each ministry setting, SAS will empower churches of any size to have God-sized impact.

Right-Sizing for Large and Multi-Staff Congregations

Earlier in the Designing Phase, we addressed how executive pastors relate to the Leadership Board in large and multi-staff churches. The same core principle applies during implementation. Simplified accountable structure depends on clear distinctions between governance and management, and those distinctions must hold not only for clergy roles but also for key staff positions with operational and financial authority. When boundaries are blurred, even well-intended structures begin to drift.

In larger congregations, this clarity is especially important for business administrators and financial staff. As churches grow more complex, these roles often expand in scope and influence. SAS requires that each position be clearly defined so that governance remains with the Leadership Board, and management remains with staff. Business administrators and financial staff oversee day-to-day operations, financial systems, reporting, and internal controls. Their work provides the information, expertise, and infrastructure necessary for faithful decision making.

These staff roles support the work of the Leadership Board, but they do not replace the board's fiduciary responsibilities. The Leadership Board retains authority for oversight, strategic direction, and alignment with the church's mission, while staff execute that work within clearly defined lanes. When these lanes are honored, staff leadership is strengthened, and boards are freed to govern rather than manage.

In the Implementing Phase, large churches benefit from establishing a clear and predictable rhythm for how business administrators and financial staff interact with the Leadership Board. Financial staff may be invited as regular (yet occasional) guests to board meetings for specific purposes, such as presenting financial reports, providing context for budget decisions, or answering technical questions. Their presence should be purposeful and well-defined, focused on informing discernment rather than shaping decisions.

This rhythm works best when financial materials are prepared in advance as part of the board packet, accompanied by clear narrative notes that highlight trends, risks, and decision points rather than raw data alone. The Leadership Board may also form short-term work teams that include financial staff to address focused tasks such as budget development, capital planning, or financial policy review. These work teams allow expertise to be fully utilized while preserving the Leadership Board's role as the governing body.

When these rhythms are practiced consistently, large churches avoid rebuilding finance committees simply by using another name. Staff are empowered to lead within their expertise, boards are equipped to govern with clarity, and the simplicity and accountability of SAS are preserved. Right-sizing the Implementing Phase in large churches is not about adding structure. It is about establishing patterns that sustain healthy leadership, shared trust, and faithful alignment with the church's mission.

Right-Sizing for Midsize Congregations

Midsize congregations, often with a full-time pastor and a mix of part-time staff and unpaid ministry leaders, experience different challenges. Many have been operating for years in a hybrid model in which staff and strong laypeople share decision making around the same table. The lines between staff (paid and unpaid, who are often congregation members) and Leadership Board members were often blurred. The SAS Implementing Phase requires deliberate boundary-setting so that the Leadership Board is not pulled back into management by habit, enthusiasm, or pressure from staff accustomed to having decision-making authority.

Staff meetings and ministry team meetings must handle operational work. Board-assigned work teams should take on detailed tasks (sometimes with staff assistance). The Leadership Board should remain focused on governance, but Leadership Boards of midsize congregations quickly find themselves reviewing curriculum choices, approving every facility request, or troubleshooting volunteer issues rather than governing. This cultural shift requires the most attention in midsize settings.

The pastor's role also shifts. Instead of chairing a committee that makes every decision together, the pastor now becomes the primary supervisor, alignment leader, vision carrier, and coach for ministry team leaders. This responsibility requires courage, clarity, and consistent reinforcement. Without it, the model devolves into a slightly streamlined version of the old committee system.

Right-Sizing for Small Churches Served by Less Than Full-Time Pastors

Small Churches Need a Right-Sized Agenda

Small churches with part-time or shared pastors experience the Implementing Phase differently. Their greatest strength is relational closeness, but that closeness often leads to meetings where every topic is discussed together. SAS asks small congregations to do something counterintuitive yet essential: separate ministry conversations from governance discussions.

I (Blake) often tell the story of a board meeting where the governing board (with twenty-plus members!) spent twice as much time discussing the type of padlock for the gate as it did on a major ministry opportunity. While the same people may be responsible for both tasks in a smaller church, the conversations must not happen in the same meeting. Governance belongs to the Leadership Board. Ministry and management belong to ministry teams or informal gatherings.

This separation is especially important when the pastor's time is limited. A right-sized agenda keeps Leadership Board meetings focused on mission, alignment, outcomes, policies, and accountability. It also protects both pastor and laity from burnout. Small churches sometimes assume that simplifying governance means packing everything into one meeting. In reality, SAS helps them discern what belongs to governance and what belongs to ministry, which ultimately strengthens both.

Right-Sizing for Cooperative Parishes and Multi-Point Charges

Cooperative parishes and multi-point charges require the most intentional right-sizing during the Implementing Phase. These ministry settings carry layered complexity by design. Multiple congregations share pastoral leadership, often share staff, and yet retain distinct (contextual and legal) identities, histories, and legal responsibilities. The challenge is not whether simplified accountable structure can work in these contexts. It can. The challenge is making sure SAS clarifies relationships rather than flattening unique differences that still matter.

The most important contextual principle is this: shared pastoral leadership does not automatically mean shared governance. Each congregation within a cooperative parish or multi-point charge remains its own local church with its own legal identity, charge conference responsibilities, trustees, and fiduciary accountability unless *The Book of Discipline* and the district superintendent have approved a different arrangement. SAS does not erase those realities. It helps churches work within them more efficiently and purposefully.

First Task: Clarifying What Is Shared and What Is Not

In cooperative parishes and multi-point charges, governance can be structured in more than one faithful way. Some charges function best with congregation-specific Leadership Boards, while others benefit from a shared or parish-level Leadership Board. The key is not which option is chosen, but whether authority, accountability, and representation are clearly understood and consistently practiced.

Option One: Congregation-Specific Leadership Boards

In some multi-point charges, each congregation maintains its own Leadership Board or governing body that fulfills the requirements of *The Book of Discipline*. In this model, Leadership Boards do not govern the other churches under their charge. They govern their own congregation's property, finances, and local ministry decisions, while the pastor provides shared leadership across the charge. Leaders from all the churches occasionally gather to submit documentation to the conference, plan a cooperative VBS or food pantry ministry, or serve as an ad hoc Staff/Pastor-Parish Relations Committee to meet with the district superintendent about an appointment change.

This approach works best when congregations have distinct identities, different financial capacities, or varied ministry contexts. It honors local ownership while requiring the pastor to maintain strong communication and coordination to keep alignment across the charge.

Confusion arises when this model is used informally without being named. When one congregation begins to assume influence over another, or when decisions appear to be made "somewhere else," resentment grows quickly. Clarity is not optional in this model. It is congregational care.

Option Two: A Shared or Parish-Level Leadership Board

In other multi-point charges or cooperative parishes, especially smaller or deeply interconnected congregations, a shared parish-level Leadership Board may be the most faithful, sustainable option. In this model, representatives from each congregation serve together on one Leadership Board that governs the shared life and ministry of the charge. There are still individual Boards of Trustees because each church remains a separate legal entity.

This approach requires intentional design and explicit approval through appropriate charge conference and district superintendent processes. Representation must be balanced, authority clearly defined, and expectations agreed upon before implementation. When done well, a parish board reduces duplication, simplifies decision making, and strengthens shared mission rather than fragmenting it.

A parish-level Leadership Board is not about efficiency alone. It is about stewarding limited leadership capacity and creating a more impactful, shared sense of ownership for the larger ministry of the whole charge, with and to the community. When congregations are small or when leadership benches are thin, this model often provides stability and critical mass when it's difficult to staff a full committee.

Coordination Without Confusion

In both models, the pastor serves as the primary integrator of mission, communication, and alignment. This does not mean the pastor replaces governance. It means the pastor helps governing leaders envision how their decisions connect to the wider ministry of the charge.

Whenever leaders of the charge or the cooperative gather in a meeting, articulate what sort of meeting it is and the authority it holds as you begin every meeting. Is it an advisory meeting? A coordination meeting to organize a particular shared ministry? Does it have the authority granted by each church to make charge-wide decisions?

Whether a cooperative parish uses congregation-specific boards or a shared parish board, the same principle applies: coordination must be intentional, and authority must be documented and transparent. SAS can encourage coordination without resorting to consolidation, but maintaining balance and communication takes effort. Regardless of the model used, one rule remains nonnegotiable: no informal or unwritten governance structures. When authority exists without being clearly outlined (and documented), SAS will quietly unravel. Complexity will return, accountability will fade, and the structure will lose its cohesiveness.

Implementation Takes Longer, and That Is Normal

Finally, cooperative parishes and multi-point charges should expect the Implementing Phase to take longer than it does in single-congregation settings. While the churches may be smaller in attendance, the situation is far more complex. Trust is built incrementally.

When done well, SAS gives cooperative parishes a shared language, clear governance and strategic lanes, and a sustainable meeting rhythm that allows each congregation to thrive.

Option Three: A Shared Parish S/PPRC Model

In some conferences, the culture and policy of multi-point charges include a shared Staff/Pastor-Parish Relations Committee (S/PPRC) across the charge. For example, each church in a three-point charge may assign representatives to serve on a single, shared S/PPRC which relates to the pastor and the district superintendent, while other governance functions remain at the congregational level.

In these cases, a congregation using a simplified accountable structure may designate members of its Leadership Board to serve as its representatives on the charge-wide or parish-wide S/PPRC. Clear expectations are essential so that those representatives can confer with and report appropriately to their Leadership Board, while honoring the confidentiality required in executive session with the attendance of the pastor.

When consultation recommendations are submitted to the bishop and cabinet, each congregation's Leadership Board should also have the ability to communicate its perspective to the district superintendent. This is particularly vital when the appointment recommendation of the shared charge-wide S/PPRC differs from that of a particular congregation within the charge, in which case, a separate "minority" report to the district superintendent may be appropriate.

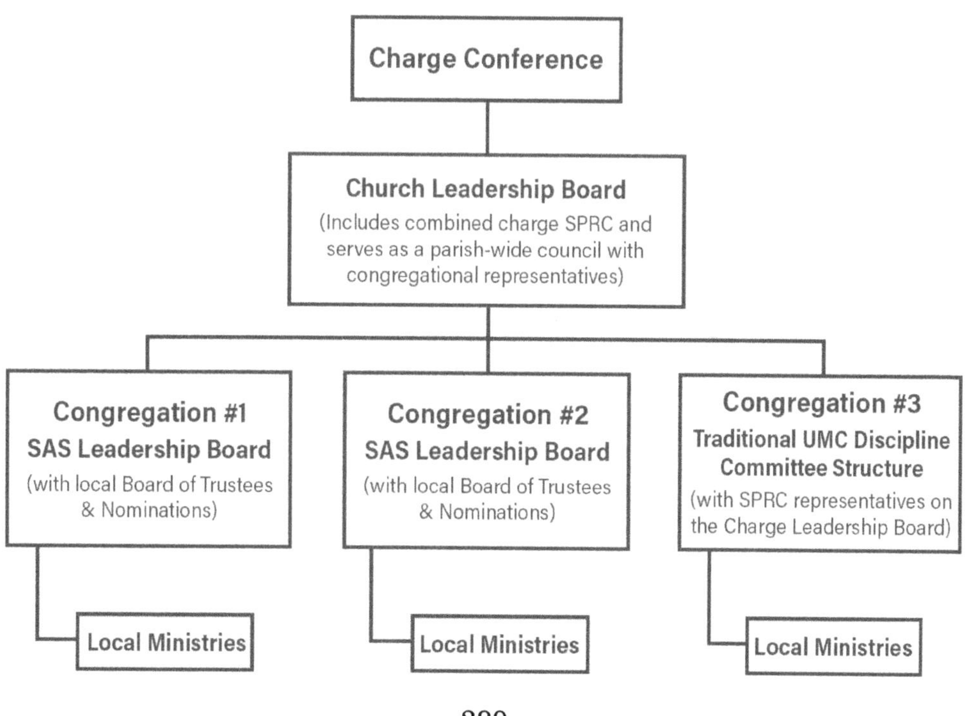

Notes

CHAPTER TWENTY-FOUR

Common Challenges in the Implementing Phase

A sense of relief and hope often accompanies the decision to move to simplified accountable structure. The vote passes. The resolution is approved. The church takes a collective breath and says, "We did it."

In reality, that is when the real work begins.

The Implementing Phase is where simplified accountable structure either takes root or quietly erodes. Most challenges do not come from opposition or bad intent. They come from fatigue, impatience, and the assumption that once the structure changes on paper, the culture will automatically follow. It will not.

Here are the most common challenges we see churches face during implementation, especially in the first year and as they move into year two and beyond.

Year One Challenges

Stopping Coaching After the Resolution Is Passed

This may be the most damaging mistake of all. Too many churches treat Authorized SAS Coaching as something needed only to "get through the vote." Once the resolution is approved, coaching is ended, budgets are redirected, and leaders assume they can handle things on their own. While we appreciate pastors acting as coaches for their churches, we find this practice to be a conflict of interest rather than a best practice.

In our experience, Authorized SAS Coaching is most valuable after the structure is in place. This is when leaders are forming new habits, navigating new authority, and unlearning old patterns. Coaching helps pastors and Leadership Boards notice drift, name tension early, and continue growing into the new structure and leadership model. Ending coaching too soon often leads to quiet regression rather than sustained transformation.

Treating the Leadership Covenant as a Form Rather Than a Practice

Many churches complete a Leadership Board Covenant early in the process and then quietly set it aside. The covenant is signed, affirmed, and then gathers dust. Accountability becomes assumed rather than actually practiced. Again and again, we have seen Leadership Boards slip into old habits, looping back into the comfort of management rather than governance and into "representative" mindsets rather than missionally accountable leadership. The Leadership Board Covenant is meant to be a living agreement that shapes attendance, preparation, boundaries, confidentiality, how leaders behave and work together, and how leaders speak with one unified voice after decisions are made.

Delaying the Creation of Guiding Principles

Another common challenge is postponing the development of Guiding Principles. Some Leadership Boards want to "just get comfortable first." Others want to get into all the action and assume they can figure things out as they go. Without Guiding Principles, decisions default to personalities, traditional practices, conflict avoidance, and preferences. Not having a set of comprehensive Guiding Principles delays the Leadership Board's shift into leading in the governance lane and prolongs its swerving into the management lane. Guiding Principles are not window dressing. They create shared expectations for how decisions are made and how authority is exercised. They also enable the Leadership Board, staff, and ministry team leaders to operate efficiently. Delaying their creation almost always creates confusion later.

Failing to Change the Conversation at the Leadership Board Table

Structural change does not automatically change the conversation at the meeting table. In the first year, Leadership Boards often continue talking about the same things in the same ways, just with fewer people in the room. Meetings drift back toward reports, operational detail, and problem-solving that belong elsewhere. If Leadership Board members are not intentionally trained and coached to focus on missional accountability, strategy, and generative questions (through the use of the recommended SAS agenda), the structure may be simplified—but the leadership will not be. For this reason, we strongly encourage

Authorized SAS Coaching to help your Leadership Board build a new governance culture.

Underestimating the Importance of Congregational Communication

Since a simplified accountable structure reduces the number of people in formal leadership roles, communication becomes more critical—not less. Many churches underestimate the amount of communication needed during the first year. Without frequent, clear, and transparent communication, members fill in the gaps themselves, and it often results in confusion and mistrust. Year one requires more communication than leaders think they need and more clarity than they think they are providing.

Year Two and Beyond Challenges

Skipping Intentional Evaluation

One of the most common mistakes churches make is assuming that if year one went well, no further evaluation is necessary. Meetings feel better. Decisions move faster. Conflict seems lower. And so the Leadership Board moves on. Without intentional evaluation in year two and beyond, small misalignments go unnoticed. Practices drift. Accountability softens. Further leadership formation opportunities are missed to shift the leadership culture. What once felt transformational slowly becomes familiar and unexamined.

Assuming the Model Will Maintain Itself

Simplified accountable structure does not run on autopilot. It requires ongoing formation, reinforcement, and attention. When Leadership Boards stop revisiting Leadership Board Covenants and Guiding Principles, stop providing SAS training and onboarding for new members, and stop using the pre-meeting packet and the recommended SAS agenda, the structure begins to hollow out. The structure remains (at least on paper in the district office), but the true transformational culture that SAS encourages begins to fade. Policies and flow charts do not maintain SAS; it is sustained by disciplined leadership.

Staying the Course

Implementation is not a single season. It is a practice over time. Churches that thrive with simplified accountable structure are not those that avoid challenges, but those that name them early and address them intentionally. When leaders remain teachable, committed to accountability, and willing to invest in ongoing formation and coaching, the structure continues to serve its purpose.

The goal is not simply to implement a new way of governing. The goal is to cultivate a leadership culture that remains aligned with Christ's mission, responsive to your unique congregational context, and grounded in trust and grace.

Afterword

During my (Blake's) season as a district superintendent, my appointment shifted from the Little Rock area into a new district where I had never served before. Early on, I discovered that roughly half of the one hundred or so congregations in the district were already using some form of simplified structure. Notice the phrasing. They were *simplified* structures, but not necessarily simplified *accountable* structures. As you now know, that distinction matters!

A few months into my tenure, charge conference season arrived, and packets began landing on my desk. Our conference had not yet taken a coordinated, conference-wide approach[49] to a simplified accountable structure. Instead, our conference had evolved over the previous decade into a governance "Wild West." Congregations had adopted leadership models drawn from nondenominational churches, business literature, nonprofit boards, or hybrid systems that looked like distant descendants of earlier versions of SAS, slowly evolving without shared guidance or accountability. It felt less like a shared ecclesial practice and more like the time of the Judges: "In those days there was no king in Israel; all the people did what was right in their own eyes" (Judges 21:25, NRSVue).

That first autumn in a new district, before we had the opportunity to teach the *why* and the *how* of simplified accountable structure, I reviewed close to fifty charge conference packets from churches using some form of a one-board model. About half of those included alternate one-board models that did not meet the minimum standards of the United Methodist *Book of Discipline*. This was not about best practices or all the specific recommendations you will find in this book. It was certainly not about whether I agreed with their intent. In fact, I

[49] Kay and I have helped several conferences begin such an approach. It's a game-changer!

applauded it. These churches were trying to lead differently, to simplify, to be nimbler and mission-focused. The problem was not their intent. The problem was compliance.

That experience clarified something for me very quickly.

The conference did not need fewer structures or looser guidelines. It needed better equipping, a shared language, understanding, and approach, and a faithful way to use simplified accountable structure within a United Methodist framework. And that responsibility rested squarely with me. As their district superintendent, I needed to invest serious time in equipping leaders to understand not just what simplified accountable structure is, but why it works and how to use it well. Without that grounding, churches were left to improvise. And improvisation, no matter how well-intentioned, is a poor substitute for shared wisdom and disciplined practice.

From the beginning of our ministry together, Kay and I have been intentional in designing and teaching a simplified accountable structure that fully meets the standards of *The Book of Discipline* while also reflecting the principles of accountable, mission-focused leadership. We are grateful that bishops, cabinets, conferences, seminaries, and our own denomination's Discipleship Ministries have used our simplified accountable structure resources, and we have become a trusted partner for churches and judicatories across the connection.

If this book has done its work, then you now understand this simple truth: structure is never neutral. It either supports missional accountability or undermines it. It either clarifies responsibility or muddles it.

Simplified accountable structure is not about doing less church. It is not about efficiency for efficiency's sake. It is not about fewer meetings on the church calendar. We created and advocate for SAS because the health of local churches trying to lead faithfully in complex times depends mightily on leadership structures that serve the mission.

The Great Commission has never changed. What must change, again and again, is our willingness to shape our structures and our methods in service of that mission.

✓ When accountability is clear, trust grows.

✓ When leadership is shared, God's gifts are used.

✓ When roles are rightly aligned, the Spirit has room to move.

✓ The mission becomes possible.

INDEX

accountability
as board culture, 166
as staff and ministry team practice, 167
cycle of, 167
defined, 159
in church leadership, 160
missional leadership and, 159
rotation as protection for, 191

adaptive leadership
defined, 169
technical shifts and, 177

agenda
checklist, 234
explanation of items, 238
meeting template, 237
packet and, 225, 231

alignment
defined, 180
strategic ministry planning and, 181

annual rhythm
for Leadership Board, 255, 267
first meeting of term, 256
onboarding and, 259
reference chart, 267

authorized coach
assignment of, by district superintendent, 35
benefits of using, 35, 70
discernment plan and, 21,35,36
discernment team and, 38
ending coaching too soon (warning), 291
not using one, 35, 70
qualifications and training, 36
role throughout all four phases, 35
year two and beyond, 272

board culture
accountability and, 166
changing conversation at the table, 172
guiding principles and, 213
honest evaluation and growth, 269
leadership covenant and, 205
rules of the road, 208
tending culture, not just structure, 127

Book of Discipline
alternative structure permission, 3, 11
charge conference and, 67
nonnegotiables, 82
pastor's role defined in, 86
rotation classes and, 79
S/PPRC requirements and, 84, 85
six-member board permitted by (smaller churches), 114

building maintenance team
difference from trustees, 98
getting started, 100

charge conference
church conference or, 67
composition of [in SAS], 90
nominations report and, 89

chartered groups
influence vs governance authority, 81
liaisons to Leadership Board, 82
representational governance warning, 81
United Methodist Men, United Women in Faith, UMYF, 81, 95

childcare ministry
financial matters and, 119, 222
personnel and, 119, 221,222
separately incorporated, 120
tuition-based ministry, 222, 224
as right-sizing consideration, 118

church conference
choosing charge conference instead, 67
preparing for, 48
resolution for, 50
vote to adopt SAS, 55, 67

Church Council
vote to explore SAS, 31

classes
terms of office defined, 78
nine-member board and, 77
rotation process for new structure, 79
six-member small church option, 114

coach
See authorized coach

communication
agenda item for, 248
commissioning and values, 276
congregational listening and, 272
example plan, 249
strategies for Leadership Board, 277
transparency and, 275
underestimating need for, 293

common challenges
in designing phase, 125
in discerning phase, 65
in equipping phase, 189
in implementing phase, 291

confidentiality
as Disciplinary obligation for S/PPRC work, 85, 249
executive session and, 249
Leadership Board covenant and, 208, 211, 212, 270
nominations and, 148

cooperative parish
designing the structure of, 117
implementation timeline and, 288
right-sizing for, 117, 286

congregational discernment
see discernment plan
building a plan, 38
discernment plan, 33
whole congregation involvement, 66

consent calendar
defined and explained, 226
packet and, 226
removing items from, 226
role in agenda preparation, 235

covenant
see leadership covenant

design phase
challenges and, 125
design basics for SAS, 80
introduction, 74
participants, 74
purpose of, 74
right-sizing and, 109
timeline, 74

discerning phase
challenges and, 65
discernment team, 37
introduction, 20
participants, 20
phasing in SAS over years (don't), 127
purpose of, 20
right-sizing and, 57
timeline, 20

discernment plan
barriers to address before adopting SAS, 34
building the congregational plan, 38
communication channels and, 40
introduction, 33
prayer team and, 39
summary report to Church Council, 41
twelve steps to discerning, 21

discernment team
assembling, 37
composition of, 37
no Disciplinary authority, 37
role of SAS coach with, 38

district superintendent (DS)
approval process, 49
authorized SAS coach and, 35
Exploration request to, 34
formal request for approval, 45
S/PPRC concerns and, 85

endowments and foundations
as right-sizing consideration, 118, 121
foundations or, 122

equipping phase
challenges and, 189
introduction, 136
participants, 136
purpose of, 136
right-sizing and, 185
timeline, 136

executive session
confidentiality in, 250
leadership posture in, 249
purpose of, 250
S/PPRC work and, 85, 250

facility use
childcare ministries and, 119
policies, 220

financial matters
current policies, 223
Leadership Board operations and, 217
meeting packet, 225,229

financial secretary
See also treasurer
role in SAS, 93
not a governing role, 93

generative work
as Leadership Board function, 164
distinguished from management work, 232

governance
defined as Leadership Board's primary role, 164
distinguished from management, 113, 164, 196
four lanes and, 196
guiding principles keeping board in governance lane, 213
inherited structure and, 3
ministry teams and, 97, 98
staying in governance lane, 109, 230, 232
steering and pedaling (bicycle metaphor and, 97

guiding principles
catalog, 215
complex associated nonprofit relationships and, 122
current policies and, 223
delaying creation of (warning), 292
supporting areas of work, 223
year two review of, 270

honorary Leadership Board members
purpose and limits, 194

human cost of change
loss of identity and belonging, 70
pastoral care and, 71

implementing phase
challenges and, 291
introduction, 202
participants, 202
purpose of, 202
right-sizing and, 283
timeline, 202

lay leader
dual role with lay member, 80
role in discernment team, 37

lay member to annual conference
dual role with lay leader, 80

Leadership Board
annual rhythms, 255, 267
as Board of Trustees, 87
as Finance Committee, 78
as S/PPRC, 78, 81, 84, 85
commissioning of, 277
covenant, 205
design basics, 80
executive session and, 249, 250
first-year learning, 155
honorary members, 194
nine-member model, 77
onboarding, 259
operations and meetings, 217
packet, 225, 227
selection criteria, 139
six-member option for small churches, 114
training, 151
vote of pastor on, 126
year two and beyond, 269

leadership covenant
expectations and accountability, 205
Leadership Board and, 205
rules of the road and, 208
use in onboarding, 259

leadership development
developing leaders and teams, 271
nominations committee and, 193
rotate leaders, 190
tools to articulate expectations, 142

meeting packet
agenda and, 225, 231
recommended contents, 227

ministry teams
governance and SAS, 98
SAS and impact, 97
staff and ministry team leader accountability, 167

misuse of SAS
authoritarian misunderstanding, 68
misunderstanding staff role, 68
misuse of model, 10
not using authorized coach, 69
phasing in SAS as, 127

multisite churches
representative governance caution, 111
right-sizing for, 57, 110, 185, 283

multi-point charge
see cooperative parish
right-sizing for, 117, 286, 288

nominations
annual process, 143
committee in SAS, 92
committee training, 139
sample report, 89

onboarding
new Leadership Board members, 259
new leaders, 154

organizational charts
cooperative parish and multi-point charge, 118
small church, 116
standard example, 102

packet
See meeting packet

pastor
ex officio role, 86
role in SAS, 126
voting and, 126

personnel
current policies, 221
staff supervision and SAS, 129

prayer team (SAS)
role in discernment process, 39
role at church conference vote, 55

quorum
Board covenant and, 208
guiding principles and, 217
nonnegotiable requirement, 87
Board of Trustees and, 87

resolution
customizing, 50

right-sizing
childcare, endowments, and nonprofits, 118
cooperative parishes and multi-point charges, 117, 286
discernment process, 57
design phase, 109
equipping phase, 185
implementing phase, 283
large and multisite churches, 57, 109, 185, 283
midsize churches, 58, 112, 186, 285
multisite churches, 110
small churches, 59, 113, 285

roles and responsibilities
agenda items, 238
four lanes defined, 196
staying in your lane, 162

rotation of leaders
as core design feature, 191
beginning rotation for the first time, 79
nonnegotiable, 83
preventing power consolidation, 191
right-sizing and, 114, 190
state laws for boards of directors and, 79

rules of the road
see leadership covenant
defined, 207
example, 208

SAS coach
See authorized coach

S/PPRC (Staff/Pastor-Parish Relations Committee)
as function of Leadership Board, 78, 81
confidentiality requirements, 84, 85
DS concerns about, 85
executive session and, 85, 250
family member restrictions, 84
membership requirements, 84

small churches
micro-churches and simplified governance, 62
real talk for, 61
six-member board option, 114

specialists
avoiding use of, 129
work teams are not, 106

staff
misunderstanding role of, 68
supervision and SAS, 129

strategic planning
in SAS Leadership Board, 181

strategic planning retreat
annual rhythm and, 258
components of, 183, 184

transparency
required in leadership communication, 275

Treasurer
guiding principles and, 219
nominations report and, 90
role in SAS, 93
not a governing role, 93

Trustees, Board of
age requirement for, 217
building maintenance team c ompared with, 98
Leadership Board as, 87

work lanes
defined, 195
four lanes described, 196
staying in your lane, 162

work teams
assignments, 104
creating, 104
leveraging leadership through, 103
not specialists, 106
using, 103

voting
by email or electronic means, 218
conference vote to adopt SAS, 55
pastor's role and, 126
quorum and, 208
simple majority rule, 55, 217
Trustee actions [age requirement for], 217

year two and beyond
challenges in, 293
evaluation and, 269
guiding principles review, 270
Leadership Board covenant review, 270
leadership development in, 271

www.ingramcontent.com/pod-product-compliance
Lightning Source LLC
LaVergne TN
LVHW081315110826
845149LV00006B/1512

9798994200827